W9-BOA-243

Economic Interaction
in the Pacific Basin

LAWRENCE B. KRAUSE AND SUEO SEKIGUCHI
Editors

Economic Interaction in the Pacific Basin

A study sponsored jointly
by the Brookings Institution
and the Japan Economic Research Center

THE BROOKINGS INSTITUTION
Washington, D.C.

Copyright © 1980 by
THE BROOKINGS INSTITUTION
1775 Massachusetts Avenue, N.W., Washington, D.C. 20036

Library of Congress Cataloging in Publication Data:

Main entry under title:
Economic interaction in the Pacific Basin.
  Includes bibliographical references and index.
  1. Pacific area—Foreign economic relations—
Addresses, essays, lectures. 2. Monetary policy—
Pacific area—Addresses, essays, lectures. 3. Pacific
area—Economic policy—Addresses, essays, lectures.
4. Pacific area—Economic conditions—Addresses, essays,
lectures. 5. Foreign trade promotion—Pacific area—
Addresses, essays, lectures. I. Krause, Lawrence B.
II. Sekiguchi, Sueo.
HF1411.E252   338.91′9   79-26006
ISBN 0-8157-5028-5
ISBN 0-8157-5027-7 pbk.

1 2 3 4 5 6 7 8 9

THE BROOKINGS INSTITUTION is an independent organization devoted to nonpartisan research, education, and publication in economics, government, foreign policy, and the social sciences generally. Its principal purposes are to aid in the development of sound public policies and to promote public understanding of issues of national importance.

The Institution was founded on December 8, 1927, to merge the activities of the Institute for Government Research, founded in 1916, the Institute of Economics, founded in 1922, and the Robert Brookings Graduate School of Economics and Government, founded in 1924.

The Board of Trustees is responsible for the general administration of the Institution, while the immediate direction of the policies, program, and staff is vested in the President, assisted by an advisory committee of the officers and staff. The by-laws of the Institution state: "It is the function of the Trustees to make possible the conduct of scientific research, and publication, under the most favorable conditions, and to safeguard the independence of the research staff in the pursuit of their studies and in the publication of the results of such studies. It is not a part of their function to determine, control, or influence the conduct of particular investigations or the conclusions reached."

The President bears final responsibility for the decision to publish a manuscript as a Brookings book. In reaching his judgment on the competence, accuracy, and objectivity of each study, the President is advised by the director of the appropriate research program and weighs the views of a panel of expert outside readers who report to him in confidence on the quality of the work. Publication of a work signifies that it is deemed a competent treatment worthy of public consideration but does not imply endorsement of conclusions or recommendations.

The Institution maintains its position of neutrality on issues of public policy in order to safeguard the intellectual freedom of the staff. Hence interpretations or conclusions in Brookings publications should be understood to be solely those of the authors and should not be attributed to the Institution, to its trustees, officers, or other staff members, or to the organizations that support its research.

Foreword

ECONOMIC INTERDEPENDENCE among countries of the Pacific basin has increased even faster than it has among nations generally. Most of the countries whose economies have grown most rapidly in the recent past, apart from those that produce oil, have Pacific shorelines; the same countries have also recorded the greatest increases in international trade. This fact suggests that the strengthened economic links among those countries have increased not only their prosperity but also their exposure to the unfavorable economic developments of the 1970s.

This study investigates the transmission of economic impulses among six countries chosen to be representative of the entire Pacific basin: Australia, Japan, the Republic of Korea, the Philippines, Thailand, and the United States. It compares their economic performance during the turbulent 1970s and examines the domestic and international effects of the economic policies pursued by individual governments.

The strength of the economic influence that Japan and the United States exert on each other has long been recognized. Its importance impressed Lawrence B. Krause, a Brookings senior fellow, and Sueo Sekiguchi, a senior economist of the Japan Economic Research Center, during their collaboration in 1973–75 as contributors to *Asia's New Giant: How the Japanese Economy Works,* edited by Hugh Patrick and Henry Rosovsky (Brookings, 1976). Krause further investigated the international transmission of economic impulses and its influence on the macroeconomic performance of individual countries in his contributions to *Worldwide Inflation: Theory and Recent Experience* (Brookings, 1977), of which he was coeditor (with Walter S. Salant). Research for the latter book stimulated Krause's desire to study the transmission of economic impulses among the countries of the Pacific basin and to put the bilateral relations between Japan and the United

States into better perspective. Krause thus found it natural to renew his collaboration with Sekiguchi, and the project culminating in the publication of this volume was undertaken jointly by Brookings and the Japan Economic Research Center.

The editors were fortunate in recruiting as contributors Ross Garnaut, professor of economics at the Australian National University; Hee-yhon Song, director of research for the Korea International Economic Institute; Romeo M. Bautista, professor of economics at the University of the Philippines; and Nimit Nontapunthawat, formerly of the economics faculty of Thammasat University and now senior economist and special assistant to the president of the Bangkok Bank.

A conference was held at the Japan Economic Research Center in June 1977, at which Yasukichi Yasuba and Chikashi Moriguchi of Kyoto University, Makoto Sakurai of the Japan Export Import Bank, and Masahiro Sakamoto of the National Institute for Research Advancement made substantial contributions that clarified issues and improved the manuscript. Parts of the manuscript were also reviewed by Yoichi Okita of the Economic Planning Agency and Ippei Yamazawa of Hitotsubashi University.

Professor Garnaut gratefully acknowledges the assistance he received from his discussions with his colleagues H. W. Arndt, W. M. Corden, P. D. Drysdale, and P. T. McCawley at the Australian National University and with the participants in a seminar in international economics at Hitotsubashi University. He also acknowledges the research assistance of Rod Sims and John Collis. Professor Bautista thanks John Power for reviewing a draft of the chapter on the Philippines.

Research assistance was also provided by Yasutoyo Shoda, Takahiko Mutoh, and Kumiko Mizutani of the Japan Economic Research Center and by Cynthia Nethercut, David Bates, and Stephen Smith of Brookings. The manuscript was edited by Alice M. Carroll, and the index was prepared by Florence Robinson.

The project was supported by grants from the National Institute for Research Advancement and the Sloan Foundation. The views expressed in this book are those of its contributors and should not be ascribed to the other staff members, officers, or trustees of the Brookings Institution, to the Japan Economic Research Center, to the National Institute for Research Advancement, or to the Sloan Foundation.

BRUCE K. MACLAURY
President, the Brookings Institution

January 1980   HISAO KANAMORI
Washington, D.C.   *President, the Japan Economic Research Center*

Contents

ix

Economic Interaction
in the Pacific Basin

CHAPTER ONE

Economic Disruption in the 1970s

THE WORLD ECONOMY in the 1970s became much more unstable than it had been in the preceding two decades. Indeed a new age of economic uncertainty seems to have commenced. Inflation has increased sharply. Economic growth has declined and unemployment has risen. Exchange rates have become much more unstable. Even international trade, the most reliable of all barometers of world economic health, has suffered a setback.

Practically all countries suffered inflation peaks in the first half of the 1970s, but some conquered inflation in the second half, while others made almost no dent at all in it. Oil exporting countries aside, many countries witnessed a sharp deceleration in their rates of economic growth, others a quite moderate decline. Exchange-rate instability by necessity affects everyone, but some countries tried for and achieved a degree of stability, while others accepted almost complete flexibility. With respect to international trade, some countries managed extremely high rates of export growth, while others suffered stagnation.

Differences in economic performance among countries can be traced to the peculiar circumstances in which each found itself and to the economic policies it adopted. As usual, policy differences reflect a host of political as well as economic factors. However, to an unusual extent, countries felt that their problems, particularly with respect to inflation, were more the consequence of disturbances arising abroad than of their own actions. For instance, in the early 1970s the United States witnessed its price and wage controls undermined by increases in world agricultural and commodity prices

1

and then suffered along with everyone else the historic rise in oil prices. Japan had a similar experience but also found its inflation moderated by the rise in the exchange value of the yen which it could not control. In smaller countries such as Norway and Sweden the belief became widespread that these economies were incapable of affecting their own price performance and thus were totally at the mercy of external forces.[1]

The world economy seems to have reached a kind of watershed in 1973–74. Obviously the change was brought on by the oil crisis. It was a time of testing for all countries. The size of the disturbance was so great, its complications so far-reaching, that the adjustment capabilities of all countries were severely challenged. Some countries proved to be quite adaptable, but others were hardly able to cope. The world instability and the inability of individual countries to control their economies have focused attention on the international transmission of economic impulses. The tendency of impulses that originate in one country or in world markets to have an impact on other countries may well be an inevitable consequence of greater economic interdependence.

The Political Context of Economic Policy

Particular national policies are chosen of course for political as well as economic reasons.[2] Economic interdependence may lead to increased real national incomes, but it has also created problems for government and certain segments of society and heightened tension in international relations. Tension has been created because governments have lost some ability to control their economies. Their short-term policies are threatened by fluctuations from abroad that are both hard to predict and difficult to recognize (in part because of lags in statistical reporting). Their medium-term policies aimed at industrial development may be frustrated or vitiated by technological or other developments abroad. Even long-term policies governing such matters as the distribution of income and wealth in their societies may be complicated by foreign involvement. For instance, the perceptions of equity and efficiency on which their policies are founded may change. When change is

1. For theoretical models and econometric tests demonstrating this external dependence, see Odd Aukrust, "Inflation in the Open Economy: A Norwegian Model," and Lars Calmfors, "Inflation in Sweden," in Lawrence B. Krause and Walter S. Salant, eds., *Worldwide Inflation: Theory and Recent Experience* (Brookings Institution, 1977).

2. See Robert O. Keohane and Joseph S. Nye, "World Politics and the International Economic System," in C. Fred Bergsten, *The Future of the International Economic Order: An Agenda For Research* (Heath, 1973).

rapid, current events are hard to comprehend and the future difficult to envision. Though governments retain political sovereignty over their own lands, their economies are affected by a wide range of events over which they have little control.[3]

Yet governments now are held responsible in the public mind for good times and bad. Inflation, unemployment, low growth, poverty, all are the fault of the government. Even natural disasters can cause people to blame the government for not taking proper precautions or failing to respond rapidly or effectively. No regime, whether democratically elected or not, can ignore public reaction to economic conditions. Governments are quick to claim credit when the economy goes well. But they are held responsible also when things go badly, even though they may attempt to place the blame elsewhere.

Governments so frequently blame foreigners for their economic troubles that when inflation is imported, their argument is not believed. Yet the domestic economy may be faced with a problem the government had not predicted or a solution whose costs in unemployment it cannot justify. Some people blame the government, which in turn becomes unhappy with its foreign economic ties. Others blame foreigners directly, adding more tension to international relations.

The complexity of economic issues increases the difficulties. In responding to the fourfold increase in oil prices in early 1974, for instance, how could a government, assuming it had the instruments to deal with domestic consequences, sort out the domestic from the international factors? The oil price rise had all of the following effects on oil importing countries: it increased domestic inflation through its effects on costs; it caused a decline in real income by deteriorating the international terms of trade as import prices rose more than export prices; it caused a substantial decline in the balance of trade; it caused a windfall to domestic energy producers (if there were any); it increased the demand for capital and labor that could substitute for energy or could be used in energy production; and it increased the prices of energy-intensive goods and services relative to other goods. In such circumstances should the government cushion the shock on the economy by slowing down the adjustment but risk misallocation of resources, or should it reinforce the price change, speeding up the adjustment but aggravating the short-run disruption? Should the government encourage saving to fight the inflation and provide the real resources to match the higher need for capital but thereby intensify the depressing effects of the decline in real incomes already suffered, or should it offset the real decline by stimulating the economy to maintain

3. Ralph C. Bryant describes the problem as a "mismatch of domains." *Money and Monetary Policy in Interdependent Nations* (Brookings Institution, 1980).

current levels of activity but run the risk of greater inflation and the worsening of the country's trade position? Should it levy increased taxes on domestic energy producers in order to capture for society some of the windfall gains but run the risk of discouraging present and future levels of domestic energy production, or should it encourage domestic energy production to increase self-sufficiency and obtain greater economic security but thereby make domestic income distribution less equal and run the risk of long-run commitment to high-cost energy and faster exhaustion of domestic energy resources?

Difficult as it may be to identify what is good for the country as a whole, choices must be made. Those choices will differ among countries as their economic and political structures differ. Natural endowments, product markets, labor markets, and financial markets affect economic responses. Though governments cannot expect other governments to behave as they do, most tend to evaluate other countries' policies in a framework relevant to their own economies. The more difficult problem of governments is not doing what is right, but knowing what is right.

Assembling a coherent national policy is not a simple matter. Most governments are organized so that different agencies represent particular constituencies and thus express different points of view in the formulation of national policies. The compromises necessary in shaping policies may well produce inconsistencies. Energy conservation as a principal instrument to fight an oil crisis, for example, might require a rise in the prices of all energy-intensive products. To offset the rise in the price of fertilizer, farmers might be given subsidies that encourage its use and therefore run counter to conservation goals.

But even assuming that a coherent and reasonably consistent policy can be determined, it will be subjected to a plethora of implementing decisions at the operating level that generally will weaken its direction and often will be at cross purposes. Top political leaders will perceive themselves to be frustrated by their bureaucracy, but the real culprit is the complexity of the issues. Those issues are made more complex by the foreign influences that impinge at many points and make policy coherence even more difficult to obtain. No wonder that governments are frustrated and political leaders ambivalent about economic interdependence.

Transmission of Economic Impulses

This study examines the questions of why inflation rates differ between countries, how much inflation is imported, what accounts for differences in growth rates, and how cyclical instability is transmitted from one country to another. It reviews the responses of six countries in the Pacific basin to a series of economic upheavals in the 1970s and analyzes the effects on their economies.[4] In a comparison of the analytical results, it indicates how disruptive particular kinds of international links may be. Finally, in considering the economic policies adopted in response to external impulses, it suggests national and regional actions that may help to spread economic benefits rather than increasing international instability.

Economic impulses are transmitted between countries through many channels.[5] The balance of payments, the accounting framework for international transactions, contains and reflects information on some of the most powerful forces in the transmission mechanism: prices of exports and imports, trade volumes, goods and services balances, capital flows, direct investment, and overall monetary balances.[6] These records of world trade and financial flows offer a means of calculating and comparing the impact of international economic fluctuations on national economies.

Each of these factors is heavily influenced by the exchange rate. It is the most important factor governing economic relations between countries. It is also the single most important price in an economy because it links all domestic prices to those in the rest of the world. A change in the exchange rate between two currencies, for instance, changes the prices of goods and services in one country relative to the other and creates expectations of further changes which may ignite capital flows. The change is seen as a rise in the value of one currency and a fall in the other. Hence it produces dissimilar economic effects. Appreciations in the exchange rate can be used to moderate increases in import prices or to restrain increases in demand for exports. Changes in goods and services balances can be restrained by appropriate exchange-rate changes.

4. An eclectic approach to macroeconomics is incorporated using Keynesian and monetary analysis, with econometric elaborations introduced occasionally. For a discussion of the mainline theories of market economies, see Alexander K. Swoboda, "Monetary Approaches to Worldwide Inflation," and William H. Branson, "A 'Keynesian' Approach to Worldwide Inflation," in Krause and Salant, *Worldwide Inflation*. Econometric investigations are described in Robert James Ball, ed., *The International Linkage of National Economic Models* (Amsterdam: North Holland, 1973).

5. For an analytical discussion of the transmission of inflation, see Walter S. Salant, "The International Transmission of Inflation," in Krause and Salant, *Worldwide Inflation*.

6. Some economists would confine balance-of-payments analysis to the overall monetary effect. See Harry G. Johnson, "Money, Balance-of-Payments Theory, and the International Monetary Problem," *Essays in International Finance*, no. 124 (November 1977).

The effects of changes in exchange rates on the domestic economy are far-reaching, and some of them occur after long lags. An appreciation, for example, will discourage exports and encourage imports, reducing profits and therefore investment in export and import-competing industries; it will also encourage investment abroad by domestic firms. The consequences of exchange-rate changes are an important factor in analyzing any economic phenomenon under a floating-exchange-rate system.

Four World Crises

Serious economic disruptions in the 1970s repeatedly outstripped the capacity of economists to describe the devastation the disruptions caused. In rapid succession, the breakdown in the Bretton Woods monetary system, the rise in raw material prices, the oil crisis, and the deep worldwide recession and weak recovery deteriorated economic performance and caused massive increases in worldwide inflation. Governments became progressively more timid because of their concern to counteract the inflation. Even in 1978 when Japan had conquered inflation and wholesale prices were falling, the government was reluctant to increase its stimulus for fear that a rise in the fiscal deficit would rekindle inflation. Other countries that tried aggressive demand-stimulating measures found that financial markets anticipated the inflationary consequences and that the result was more inflation rather than real growth. The disruptions affected not only single countries but all countries and led to structural changes of varying importance.

The Breakdown of the Bretton Woods System

From the end of World War II until March 1973 the international monetary system was governed by a set of rules and understandings designed to prevent a return of the monetary chaos of the 1930s.[7] Under the Bretton Woods agreement, countries were obliged to establish par values for their currencies (in terms of either gold or the U.S. dollar) and to defend those values by intervening in the foreign-exchange market. To prevent the exhaustion of international reserves, the International Monetary Fund stood ready to help deficit countries. But the heart of the system was the obligation of countries—both deficit and surplus—to make internal economic adjust-

---

7. See Lawrence B. Krause, *Sequel to Bretton Woods* (Brookings Institution, 1971); Robert Solomon, *The International Monetary System 1945–1976: An Insider's View* (Harper and Row, 1977); and Thomas D. Willet, *Floating Exchange Rates and International Monetary Reform* (Washington: American Enterprise Institute, 1977).

ments to correct disequilibriums in their balance of payments. The costs in unemployment and forgone output in deficit countries and in inflation in surplus countries were so high that most refused to make internal adjustments. Borrowing abroad could relieve the pressure on deficit countries (as lending could for surplus countries), but eventually revaluation of the currency was the solution most countries chose.

For twenty years or so, the system worked well. The world economy prospered and the volume of international trade grew extremely fast. Par value changes—most often devaluations—did upset financial markets from time to time, and the dollar tended to be appreciated as a result of them. As commercial activity became increasingly complex, governments found they had to liberalize exchange controls and other restrictions on capital transactions. Freer movements of capital eventually led to both private and official speculation in currencies, thus helping to undermine the Bretton Woods system.

As American indebtedness grew in the 1960s, confidence in the dollar waned. In an effort to correct the Bretton Woods system's failure to provide for the orderly growth of international reserves, the International Monetary Fund was empowered to create its own reserves of special drawing rights (SDRs) in 1970. That was inadequate to prevent the collapse of the system. The major flaw in the system was its lack of a gradual and automatic mechanism for adjusting payments imbalances. When the dollar became overvalued, there was no practical way for the United States to devalue its own currency or force other countries to appreciate theirs.

In a sense, the breakdown of the Bretton Woods system was inevitable. With the growing economic strength of Europe in the early 1960s and of Japan later in the decade, the United States lost its predominant position and the system lost its mainstay. Unfortunately the efficiency of the Bretton Woods system eroded slowly and the decline was marked by a number of monetary crises. The process of disintegration was much more disruptive for the world economy than the change to a new system itself.

The first sign of significant trouble, in the mid-1960s, was the failure of official gold reserves to match the growth in international reserves. Between 1953 and 1965, total international reserves had grown 2.5 percent a year, with gold providing 40 percent, IMF deposits 20 percent, and foreign-exchange accumulations 40 percent of the growth. Thus some balance was maintained among different reserve assets. While international reserves continued to grow at 2.4 percent annually from 1965 through 1969, official gold reserves actually declined. The process of disintegration speeded up between 1969 and 1971; international reserves expanded at a gigantic 17.9 percent annual growth rate and became an inflationary force in the world economy.

The explosion of world reserves was the inevitable result of the U.S. overall balance-of-payments deficits which the system could neither accommodate nor control. Finally in March 1973 the major countries gave up trying to maintain fixed-exchange-rate parities. A new system of managed, floating exchange rates evolved pragmatically. Gradually the governments of the major industrial countries reached general understandings as to what constituted proper intervention by central banks in exchange markets. Most of them tended to intervene to support their currencies when they were under market pressure. Smaller countries usually pegged their currencies to those of larger countries.

The Rise in Raw Material Prices

The second crisis of the 1970s began while the Bretton Woods system was disintegrating. Raw material prices had been remarkably stable since the end of the Korean War. The UN overall index of commodity prices was at the same level in 1970–71 as it was in 1953–54 (table 1-1). Furthermore the components of the index showed the same stability, although primary metal ores had increased somewhat more than the average and nonfood agricultural products somewhat less. Not since the early 1900s had there been a comparable period of price stability.

The balance between supply and demand for particular commodities explains this period of price stability, but certain other factors contributed to the supply growth, the changes in which helped cause the subsequent price explosion. The 1950s and 1960s saw the rise of multinational corporations and their domination of the entire product chain from exploration and discovery to finished products. These corporations proved to be an efficient organizing instrument that helped to maintain price stability by creating new supplies in advance of actual demand. The large increase in raw materials demanded by Japan in these decades was handled expeditiously through long-term contracts between Japanese trading firms and multinational companies producing principally in Australia.

In the mid-1960s, growing nationalism in developing countries plus concern in Australia and Canada about the long-run implications of natural-resource-led growth coupled with resentment against some multinational corporations began to disrupt this efficient mechanism. The most extreme reaction was in Chile, but changes were evident throughout the world. Because of the long gestation time for many natural-resource projects, the inhibitions on the supply mechanism were not felt until the 1970s.

No doubt the stability of raw material prices contributed greatly to con-

Table 1-1. *UN Price Indexes for Primary Commodities, 1953–77*
Index, 1963 = 100

| Year | All commodities | Agricultural commodities | | Metal ores |
		Food	Other	
1953	107	106	111	98
1954	111	116	111	96
1955	107	104	113	100
1956	107	104	112	107
1957	109	106	111	109
1958	102	102	98	102
1959	99	94	103	99
1960	99	92	105	100
1961	97	91	101	102
1962	96	94	97	100
1963	100	100	100	100
1964	103	105	102	108
1965	103	103	103	114
1966	104	105	104	105
1967	101	104	96	109
1968	100	102	96	108
1969	104	106	101	114
1970	108	111	100	122
1971	115	117	105	126
1972	130	132	120	134
1973	188	191	184	161
1974	295	248	219	216
1975	312	239	192	255
1976	321	235	214	259
1977	353	266	230	265

Source: United Nations, *Monthly Bulletin of Statistics*, vols. 11–32 (September 1957–November 1978).

tainment of world inflation. In a real sense, all countries benefited from world price stability, but some benefited more than others. Industrial countries that rely on imported raw materials were particularly well served since it permitted them to improve their terms of trade and gain more real income from international trade. Raw material exporters, however, had the reverse experience since their terms of trade deteriorated somewhat and their real income was less than it would have been if the same volume of exports could have been sustained without the price deterioration.

Prices changed dramatically in 1972, the UN index for all commodities increasing at a 28.6 percent annual rate in the first quarter.[8] Furthermore all

8. Quarterly data are from United Nations, *Monthly Bulletin of Statistics*, various issues.

components of the index increased; the inflation thrust was pervasive and increases for the year were much above other years. Yet 1972 was just a warm-up for 1973, when the price index for all commodities soared 53.7 percent for the average for the year, but increased 72.4 percent from the fourth quarter of 1972 to the fourth quarter of 1973. Food was a leader, as it was in 1972, but its increases were surpassed by those of nonfood agricultural commodities. In 1974 the overall index grew at an even higher rate of 56.9 percent (but "only" 46.1 percent fourth to fourth quarters). While this increase was dominated by the explosion of crude oil prices, the other components also increased greatly, particularly in the early part of the year. Not until the onset of the severe worldwide recession was the inflation of raw material prices halted. Meanwhile, prices of manufactured goods in international trade, which had been quite stable through 1971, increased 15–20 percent in 1972 and 1973 and 25 percent in 1974. Nevertheless the terms of trade moved against industrial countries because the rise of raw material prices was even greater.

One of the many factors that contributed to the raw material price explosion was the unique degree of synchronization in the expansion of all the major industrial countries.[9] Another was a shortfall in the production of agricultural crops. Food prices rose spectacularly, and farmers shifted production to grains, which resulted in a deficit of nonfood agricultural products and a rise in their prices. Prices seem also to have risen because users of commodities built up precautionary inventories. And the intense speculation in commodities that developed in this period added to inflationary pressures.

The consequences of the rise in commodity prices for importers and exporters alike were profound. Social, political, and economic trends in the advanced countries made their economies prone to general inflation.[10] In particular, labor markets had become more inflexible as more workers gained real income protection through wages indexed to the cost of living and through job security provided by custom, law, and government economic policy. Increases in food prices thus quickly generated inflationary pressure. In developing countries the price rises affected imported goods for which there were no substitutes and little leeway to reduce consumption.

The inflationary pressures also hit exporters of raw materials whose economies were unable to satisfy the domestic demand stimulated by increased

9. Richard Cooper and Robert Lawrence found that raw material prices, excluding petroleum, rose faster in 1972–74 than in any other period measured by the Economist index since 1860. "The 1972–75 Commodity Boom," *Brookings Papers on Economic Activity, 3:1975*, pp. 671–715.

10. Krause and Salant, *Worldwide Inflation*.

incomes. Improvement in the balance of payments of commodity exporters induced them to increase imports; world trade was thus stimulated and the volume of manufactured exports increased markedly. The explosion of raw material prices was not sustainable and prices ultimately collapsed in the world recession.

The Oil Crisis

The oil crisis was immediately and correctly perceived as a disruption of major proportions, equivalent in its effects to a world conflict. Crude oil prices, which during the 1950s had been relatively stable and in the early 1960s had declined, began to climb in 1967. With world energy use during the 1960s expanding by 5.4 percent a year, and petroleum demand by 7.6 percent, the Organization of Petroleum Exporting Countries (OPEC) was finally able to exercise some control over the price of oil.[11] By 1973 its members had become adept at judging the world oil market and pushing prices up when market conditions permitted it.

The renewal of hostilities in the Middle East in October 1973 precipitated the oil crisis. The Arab members of OPEC declared that they would sharply and progressively reduce their output of oil and embargo shipments to certain countries, principally the United States and the Netherlands. Spot prices of petroleum rose so dramatically that by the end of the embargo, oil exporters could insist on a fourfold increase in price—the price of Saudi Arabian crude oil which averaged $3.27 a barrel in 1973 ($2.59 in the first quarter of 1973) rose to $11.58 a barrel in 1974.

Control over world oil supplies by OPEC was made easy by the fact that the OPEC governments had only to capture control of the industrial mechanism dominated by eight major corporations and turn it to their own purposes. In the United States and Canada, production of oil was approaching its limit with existing investment and incentives, and thus the United States sought imports both to replace an ebbing domestic production and to provide for growth in demand.

The immediate impact of the increase in oil prices for oil-importing countries was a rise in domestic inflation. Inflation was fueled directly through increased prices of petroleum to consumers and indirectly as higher energy prices caused producers of all other products to raise prices. Workers' de-

11. See Joseph A. Yager and Eleanor B. Steinberg, "Trends in the International Oil Market," in Edward R. Fried and Charles L. Schultze, eds., *Higher Oil Prices and the World Economy* (Brookings Institution, 1975). The major oil-exporting countries, led by Venezuela, formed OPEC in 1960 in order to prevent the erosion of oil prices.

mands for higher wages to compensate for the increase in their cost of living perpetuated the inflation. Economic activity was also restrained since a large share of consumer income was being spent on energy bills and petroleum imports. It was further restricted by governments' policies necessary to contain inflation and to accommodate the decline in income resulting from the deterioration in their terms of trade.

The disturbance of the balance of payments is apparent in the leap in the current-account surplus of OPEC countries from only $7.0 billion in 1973 to $67.8 billion in 1974 (it went down to about $40 billion in 1975 and 1976). Oil-importing countries had to suffer a corresponding deterioration in their current accounts. The accumulation of assets by which OPEC financed its surplus meant, of course, an increase in liabilities for oil-importing countries. The cumulative total for 1974 through 1977 was $185 billion.

In a larger sense, the oil crisis caused a shift in the distribution of economic power in the world. With increased real incomes the OPEC countries became an important economic and political force in the world. Their relative advance was mainly at the expense of the old industrial countries and the really poor developing countries. Higher-income developing countries (such as the Republic of Korea, the Philippines, and Thailand) showed greater ability to adjust to the oil crisis than the industrial countries and were able to improve their position relative to all except the OPEC countries.

The Worldwide Recession and Weak Recovery

Policymaking was confused during 1974 because of the simultaneous inflationary and deflationary impacts of the oil crisis. Thus monetary policy in the major industrial countries, which had been tightened in reaction to the 1972–73 expansion, remained tight long after the cyclical peak had been passed. What resulted was the longest and deepest recession since World War II. Industrial production of countries in the Organization for Economic Cooperation and Development peaked in the fourth quarter of 1973 and either failed to rise or actually declined during the following six quarters (table 1-2)—fully twice the length of a typical recession. The OECD as a whole showed no growth in gross domestic production in 1974 or 1975, as small advances in one region were counterbalanced by declines elsewhere. As is to be expected, the decline in output led to record unemployment. As compared to the 1965–74 average, unemployment was up 60 percent in Canada, 100 percent in the United States and Japan, 150 percent in France, the United Kingdom, and Italy, and almost 400 percent in West Germany.

Table 1-2. *Indexes of Industrial Production of OECD Countries, by Year and Quarter, 1971–77*

Index, 1970 = 100

| Year and quarter | Organization for Economic Cooperation and Development[a] | | | |
	All members	European members	United States	Japan
1971	101	102	100	103
First	101	102	99	103
Second	101	102	100	102
Third	102	103	100	103
Fourth	102	103	101	104
1972	108	107	108	110
First	104	105	103	106
Second	107	106	107	108
Third	109	107	109	111
Fourth	113	111	113	116
1973	118	116	118	127
First	115	113	115	122
Second	117	115	117	127
Third	119	117	119	129
Fourth	120	118	119	132
1974	119	117	117	123
First	120	119	117	130
Second	120	119	118	127
Third	119	118	118	122
Fourth	115	113	116	115
1975	110	110	109	110
First	108	111	105	107
Second	108	109	106	110
Third	111	108	112	112
Fourth	114	113	114	113
1976	120	117	120	122
First	117	115	118	117
Second	119	117	120	121
Third	120	117	121	124
Fourth	122	120	122	125
1977	124	120	127	126
First	124	122	124	126
Second	124	120	127	126
Third	124	119	128	126
Fourth	125	120	129	128

Source: Organization for Economic Cooperation and Development (OECD), "Industrial Production," in *Main Economic Indicators*, various issues. Figures are seasonally adjusted.

a. Members of the OECD are Australia, Austria, Belgium, Canada, Denmark, Finland, France, Germany, Greece, Iceland, Ireland, Japan, Luxembourg, Netherlands, New Zealand, Portugal, Spain, Sweden .Switzerland, Turkey, United Kingdom, and United States.

The recovery that followed this severe recession was weak and faltering. Industrial production in Japan, the United States, and Europe returned slowly to its previous cyclical peaks. None of the industrial areas with the possible exception of the United States was able to sustain an expansion long enough to compensate for the slack created in their economies during the downturn.

The depth of this recession was no doubt due in major part to the severity of the preceding inflation and the lack of internal instruments to deal with externally prompted inflation. Also domestic measures could not easily offset the decline in real income caused by the oil price rise. Furthermore, the decline in the volume of world trade in 1975 caught many governments by surprise. Since exports constitute a major share of output in most countries (with the exception of the United States), the loss of demand was significant.

Some of the same factors explain why the subsequent recovery was weak. The high and seemingly intractable inflation rate made governments very cautious in making economic policy. Balance-of-payments deficits brought about by high-priced oil imports caused many countries to wait for export-led growth; only Japan succeeded in capturing it. Industries that had been operating well below their preferred levels of utilization failed to make the private plant and equipment investments that usually helped to raise growth rates.

In the recession and its aftermath, industrial countries suffered substantial losses in the form of forgone output. Generous unemployment and welfare benefits cushioned the burden for some of the workers made idle by the slowdown, but for temporary workers and new entrants into the labor force the burden was not relieved. Commodity prices in international trade declined sharply, worsening the terms of trade and real welfare of countries dependent on such exports. The growth of international trade, which had been expanding by about 8 percent a year, slowed to only 3.9 percent in 1974 and declined 3.3 percent in 1975. There was a recovery in 1976 as trade expanded by 11.6 percent, but the growth rate declined to 4.2 percent in 1977. Thus the mechanism for spreading economic progress to many parts of the world was impaired. Protectionist pressures increased in many countries, restraining imports somewhat and introducing an uncertainty into trading arrangements that undermined the willingness of private entrepreneurs to risk investment in export industries. Finally in the industrial countries there seemed to be a loss of faith in the ability of government to solve economic problems. In small measure this was reminiscent of the sentiment that was so widespread in the 1930s.

Table 1-3. *Growth Rates of Six Pacific Basin Countries, 1964–77*

	Percent change in gross national product[a]								
Country	1964–1969	1970	1971	1972	1973	1974	1975	1976	1977
Australia	5.4	5.0	5.5	3.5	6.2	2.5	1.7	3.5	1.6
Japan	10.4	10.9	7.4	9.1	9.8	−1.3	2.5	6.0	5.1
Korea	10.6	8.6	9.8	7.3	16.4	8.8	8.8	15.0	9.8
Philippines	5.0	4.3	5.8	4.9	9.7	6.3	5.9	6.7	6.1
Thailand	8.8	7.5	4.7	5.3	9.3	5.0	7.7	8.2	6.2
United States	4.3	−0.3	3.0	5.7	5.5	−1.4	−1.3	6.0	4.9

Source: International Monetary Fund (IMF), *International Financial Statistics*, vols. 31 (May 1978), 32 (July 1979).

a. Change in gross domestic product of Australia, Korea, and Thailand.

The Pacific Basin

Countries in the Pacific basin, however, continued to grow quite rapidly in the 1970s (table 1-3). The Pacific basin is the most dynamic region of the world. Though the region has no supranational political institution, nor even a clearly identified sense of geography, a complex series of economic relationships has evolved there.[12] The six countries that are the subject of this study juxtapose a variety of economic structures: resource-rich advanced countries (the United States and Australia), a resource-poor developed country (Japan), resource-rich developing countries (Thailand and the Philippines), and a resource-poor developing country (the Republic of Korea).[13] The United States and Japan of course have worldwide economic interests, but the center of economic gravity for both countries is shifting toward the Pacific basin. Australia is enlarging its economic ties there, and the other three countries' trade is largely Pacific oriented. Complex economic

12. For recent studies of the region, see Federal Reserve Bank of San Francisco, *Central Bank Macroeconomic Modeling in Pacific Basin Countries, Proceedings of the First Pacific Basin Central Bank Conference on Econometric Modeling, May 27–29, 1975* (Federal Reserve Bank of San Francisco, 1978); and Lawrence B. Krause and Hugh Patrick, eds., *Mineral Resources in the Pacific Area, Proceedings of the Ninth Pacific Trade and Development Conference* (Federal Reserve Bank of San Francisco, 1978). Also see reports of the other Pacific Trade and Development conferences.

13. Other countries often included in this regional economic grouping are Canada, China, Hong Kong, Indonesia, Malaysia, New Zealand, Papua New Guinea, and Singapore. The countries examined here were selected for their size, importance in the region, and special characteristics. Latin American countries might also be included as part of the Pacific basin.

Table 1-4. *Income and Population of Six Pacific Basin Countries, 1976*

Item	Australia	Japan	Korea	Philip- pines	Thailand	United States
Gross domestic product (billions of dollars)	71.3	562.2	25.4	17.8	16.3	1,685.7
Gross national product per capita (dollars)	6,990	5,090	700	420	380	7,880
Population (millions)	13.9	112.8	35.9	43.3	43.0	215.1
Population growth, 1960–75 (percent per year)	1.8	1.1	2.3	3.0	3.1	1.1

Sources: IMF, *International Financial Statistics*, vol. 31 (November 1978); *World Bank Atlas 1978.*

relationships are evolving among all these countries, and they display the tensions typical of economic interdependence.

The United States is the largest and richest of the countries. It is also the slowest growing with respect to both population and gross national product (tables 1-3 and 1-4). Its international involvement as measured by exports of goods and services as a percentage of gross national product (table 1-5) is less than the others' but it has been rising rapidly since 1965. The United States is the largest exporter and importer of goods both with the other countries in this study and in the Pacific basin as a whole (table 1-6). How-ever, the share of its trade that is Pacific oriented is somewhat less than the others'.[14] While the United States does export highly sophisticated manufac-tured goods and import raw materials and labor-intensive products, it does not fit the pattern of a typical advanced industrial country. Because services have replaced manufacturing as the dominant employer in the society, the United States is better described as a postindustrial country.

Japan more nearly fits the definition of an advanced industrial country. It has achieved a high level of per capita income (table 1-4) and its industrial production is second only to that of the United States. Without question Japan has been the fastest growing advanced country in the world over the last decade or so. Its involvement in the world economy, somewhat below European countries', has been rising rapidly. Its exports and imports are sub-stantially oriented toward the Pacific basin, and especially the countries in this study. Unlike the United States, which runs a deficit with its Pacific basin trading partners, Japan tends to maintain a balance or surplus in its regional trade. The structure of its trade is unambiguous; it exports manufactured

14. Trade values are measured in current prices so the analysis of trade shares is somewhat distorted by the gigantic rise in oil prices in 1974.

Table 1-5. *Measures of International Involvement of Six Pacific Basin Countries, 1950–77*

Country	Goods and services exports as a percentage of GNP						
	1950	1955	1960	1965	1970	1975	1977
Australia	15	13	14	15	18	16	17
Japan	n.a.	8	9	11	13	15	18
Korea	2	1	2	5	15	28	36
Philippines	17	17	13	17	14	19	19
Thailand	24	20	17	19	17	19	22
United States	4	4	5	5	6	8	7

Sources: World Bank, *World Tables 1976;* Hugh Patrick and Henry Rosovsky, eds., *Asia's New Giant: How the Japanese Economy Works* (Brookings Institution, 1976), p. 399; OECD, *Main Economic Indicators,* March 1979; IMF, *International Financial Statistics,* vol. 32 (July 1979).
n.a. Not available.

products and imports raw materials. Indeed Japan's heavy dependence on imports of raw materials and food is one of its major characteristics and dominates its view toward the world economy.

Australia, the smallest country by population in this study, is by the other measures in table 1-4 among the largest. It is third in total income and second in per capita income. It also is second to the United States in the slowness of economic growth. Australian international economic involvement has been quite high and relatively unchanged since 1950. Having once been heavily oriented toward Europe, and Great Britain in particular, Australian trade is now directed toward the Pacific basin. Australia typifies an advanced nonindustrial country in that it exports primarily agricultural and mining products and imports manufactured goods. But it has a large secondary manufacturing sector which is very important in terms of employment.

The Republic of Korea without doubt is the most dynamic country in the Pacific basin. Though it is still poor by the standard of advanced countries, its aggregate and per capita incomes have been growing very rapidly. Korea may well be the fastest growing non-oil-producing country in the world. One of the most remarkable aspects of the Korean "economic miracle" is the phenomenal rise in Korea's international involvement; from a very low ratio through 1965, its exports of goods and services as a share of gross national product had risen by more than seven times by 1977 (table 1-5). No comparable experience has been measured elsewhere. Korean trade is heavily oriented to the Pacific basin, and like the Philippines, Korea has an export and import concentration near 70 percent. Much like Japan, it has a limited natural-resource base and must depend on manufacturing as the source for both economic growth and exports.

Table 1-6. *Distribution of International Trade of Six Pacific Basin Countries, 1970,*
Millions of dollars and, in parentheses, percent of worldwide less OPEC exports or imports

Country and year	Exports				
	Worldwide		Pacific basin		
	Total	Less OPEC	Study countries	Other	Total
Australia					
1970	4,788	4,677	1,967 (42.1)	932 (19.9)	2,899 (62.0)
1973	9,576	9,298	4,488 (48.3)	1,780 (19.1)	6,268 (67.4)
1977	13,333	12,614	6,102 (48.4)	2,259 (17.9)	8,361 (66.3)
Japan					
1970	19,318	18,347	8,326 (45.4)	3,021 (16.5)	11,347 (61.8)
1973	37,008	34,319	13,905 (40.5)	6,364 (18.5)	20,269 (59.1)
1977	81,126	69,253	29,015 (41.9)	11,595 (16.7)	40,610 (58.6)
Korea					
1970	839	823	640 (77.8)	70 (8.5)	710 (86.3)
1973	3,225	3,147	2,315 (73.5)	357 (11.3)	2,671 (84.9)
1977	10,048	8,807	5,508 (62.5)	951 (10.8)	6,459 (73.3)
Philippines					
1970	1,043	1,040	891 (85.7)	43 (4.2)	934 (89.8)
1973	1,886	1,869	1,415 (75.7)	130 (7.0)	1,545 (82.7)
1977	3,151	3,094	1,936 (62.6)	232 (7.5)	2,168 (70.1)
Thailand					
1970	710	674	283 (42.0)	195 (28.9)	478 (70.9)
1973	1,563	1,460	607 (41.6)	479 (32.8)	1,087 (74.4)
1977	3,489	3,053	1,100 (36.0)	948 (31.0)	2,048 (67.1)
United States					
1970	43,231	41,313	6,797 (16.5)	10,741 (26.0)	17,538 (42.5)
1973	71,347	67,907	11,740 (17.3)	18,554 (27.3)	30,294 (44.6)
1977	120,166	106,684	16,635 (15.6)	31,756 (29.8)	48,391 (45.4)

Sources: IMF, *Direction of Trade Annual, 1970–1976, 1971–1977.*

The Philippines, along with Korea and Thailand, is a middle-income developing country. In terms of population it is rather large and growing rapidly. The Philippines' economic growth has also been high and rather stable. Its international economic involvement has been about the same as Australia's and, like that country's, has not changed very much. Philippine trade, to a remarkable extent oriented to the Pacific basin, is dominated by raw materials (especially minerals) on the export side and by manufactured goods and fuel on the import side. The government has followed an import-replacement industrialization policy for some time, so manufactured imports tend to be restricted to goods not easily produced domestically.

1973, and 1977

	Imports			
Worldwide		Pacific basin		
Total	Less OPEC	Study countries	Other	Total
4,540	4,363	1,745 (40.0)	490 (11.2)	2,235 (51.2)
6,876	6,679	2,818 (42.2)	901 (13.5)	3,719 (55.7)
12,233	11,323	5,136 (45.4)	1,867 (16.5)	7,003 (61.8)
18,881	16,046	8,025 (50.0)	2,539 (15.8)	10,564 (65.8)
38,323	31,242	15,206 (48.7)	7,027 (22.5)	22,233 (71.2)
71,328	46,149	21,618 (46.8)	12,568 (27.2)	34,186 (74.1)
1,984	1,856	1,455 (78.4)	171 (9.2)	1,626 (87.6)
4,240	3,836	3,074 (80.2)	475 (12.4)	3,550 (92.5)
10,814	8,502	6,722 (79.1)	943 (11.1)	7,666 (90.2)
1,206	1,105	782 (70.7)	117 (10.6)	898 (81.3)
1,790	1,591	1,160 (72.9)	122 (7.6)	1,282 (80.6)
4,270	3,428	2,210 (64.5)	536 (15.6)	2,746 (80.1)
1,298	1,231	729 (59.2)	101 (8.2)	830 (67.4)
2,032	1,913	1,094 (57.2)	181 (9.5)	1,276 (66.7)
4,615	3,885	2,213 (57.0)	439 (11.3)	2,653 (68.3)
42,452	40,795	7,894 (19.4)	14,180 (34.8)	22,074 (54.1)
73,592	68,917	13,267 (19.3)	24,141 (35.0)	37,408 (54.3)
156,708	121,702	26,402 (21.7)	44,396 (36.5)	70,798 (58.2)

Thailand has a slightly lower level of per capita income than the Philippines and shares with it a population growth rate of roughly 3 percent a year. Nevertheless Thailand is a rapidly growing country. Despite special problems associated with the ending of American military expenditures after the Vietnam War, Thailand sustained a reasonably high rate of economic advance even after the oil crisis. Thailand's international involvement is fairly high but shows no tendency to rise further. Thai trade, most of it within the Pacific basin, is composed of natural resources, primarily from agriculture, on the export side and mainly manufactured products on the import side.

Prelude to the 1970s in the Pacific Basin

For the countries of the Pacific basin the latter half of the 1960s was a time of substantial economic progress (table 1-3). The United States experienced a rapid growth rate of 4.3 percent a year between 1964 and 1969 and unemployment averaged less than 4 percent. Japan's growth was a truly outstanding 10.7 percent a year and while the annual rise in consumer prices averaged 5.3 percent a year, the rise in wholesale prices was only 1.6 percent (table 1-7). For Australia this was a golden period as its economy grew by 5.4 percent a year, the unemployment rate was held to an exceptionally low level, and the inflation rate (consumer prices) was a very moderate 3 percent. The Korean economy reached the remarkable growth rate of 10.6 percent under the country's first five-year plan, and open inflation, while serious, was held to an acceptable 11.9 percent rate. The Philippines' growth rate of 5.0 percent annually was quite respectable even though potential growth may have been a bit higher. Philippine inflation was very moderate, with consumer prices rising 3.6 percent a year and wholesale prices 2.2 percent. Thailand's extremely rapid economic growth rate of 8.8 percent a year made it among the fastest growing countries in the world between 1964 and 1969, while consumer prices increased only 2.5 percent a year.

Table 1-7. *Percent Change in Consumer and Wholesale Price Indexes of Six Pacific Basin Countries, 1964–77*

Country	1964–1969	1970	1971	1972	1973	1974	1975	1976	1977
				Consumer price index					
Australia	3.1	4.0	6.1	5.9	9.3	15.1	15.0	13.6	12.3
Japan	5.3	7.7	6.1	4.5	11.7	24.5	11.8	9.3	8.1
Korea	11.8	12.7	12.1	12.0	3.0	23.7	26.2	15.4	10.3
Philippines	3.6	14.0	15.0	10.0	14.0	33.6	8.2	6.2	7.9
Thailand	2.5	0.9	2.0	3.9	11.7	23.3	4.1	5.0	8.4
United States	3.4	5.9	4.3	3.3	6.2	11.0	9.1	5.8	6.5
				Wholesale price index					
Australia	n.a.	4.4	4.8	4.9	8.6	15.2	15.0	11.4	10.1
Japan	1.6	3.7	−0.8	0.8	15.8	31.4	3.0	5.1	1.8
Korea	8.0	9.2	8.6	14.0	7.0	42.1	26.6	12.1	9.0
Philippines	2.2	23.6	15.7	13.1	23.7	47.8	5.4	9.2	9.9
Thailand	4.6	−0.5	0.3	7.9	22.8	28.8	3.7	3.9	5.4
United States	2.4	3.6	3.3	4.4	13.1	18.8	9.3	4.6	6.1

Source: IMF, *International Financial Statistics*, vol. 31 (May 1978).
n.a. Not available.

Closer inspection of each of the countries, however, reveals tendencies that would make such progress unsustainable even during the latter 1960s. The United States was pressing on the limits of its economic resources and inflationary forces were heating up. Pressure was coming from the expansion of the federal budget to fight the Vietnam War, but a political consensus on how to pay for that unpopular war was hard to achieve. Japan was developing a structural balance-of-payments surplus and a substantial undervaluation of the yen. Private investment in traded-goods industries was speeding up and was being misallocated because of the undervalued currency. The rapid growth of Australia during this period was propelled by expansion of the large-scale, high-productivity mining sector. Continuation of mineral development depended both on Australia's willingness to have its natural resources exploited (in part by multinational firms) and on the ability of Japanese mineral-processing industries—Australia's principal export customers—to grow at an exponential rate. Furthermore the rapid expansion of mineral exports combined with replacement of petroleum imports by domestic production created a structural surplus in Australia's overall balance of payments that made an adjustment of some kind inevitable.

The extraordinary growth of the Republic of Korea was heavily dependent on expanding exports. Fortunately there was strong foreign demand during the latter 1960s and plentiful financing, fed in part through foreign borrowing, to expand industrial capacity. Korea's international involvement was still so small that domestic factors determined how fast its exports could advance and the economy was fairly well insulated from external instability. The rapid growth accompanied by excessive domestic monetary expansion caused strong inflationary pressures. Even though the Korean economy was attuned to high inflation rates, direct price controls—principally on rice— were adopted to suppress the inflation. The exchange rate was not devalued as required which artificially maintained cheap imports. But inflation cannot long be suppressed without causing severe structural damage; something had to change.

There were several indications in the Philippines that the economic situation of the 1960s could not be sustained. In the first place the growth rate of the economy itself was not fully adequate. It has been suggested that not enough investment was being directed toward rural development, particularly toward agriculture, and that too much reliance was placed on import replacement to sustain industrial development. As Philippine import growth outpaced export growth, the deficit on the trade balance required foreign borrowing and led to problems in servicing short-term debts. Foreign direct investment, however, was being withdrawn because of the uncertain political situation and the prospective ending of the Laurel-Langley agreement governing the status of U.S. investment in the Philippines.[15] Finally in February 1970, before the world monetary system began to fail, the external situation led to the floating of the Philippine peso and its rapid depreciation during that year.

The excellent overall performance of the Thai economy during 1964–69 was not achieved without reliance on some very destabilizing factors. The massive expansion of the American military presence during this period with its significant economic and social consequences was one destabilizing factor. Growth was concentrated in industrial and commercial development in a few urban centers, to the detriment of agriculture (particularly in remote areas) despite government interest in promoting agriculture. The result was urban congestion and an increasingly unequal distribution of personal incomes. Furthermore the balance of payments was evolving in an unhealthy direction. Small trade deficits during the early 1960s had been more than offset by surpluses on services and inflows of direct investment; toward the end of the decade not even a growing service surplus could offset the deficit caused by a rapidly deteriorating trade balance. The difficulty stemmed from the stagnation of Thai exports. The trade balance would have been even worse had it not been for an improvement in the Thai terms of trade. But, unfortunately, the terms of trade were reversed in 1970. Thus certain elements of instability were apparent in all of the economies even before the four international shocks of the 1970s.

15. The agreement between the Philippines and the United States was designed to ease economic adjustments from the time of decolonization to 1974.

CHAPTER TWO

The End of U.S. Hegemony

HISTORICALLY, economic policymaking in the United States has responded only to domestic conditions. That may have been reasonable when economic events in other countries had little effect on the U.S. economy. The seemingly provincial U.S. approach was not resented by most other countries as long as the United States served as a fixed point against which they could gauge their prospects and plan their policies. From a wealth of published data other countries could forecast U.S. economic developments and anticipate U.S. policy actions. They could then plan their policies without fear of disturbing either the economy or the policies of the United States. Once the United States lost the leeway it had to suffer a deterioration in its balance of payments or in the value of the dollar without initiating a policy response, other sovereign nations were faced with the problem of determining their policies without a reliable system against which to judge them.

The U.S. Economy in the 1970s

The United States entered the decade of the 1970s with substantial inflationary pressure resulting from excess demand. The economy was pressed into producing above its full-employment capacity from 1965 through 1969 (table 2-1) as increased military expenditures were heaped on an expanding private economy. Price increases were moderated in part by a 55 percent rise in volume of imports from 1965 to 1969 (and 68 percent increase in value) and a decline in the net goods and service balance from $7.1 billion to less than $2 billion. Thus the rest of the world was a stabilizing factor for the U.S. economy during this period.

23

Table 2-1. *Gap between Potential and Actual U.S. Gross National Product, 1954–77*

Billions of 1972 dollars

| Year | Gross national product | | |
	Potential	Actual	Gap
1954	629.7	613.7	16.0
1955	651.4	654.8	−3.4
1956	673.9	668.8	5.1
1957	697.2	680.9	16.3
1958	721.3	679.5	41.8
1959	746.2	720.4	25.8
1960	771.9	736.8	35.1
1961	798.6	755.3	43.3
1962	826.4	799.1	27.3
1963	857.1	830.7	26.4
1964	890.3	874.4	15.9
1965	925.0	925.9	−0.9
1966	960.8	981.0	−20.2
1967	996.3	1,007.7	−11.4
1968	1,031.7	1,051.8	−20.1
1969	1,068.3	1,078.8	−10.5
1970	1,106.2	1,075.3	30.9
1971	1,145.5	1,107.5	38.0
1972	1,186.1	1,171.1	15.0
1973	1,227.0	1,235.0	−8.0
1974	1,264.2	1,217.8	46.4
1975	1,302.1	1,202.3	99.8
1976	1,341.1	1,271.0	70.1
1977	1,381.4	1,332.7	48.7

Source: *Economic Report of the President, 1978, 1979.*

The United States financed its overall balance-of-payments deficit through the issue of dollar liabilities, and surplus countries were thus forced either to accept the dollars or revalue their currencies. Economic policy was finally directed to the inflation in the spring of 1968 when taxes were raised, followed by adoption of a restrictive monetary policy at the end of the year. In 1970 the anti-inflationary policy took hold and real income of the country declined. Unemployment rose rapidly from 3.5 percent to close to 6 percent by the year's end. In the face of the growing recession, the government shifted gears and turned its policies toward stimulation. Monetary policy was made easier and fiscal policy also became less restrictive with the reduction of the full-employment budget surplus by $5 billion. Nevertheless attempts to reflate the economy were restrained because of concern about inflation. The restrictive policies of 1968 and 1969 had stopped the growth of the real economy in 1970 but hardly reduced the inflation rate (as measured by the GNP deflator which rose at a 5.5 percent annual rate) at all. The stagflation of 1970 set the stage for the abrupt shift in economic policy the following year and marked the beginning of the end of the Bretton Woods system.

In the early months of 1971 the economy seemed to be on the path to recovery, but as the temporary stimulus from the ending of a major strike in the automobile industry ebbed, the economy began to falter. Unemployment remained stubbornly close to 6 percent. Inflation was reduced in the first quarter but then refused to fall further. Furthermore the balance of payments, which had been a worry for a number of years as U.S. competitiveness faltered, began to deteriorate rapidly. With the recovery in domestic output, imports began to rise quickly and for the first time since 1893 the United States incurred a balance-of-trade deficit (beginning in the second quarter). Moreover, a decline in short-term interest rates relative to those abroad encouraged private capital to move out of the United States, and there were also signs of a speculative outflow.

American policymakers surveying the economy during the summer faced a dilemma: the low rate of growth and the high unemployment rate indicated that the economy needed more stimulus. But the Nixon administration, with an election due in 1972, was not prepared to stick with a policy that would worsen the inflation and balance-of-payments problems. Its response was the New Economic Policy of August 15, 1971. To handle the balance-of-payments problem, the United States suspended the convertibility of the dollar into gold or other reserve assets for official holders. A temporary surcharge was imposed on imports and it was announced that the United States sought a devaluation of the dollar. These moves provoked a massive flow of capital out of the United States and the official settlements recorded a staggering $30 billion deficit for the year. Although it was not their intention, these acts set the stage for ending the Bretton Woods system.

The U.S. Balance of Payments and the Breakdown of Bretton Woods

The United States was undoubtedly more responsible than any other country for ending the Bretton Woods system. It was by far the largest economy and the dollar was the key currency in the system. Nevertheless the United

States was not solely to blame for the disintegration and was less culpable than some others for prolonging the process. Since the cornerstone of the system was the fixed-exchange-rate regime, and since countries were required to state par values for the currencies and then defend them in the exchange market, the system required that countries correct their balance-of payments disequilibriums primarily through internal means. Corrective action frequently depended on policy decisions that conflicted with domestic goals.

Governments were often able to avoid difficult problems during the early years of U.S. hegemony after World War II because the United States managed its strong balance-of-payments surplus by giving financial transfers (the Marshall Plan), opening its market to other countries, and permitting other countries to discriminate against American goods and services. Moreover, many countries devalued their currencies in terms of dollars, which acted to appreciate the dollar itself.

As European countries and Japan regained their economic strength, the underlying surplus of the United States was corrected, but without an automatic adjustment mechanism, equilibrium proved hard to sustain. About 1965 the United States began to develop an underlying balance-of-payments deficit whose correction proved impossible under the Bretton Woods system. For two decades while the dollar was the key currency, American traders had been free of worry about exchange-rate risks, American balance-of-payments deficits had been almost automatically financed, and American financial institutions had easily spread their activities to other countries. As the dollar became more and more overvalued, however, the disadvantages of the Bretton Woods system became more evident. The United States was responsible for maintaining the stability of the financial system and that responsibility proved to be incompatible with efforts to devalue the dollar.

The growing overvaluation of the dollar began to impinge on the economy at a number of points. Export markets were lost and import penetration became severe. American firms devoted an increasing share of their productive capital to other countries through direct investment. As long as the economy had excess demand, the problem was manageable and even helped to contain inflation. When overvaluation became a problem after the 1970 recession, the United States attempted to devalue the dollar. Although the depreciation of the dollar began in June 1970, the devaluation was small until August 15, 1971. Thereafter the pace quickened, the dollar depreciating about 8 percent after the Smithsonian agreement in December 1971 and a further 2 percent in March 1972. The dollar's value was stabilized for close to a year but then fell 15 percent from the May 1970 level with the monetary upset in February

1973. The Bretton Woods system finally collapsed with the end of fixed exchange rates in the following month.

The U.S. Inflation and the Rise of Raw Material Prices

Reducing the U.S. balance-of-payments deficit was just one of the objectives of the New Economic Policy of August 15, 1971. Its major domestic purpose was to stimulate the economy while slowing inflation. To fight the inflation, an incomes policy was instituted which in its first phase froze prices and wages for ninety days and in its second severely limited price and wage increases.[1] To boost the economy, tax reductions were enacted in December in the Revenue Act of 1971 and monetary policy was eased during the course of 1972. The economy performed very well in 1972.[2] During the year real output expanded by 7.5 percent, much above the growth of potential GNP, so that the GNP gap was reduced and unemployment declined. The expansion was fueled by stimulative fiscal policy—the full employment budget shifted into deficit—and the easing of monetary policy in the first half of the year. Despite the rapid growth of income, inflation was reduced under the controls program. Even the balance-of-payments performance was reasonably hopeful given the domestic expansion.[3] The deficit in the current account peaked in the first half of the year and then improved. The official settlements improved substantially but continued to show a large deficit.

Nevertheless the controls program had its shortcomings. The economic picture was clouded by the knowledge that inflation was being restrained not cured, particularly since the pace of monetary expansion was inconsistent with stable prices. Also, certain prices that could not be controlled—principally auction prices of domestic agricultural products and import prices for raw materials—rose dramatically. Furthermore, because the costs of the controls program, in the form of retardation and distortion of economic activity and inequities of various types, would become greater the longer the

1. During the control period, price increases were less than expected given wage increases, but wage increases were about what would have been expected given the actual path of price changes. Robert Gordon, "The Response of Wages and Prices to the First Two Years of Controls," *Brookings Papers on Economic Activity, 3:1973.* (Hereafter *BPEA.*)

2. Some political scientists point to the fact that 1972 was a presidential election year as evidence that the U.S. economy follows a four-year political cycle. See Edward Tufte, *Political Control of the Economy* (Princeton University Press, 1978).

3. The current account of the balance of payments may well deteriorate immediately after a devaluation when measured in the currency of the devaluing country, although it does not follow a J curve automatically. Stephen P. Magee, "The Welfare Effects of Restrictions on U.S. Trade," *BPEA, 3:1972.*

controls remained in effect, a much less restrictive third phase of the price control program was introduced at the end of the year.

Domestic economic policy in the United States was too expansionary in 1972–73 and thus the major cause of the subsequent inflation. The false sense of security concerning inflation that price controls induce encourages an excessively stimulative policy. When controls are given up, as they must be in order to avoid even greater economic damage, the suppressed inflation bursts forth and the earlier economic gains are lost. Thus the United States faced a serious problem of inflation even without the many and serious external complications.

The explosion of raw material prices during 1972–73 had an important impact on the United States because it is a producer and exporter of commodities as well as a consumer and importer and domestic prices for agricultural products are determined by world markets. The UN price index of all internationally traded commodities (based on 1970) which had stood at 108 in the fourth quarter of 1971 had reached 219 by the fourth quarter of 1973. (Actually, raw material prices had been rising since 1969, but double-digit increases did not begin until 1972.)

One factor in the price rise was the sharp increase in demand for primary commodities by producers of industrial goods in the United States, Europe, and Japan. Demand in the United States resulted from an unusually high rate of real growth—from the first quarter of 1972 it averaged 7.5 percent for five quarters (table 2-2), twice the rate of growth of its potential. On the supply side, U.S. prices were affected by the shortfall in the output of grains in the rest of the world in 1972. The American corn crop had been reduced by blight in 1970–71, but most of the variance of output had been absorbed through inventory reductions. World demand for U.S. exports, however, led to substantial price increases since U.S. grain inventories were low. Speculation added to the price increases as commodity trade became an appealing investment.

The United States and the Oil Crisis

Inflation and concern about it dominated the U.S. economy in 1973. The growth of real output decelerated as the economy reached full capacity.[4] Excess demand combined with the ending of price controls gave a decided upward push to prices, as did continuing rises in the prices of imported commodities. When the uneasy truce in international capital markets was broken,

4. The economy operated above its potential in 1973 (see table 2-1), although this was not realized at the time.

Table 2-2. *Percent Change in U.S. Gross National Product and Exports and Imports of Goods and Services, by Year and Quarter, 1970–77*

Year and quarter	GNP	Exports	Imports
1970	−0.3	7.9	3.5
First	−1.4	17.4	4.3
Second	0.2	3.0	3.0
Third	2.9	−1.8	−8.4
Fourth	−3.9	−7.7	5.5
1971	3.0	1.2	4.3
First	9.2	8.5	0.6
Second	2.9	9.5	27.9
Third	2.8	8.7	1.7
Fourth	3.4	−35.1	−22.6
1972	5.7	7.1	10.9
First	7.6	39.1	57.5
Second	7.9	−5.7	−12.0
Third	5.2	20.7	4.3
Fourth	8.5	20.2	18.7
1973	5.5	20.3	5.3
First	9.5	39.0	18.9
Second	0.4	8.0	−7.8
Third	1.7	9.7	−7.5
Fourth	2.0	10.9	−6.6
1974	−1.4	6.4	−3.5
First	−4.0	9.7	1.0
Second	−1.9	1.7	0.0
Third	−2.5	−6.9	−7.7
Fourth	−5.5	10.5	1.0
1975	−1.3	−3.3	−12.6
First	−10.0	−19.1	−37.3
Second	6.3	9.8	−37.0
Third	10.9	12.4	29.3
Fourth	3.0	12.9	20.8
1976	5.7	6.5	19.3
First	8.5	0.9	33.3
Second	4.9	8.6	13.0
Third	3.8	11.8	13.6
Fourth	1.2	−2.9	11.2
1977	4.9	2.4	10.2
First	6.0	−0.8	8.1
Second	5.8	7.4	9.3
Third	5.7	7.6	1.4
Fourth	3.3	−19.0	21.3

Sources: U.S. Department of Commerce, *Business Conditions Digest*, November 1977, November 1978, and *Survey of Current Business*, vol. 58 (September 1978).

resulting in further loss of confidence in the dollar, a second dollar devaluation, and finally the suspension of the par value system in March, policymakers designed a long-term strategy to resist inflation.

Their hopes of success were crushed by the renewal of hostilities in the Middle East and the ensuing energy crisis. In terms of its economic consequences, the crisis probably affected the United States less than many countries, but the disruption it caused with respect to prices, real output, and financial markets was nevertheless substantial.

Once the Arab embargo on shipment of oil to the United States ended, the most serious problem became the rise in oil prices. The price of imported crude oil, which once had been lower than that of domestic oil, went above it because domestic oil was constrained by a complicated control system. The price of domestic oil was allowed to rise but not to the international level. The rise in oil prices increased domestic inflation, raised the relative price of energy, and worsened the terms of trade of the United States. The relative rise in oil prices induced further inflation as higher energy costs were passed along into higher product prices and subsequently into higher wages.

The rise in oil prices also affected the level and distribution of real output in the United States. The deterioration in the terms of trade reduced real income and caused a decline in domestic output as consumers diverted larger portions of their income to energy. In the short run, purchases of automobiles were particularly depressed. There was a secondary contraction of domestic output as monetary policy did not accommodate the induced inflation.[5] The crisis not only involved a transfer of income to foreign oil producers but also a shift of income to domestic energy producers. Furthermore, producers saved a larger share of their marginal income than consumers which depressed current output. The rise in the price of oil may have caused losses (measured in 1973 prices) as high as $20 billion in 1974, $50 billion in 1975, and $67 billion in 1976.

The American-owned multinational energy companies were major actors in the worldwide energy drama. When the petroleum-producing countries nationalized the properties of the oil companies, they retained the companies as operators of the facilities under profitable service contracts. Profits realized on oil inventories were part of the reason that U.S. earnings on foreign investment rose sharply in 1974. Thus the U.S. balance-of-payments deterioration was eased by the profits of American oil companies, but those

5. George L. Perry, "The United States," in Edward R. Fried and Charles L. Schultze, eds., *Higher Oil Prices and the World Economy: The Adjustment Problem* (Brookings Institution, 1975).

profits were unhelpful in the political process of designing an energy policy for the United States.

The United States and the World Recession and Weak Recovery

The recession that began in the United States in 1974 was the longest and most severe since the Great Depression of the 1930s. Output declined for five consecutive quarters, almost twice the length of the typical postwar downturn. As seen in table 2-1, actual GNP fell short of potential by $99.8 billion in 1975—almost 8 percent of total U.S. output. Unemployment rose from 4.6 percent in October 1973 to 8.9 percent in May 1975. Also the nature of the unemployment problem changed, with the labor force including a rising proportion of nonwhite workers, women, and teenagers, whose spells of unemployment are more frequent and longer than normal. The liberalization of unemployment compensation along with the compositional shift in the economy increased the natural rate of unemployment. This rise in the rate of unemployment at which significant inflationary pressures are generated from labor shortages complicated policymaking during the subsequent recovery. A further significant aspect of this recession was its simultaneous appearance in other countries signaling the perpetuation of the pattern of synchronization that characterized the previous upswing.

The downturn of the American economy grew out of the previous expansion. Actual GNP exceeded potential in 1973 by $8 billion with all the consequences typical of an overheated economy. Spot shortages occurred in product markets; delivery schedules were lengthened and were still missed; labor markets tightened and skilled labor was critically short in many parts of the economy. Since the economy hit capacity ceilings, a slowdown was inevitable. However, the situation was aggravated and the subsequent downturn intensified because of the breakdown of the international monetary system, the explosion of raw material prices, and the stagflation brought on by the oil crisis. These international factors so undermined confidence in the economy that personal consumption was reduced (household savings rate rose sharply) and business investment declined.

In 1974 the monetary authorities took a stand against inflation, driving interest rates so high that construction activity collapsed. Fiscal policy automatically became more restrictive as inflation pushed people into higher marginal tax brackets. The authorities even proposed a small tax increase despite the fact that the economy was already nine months into a recession—evidence that inflation was at that moment of greater concern than unemployment. With the recession continuing, unemployment began to rise rapidly in the second half of 1974 and policy changed. Monetary policy was eased and short-term interest rates began to decline in August. By the end of the year the government proposed a personal tax reduction with strong congressional backing.

The United States was not the only country that was depressed. Germany and Japan were too, and this caused the world economy to worsen. All other oil-importing countries were also depressed by the same international developments, and the recession in the three major countries increased the weakness of other industrial countries and of developing countries as well. Real imports of the United States stagnated in 1974 and declined by 12.6 percent in 1975 (table 2-2). In fact, total world trade volume in 1975 declined for the first time since World War II. Thus the reduction in international trade spread the recession to other countries. And as commodity prices began to decline, the recession's effect on primary-producing countries became more pronounced.

The spread of the recession outward from the United States helped mitigate deflationary pressures in the United States (and even more so in Japan). Between the second quarters of 1974 and 1975, U.S. net exports rose by $10 billion while real GNP declined by $43 billion (both in 1972 dollars). Without the cushioning rise of net exports, the decline in real output would have been greater. Similarly the decline in raw material prices helped stem the double-digit inflation, setting the stage for stimulative policy measures.

Although monetary policy had already been eased, fiscal policy was chosen as the principal instrument to revive the economy of the United States. Thus a substantial tax reduction in the form of a personal tax cut and liberalized investment credits was given in the second quarter of 1975 and government expenditures were increased. The economy responded immediately. The ensuing recovery was among the longest peacetime expansions ever recorded. The number of new jobs created increased at a rate of over 3 percent a year, leading to a truly remarkable rise in employment from 83 million at the bottom of the recession to almost 96 million by the end of 1978. Despite the improvement in the economy, long-term concerns remained. How was inflation to be conquered? Was the mix between government and private expenditures becoming too heavily weighted on the government side? How were private plant and equipment expenditures to be made adequate for the needs of the economy? How was the high rate of unemployment ever to be reduced? How was balance-of-payments equilibrium to be achieved? All of these questions became more pressing even as the economic recovery was prolonged.

Channels of Economic Instability

Like other countries, the United States transmits and receives impulses from abroad. Because its economy is so much larger than other countries', and less dependent on world trade than most, the United States is generally seen as a sender rather than a receiver of economic impulses. The United States is increasingly affected by foreign economic factors, however. The results of outside disturbances can be dramatic, as the impact of the oil crisis proved.

The Exchange Rate and Monetary Balance

Under a fixed-exchange-rate system the overall balance in the balance of payments is a powerful force linking countries together. If excessive monetary expansion is reflected as a large deficit in one country's overall balance of payments, its trading partners show a corresponding surplus. To prevent an appreciation of its currency, each of the surplus countries must sell its currency for that of the deficit country. The very act of intervening in the exchange market, however, creates more money in the surplus country—in fact it is high-powered money that can be used by the banking system to expand credit further.

During the regime of fixed exchange rates, the U.S. official settlements balance was a particularly potent means of transmitting economic impulses.[6] World official monetary reserves rose when the United States was in deficit and fell when the United States was in surplus (table 2-3). During the 1950s and 1960s, world reserves grew at a very modest pace. From the beginning of 1970 through the third quarter of 1971, world reserves increased by $39.8 billion, reflecting new issues of special drawing rights and the growth both of the Eurodollar market and of the cumulative U.S. deficit to $33.7 billion. The deterioration of the U.S. official settlements was caused mainly by capital flows; indeed during 1970 the current account improved. Even when the current and capital accounts were moving in the same direction, the magnitudes in the latter were larger.

Along with the increasing U.S. deficit there was a monetary explosion,

6. The official settlements balance of the balance of payments is the link among countries that monetarists stress. See Alexander K. Swoboda, "Monetary Approaches to Worldwide Inflation," in Lawrence B. Krause and Walter S. Salant, eds., *Worldwide Inflation: Theory and Recent Experience* (Brookings Institution, 1977), pp. 9–50.

Table 2-3. *U.S. Official Settlements Balance and World Monetary Reserves, by Year and Quarter, 1970–77*

Year and quarter	Growth of U.S. money supply (percent)[a]		U.S. official settlements balance (millions of dollars)	U.S. interest rates (percent)		World reserves (millions of SDRs)	
	M_1[b]	M_2[c]		Commercial paper (4–6 months)	Eurodollar deposits (3 months)	Level	Change[a]
1970	3.9	4.1	−9,838	7.72	8.51	86,011	8,565
First	3.5	1.4	−1,974	8.56	9.40	81,300	3,561
Second	4.8	6.8	−2,067	8.17	8.86	83,845	2,545
Third	5.0	10.1	−2,611	7.84	8.33	86,955	3,110
Fourth	5.7	9.9	−3,186	6.29	7.45	91,945	4,990
1971	6.7	11.6	−29,753	5.11	6.58	123,237	37,226
First	7.1	13.9	−4,718	4.59	5.52	99,390	7,445
Second	9.3	14.0	−6,462	5.04	6.70	104,975	5,585
Third	6.8	8.1	−12,703	5.74	7.66	117,560	12,585
Fourth	2.8	7.7	−5,870	5.07	6.41	121,705	4,145
1972	7.1	10.6	−9,721	4.69	5.46	146,770	23,533
First	7.8	12.0	−2,506	4.06	5.22	128,755	7,050
Second	7.4	9.8	−741	4.58	4.98	135,120	6,365
Third	8.3	10.8	−5,590	4.94	5.50	141,630	6,510
Fourth	9.1	10.4	−1,517	5.33	5.94	146,255	4,625
1973	7.5	9.6	−5,072	8.15	9.24	152,265	5,495
First	8.2	9.7	−9,993	6.28	7.37	148,595	2,340
Second	5.6	7.9	769	7.47	8.47	151,465	2,870
Third	5.2	7.6	939	9.87	11.00	155,898	4,433
Fourth	5.3	9.0	2,978	8.98	10.15	152,301	−3,597

1974	5.5	8.4	−9,476	9.87	11.01	180,177	27,912
First	7.2	10.2	1,406	8.30	9.04	155,402	3,101
Second	4.7	7.1	−4,048	10.46	11.26	165,375	9,973
Third	3.6	6.1	−1,683	11.53	12.96	177,421	12,046
Fourth	4.3	6.5	−4,049	9.05	10.43	180,338	2,917
1975	4.4	7.7	−6,564	6.33	6.99	194,458	14,281
First	2.1	6.3	−2,194	6.56	7.43	184,435	4,097
Second	6.3	9.8	−1,415	5.96	6.38	186,058	1,623
Third	6.8	8.9	3,064	6.67	7.19	190,367	4,309
Fourth	2.9	6.7	−1,918	6.12	6.79	194,296	3,929
1976	5.3	9.9	−15,552	5.35	5.58	222,357	27,899
First	4.7	10.6	−3,132	5.29	5.54	202,279	7,983
Second	6.9	10.0	−2,515	5.57	5.86	207,374	5,095
Third	3.8	8.7	−2,602	5.53	5.68	213,218	5,844
Fourth	7.4	12.7	−7,175	4.99	5.25	222,144	8,926
1977	7.3	10.7	−36,559	5.60	6.00	244,848	22,491
First	7.0	10.9	−5,346	4.81	5.11	228,759	6,615
Second	8.3	9.1	−7,848	5.24	5.56	239,035	10,276
Third	8.1	9.9	−8,414	5.81	6.21	249,211	10,176
Fourth	7.4	8.1	−15,219	6.59	7.11	262,837	13,626

Sources: U.S. Department of Commerce, *Survey of Current Business*, various issues; Council of Economic Advisers, *Economic Indicators*, various issues; International Monetary Fund, *International Financial Statistics*, September 1978.
a. Change over twelve-month period.
b. Currency in hands of public plus demand deposits in commercial banks.
c. Time deposits in commercial banks plus M1.

with reserves growing 11 percent in 1970, 43.3 percent in 1971, and 19 percent in 1972. This monetary explosion was a major cause of worldwide inflation.[7] Some of the growth in international reserves could have been avoided if the Bretton Woods system of fixed exchange rates had been abandoned shortly after August 15, 1971. Of the total cumulative $60 billion deficit of the United States as of March 1973, about $40 billion was incurred after August 1971. If the floating-exchange-rate system had been in operation, changes in exchange rates could have alleviated much of the pressure that forced central banks to intervene in the foreign-exchange market during that period. The United States probably would have been willing to see the dollar decline at that time since the New Economic Policy was formulated in part to free U.S. economic policy from the constraint of the balance of payments.

The U.S. official settlements balance remained in deficit until the abandonment of fixed exchange rates. Then the account swung around and the United States had a surplus from the second quarter of 1973 through the first quarter of 1974. Beginning in this period and certainly following it, world reserve growth and the U.S. official settlements deficit were in part decoupled. Other sources of reserve growth, including loans from the International Monetary Fund and the growth of Eurocurrency markets, became more important. In 1975, however, the U.S. official settlements balance and world reserve growth were tied together again. As central banks attempted to fix exchange rates, the semblance of a Bretton Woods system was recreated with all its difficulties.

After the end of the Bretton Woods system, the dollar went through a number of cycles (table 2-4). It declined till July 1973, then advanced to a peak in January 1974. In a second cycle it declined to a trough in May 1974 and then appreciated to a peak in September 1974. It reached a third trough in March 1975 and then a high in September 1975. These cycles at first showed some tendency to be damped, as if a learning process were taking place or an existing disequilibrium were being overcome in stages that could eventually reduce the swings in values.[8] After September 1975 the dollar remained quite stable until the last quarter of 1977.

It is clear, however, that the dollar became overvalued during 1975. From the beginning of floating in March 1973 until September 1975 the United States ran a cumulative balance-of-payments deficit on official settlements of only $4 billion—roughly the equivalent of OPEC surplus countries' desired

7. Harold Van B. Cleveland and W. H. Bruce Brittain, *The Great Inflation: A Monetary View* (Washington: National Planning Association, 1976).

8. The turning points were generally related to changes in relative short-term interest rates, although the failure of the Herstatt Bank in Germany and the Franklin National in the United States in 1974 also played a part.

Table 2-4. *Percent Change in U.S., Australian, and Japanese Effective Exchange Rates, by Year and Month, 1970-77*[a]

Year and month	Percent change in effective exchange rate			Year and month	Percent change in effective exchange rate		
	United States	Australia	Japan		United States	Australia	Japan
1970	−1.43	−0.92	0.23	1974	−16.77	12.94	12.49
January	−0.31	−0.56	0.62	January	−11.81	20.06	11.73
February	−0.32	−0.42	0.60	February	−13.59	18.09	13.34
March	−0.39	−0.42	0.61	March	−15.23	15.54	16.10
April	−0.46	−0.44	0.41	April	−16.31	13.89	17.21
May	−0.43	−0.46	0.18	May	−17.09	13.34	16.03
June	−1.61	−0.82	−0.05	June	−16.16	14.54	14.94
July	−1.81	−1.07	−0.19	July	−15.51	15.40	11.84
August	−2.26	−1.34	0.04	August	−14.20	17.98	8.12
September	−2.47	−1.49	0.09	September	−13.66	15.42	10.04
October	−2.30	−1.41	0.16	October	−14.06	3.82	10.93
November	−2.38	−1.34	0.14	November	−14.47	3.61	10.18
December	−2.43	−1.31	0.16	December	−15.16	3.54	9.38
1971	−4.24	−1.07	2.01	1975	−14.35	3.08	11.18
January	−2.72	−0.80	−0.13	January	−15.99	3.48	8.77
February	−2.98	−0.46	−0.15	February	−16.82	3.32	11.15
March	−3.02	−0.43	−0.15	March	−17.35	3.30	12.19
April	−2.95	−0.45	−0.12	April	−16.20	3.27	11.34
May	−3.24	−0.66	−0.30	May	−15.95	3.17	11.61
June	−2.91	−0.69	−0.31	June	−15.91	3.20	10.87
July	−3.02	−0.79	−0.38	July	−13.85	3.39	11.53
August	−3.83	−0.70	−0.35	August	−12.34	2.70	12.32
September	−5.36	−1.63	4.28	September	−11.88	2.51	11.95
October	−6.34	−1.85	6.05	October	−11.96	2.27	11.15
November	−6.57	−2.03	6.75	November	−12.24	2.34	11.02
December	−7.95	−2.09	8.91	December	−11.69	2.40	10.26
1972	−10.16	−3.33	13.98	1976	−11.59	0.87	14.70
January	−8.86	−2.28	10.80	January	−12.01	2.42	10.48
February	−9.75	−3.66	13.20	February	−12.24	2.36	11.55
March	−10.28	−4.17	13.98	March	−11.71	2.36	12.56
April	−10.24	−3.98	13.63	April	−11.35	2.18	13.52
May	−10.47	−3.96	13.22	May	−11.27	2.22	13.74
June	−10.87	−4.05	13.89	June	−11.18	2.16	13.93
July	−10.60	−3.57	14.63	July	−11.53	2.14	15.58
August	−10.55	−3.50	14.64	August	−11.54	−2.28	16.99
September	−10.44	−3.41	14.74	September	−12.23	2.04	18.12
October	−10.23	−3.10	14.98	October	−12.08	2.22	16.68
November	−9.96	−2.81	15.13	November	−11.46	0.56	15.45
December	−9.65	−1.36	14.92	December	−10.47	−12.53	17.73
1973	−15.72	7.70	21.24	1977	−11.04	11.61	29.04
January	−9.72	3.87	13.88	January	−11.03	−10.79	19.43
February	−13.26	5.56	21.11	February	−10.60	−10.69	21.49
March	−15.77	6.39	26.17	March	−10.27	−10.56	23.54
April	−15.03	7.39	24.79	April	−10.68	−10.70	25.68
May	−15.64	6.59	24.62	May	−10.74	−10.67	24.58
June	−17.15	5.14	23.22	June	−10.72	−10.79	26.69
July	−18.70	4.06	21.66	July	−11.41	−10.88	30.03
August	−17.60	5.02	22.40	August	−10.52	−11.91	29.74
September	−17.51	9.35	21.81	September	−10.35	−11.82	29.96
October	−17.97	10.21	20.95	October	−10.91	−12.51	35.62
November	−15.77	13.58	17.11	November	−11.75	−13.56	40.62
December	−14.56	15.28	17.21	December	−13.50	−14.47	41.43

Source: Morgan Guaranty Trust Co. of New York, *World Financial Markets*, August 1976 through January 1978.

a. Based on pre-June 1970 parities with fifteen major currencies weighted according to bilateral trade in manufacturing with each country.

investment in liquid U.S. assets. From the fourth quarter of 1975 through the first quarter of 1978, the deficit became progressively larger. At first the negative effect on the value of the dollar was small because central banks of non-OPEC countries—principally Japan and Germany in 1976 and Japan, the United Kingdom, and Italy in 1977—were buying dollars to keep down the value of their own currencies; but they were thereby raising the value of the dollar above its equilibrium. Overvaluation of the dollar was one of the factors that led to the deterioration of the U.S. trade and current accounts in 1976 and 1977. By the fourth quarter of 1977 the U.S. balance-of-payments deficit had become so large that the dollar's value could not be held up any longer despite heavy government intervention. Hence the dollar depreciated by 3.25 percent in that quarter and further in 1978.

Starting with the beginning of floating, the policy of the United States was that the value of the dollar should be determined solely by supply and demand for currency in the foreign-exchange market and government intervention should be limited to ensuring orderly markets. Thus if the dollar rose or fell in an orderly fashion, the United States was prepared to accept the market's judgment. This policy was followed even after the dollar had declined at the end of 1977 and a disorderly market had appeared in early January 1978. However, when the dollar dropped further in mid-1978, the policy was changed as the devaluation of the dollar was seen as a factor increasing domestic inflation and was greatly resented by other countries.[9] Despite the new policy, the dollar dropped sharply during October 1978. This swiftly brought forth a new batch of measures on November 1, 1978, as the decline of the dollar was seen to be undermining domestic financial markets. The measures included a decided tightening of domestic monetary policy and more aggressive intervention in foreign-exchange markets made possible by a pool of assets of $30 billion assembled for that purpose. The October decline was quickly reversed in November 1978.

The change in American policy meant that the United States would prevent a sharp decline of the dollar that it viewed as undesirable. It also meant that Japan and other countries would not be able to determine the value of their own currencies without concurrence from the United States. That had only been possible because of the passive attitude of the United States toward the value of the dollar. In the future the United States is likely to resist efforts of other countries to overvalue the dollar.

9. In August 1978 the president announced that he was concerned about the value of the dollar and he directed the chief economic policymakers to design a program to strengthen the dollar. This position was reiterated when the president addressed the annual meeting of the International Monetary Fund in September 1978.

Changing Trade Prices

Even after a number of years of excess demand during the late 1960s, inflation in the United States during 1969 and 1970 was not very high by later standards. Nevertheless, the rate of price increase and its tendency to accelerate during the 1970 recession and early in the subsequent recovery were viewed with alarm. The temporary price freeze initiated on August 15, 1971, and the price control program that followed it did suppress the inflation, as changes in the consumer price index and the wholesale price index for manufactured goods indicate (table 2-5). When price controls were relaxed in 1973 and the economy reached capacity ceilings, the suppressed inflation burst forth and double-digit price increases were recorded even before oil prices rose.

The first evidence of double-digit inflation appeared in import prices for food early in 1972 at the same time that the domestic WPI for farm products rose, indicating that the problem was worldwide. After a short lag, export prices for food also advanced sharply. As seen in the annual data, import prices increased before domestic or export prices, reflecting the devaluation of the dollar among other things. Even in 1973 when domestic prices were advancing rapidly with the easing of price controls, the prices of internationally traded goods were increasing even faster—just the reverse of the previous twenty years.[10]

Inflation continued to accelerate in 1974, the largest increases being for imported industrial raw materials, including petroleum. The increases can be traced through the WPI for manufactured products and finally the GNP deflator.[11] Just as agriculture led the upsurge of inflation, so it led on the downside. Some price declines in the WPI for farm products were recorded in 1974, reflecting the return to more normal production patterns and the be-

10. About half of the increase in a specially defined U.S. wholesale price index between November 1972 and August 1973 has been attributed to the combined impact of dollar devaluation and world agricultural price increases, with the latter variable being the more important determinant. Econometric study by William Nordhaus and John Shoven, "Inflation 1973: The Year of Infamy," *Challenge,* May–June 1974, pp. 14–22; summarized in Michael E. Levy, "International Influences on U.S. Inflation, 1971–1976," prepared for the Office of Economic Research, U.S. Department of Commerce, contract 6-36235 (September 7, 1977).

11. About 20 percent of the rise in the U.S. personal consumption deflator (which is similar in behavior to the CPI) between the third quarter of 1971 and the second quarter of 1974 is estimated to have been caused by the rise in world prices of raw materials (other than oil). Econometric study by Richard Berner and others, "International Sources of Domestic Inflation," in Joint Economic Committee, *Studies in Price Stability and Economic Growth,* Paper 3, 94 Cong. 1 sess. (GPO, 1975); summarized in Levy, "International Influences."

Table 2-5. Percent Change in Various U.S. Price Indexes, by Year and Quarter, 1970–77

Year and quarter	Chain (GNP deflator)	Consumer	Wholesale		Export[a]		Import		
			Manufactured goods	Farm products	Merchandise	Food, feeds, and beverages	All	Food, feeds, and beverages	Industrial materials and supplies
1970	5.3	4.7	3.7	1.8	5.7	3.3	6.3	10.1	3.6
First	5.8	3.8	5.4	11.9	-4.4	9.2	1.8	13.1	2.7
Second	5.1	5.2	2.5	-8.0	4.0	4.5	2.9	10.9	3.5
Third	3.5	3.1	3.1	-0.6	1.4	11.0	9.4	5.5	6.9
Fourth	5.6	4.4	1.9	-13.8	1.4	11.5	2.8	-0.3	-1.1
1971	5.0	3.4	3.4	1.7	3.2	6.2	5.2	0.3	3.1
First	6.8	1.7	3.9	18.6	12.6	11.1	8.8	-2.4	3.4
Second	4.6	5.7	4.1	10.6	-1.7	4.1	1.0	-2.7	1.5
Third	3.4	2.3	4.5	-19.0	-3.8	1.1	3.4	0.0	6.3
Fourth	2.1	2.9	0.0	19.2	4.9	-11.4	5.8	2.4	5.1
1972	4.1	3.0	3.5	10.7	3.0	5.2	7.4	7.1	6.2
First	5.4	2.9	5.7	13.5	5.6	5.7	7.4	4.4	5.1
Second	2.9	3.2	3.7	11.9	2.7	9.0	12.8	16.2	10.4
Third	4.0	3.8	4.0	27.7	0.7	7.0	5.4	12.7	4.9
Fourth	4.3	3.5	3.5	30.0	12.9	30.6	9.4	13.5	6.2
1973	6.0	7.4	9.6	41.0	16.8	54.6	17.8	22.5	20.0
First	6.4	-3.7	14.3	57.4	15.5	64.8	15.1	15.8	16.6
Second	7.1	9.5	15.9	53.5	18.7	56.6	34.0	33.9	26.3
Third	8.1	10.8	10.2	42.8	27.3	83.9	15.0	12.2	26.5
Fourth	8.5	9.7	5.8	-20.6	27.6	36.6	35.0	53.6	59.2

1974									
First	9.9	12.0	19.3	6.5	27.0	37.7	50.4	25.2	99.6
Second	10.7	15.6	25.4	15.6	32.7	45.0	65.5	4.0	176.0
Third	11.2	9.6	22.0	−59.7	14.5	−2.4	55.5	29.6	80.7
Fourth	12.8	12.7	28.9	31.0	26.6	0.3	26.8	35.6	20.3
	12.7	10.2	8.2	7.3	24.9	49.1	14.2	32.9	5.3
1975									
First	9.4	8.9	11.0	−0.5	11.8	−2.6	8.0	2.6	3.9
Second	9.5	6.0	2.8	−27.6	13.6	−6.1	4.1	1.8	0.3
Third	6.5	6.7	5.5	31.3	−2.6	−36.0	3.4	−12.1	−7.6
Fourth	7.4	6.6	6.8	22.5	−2.4	−16.1	−14.0	−44.9	−13.5
	6.1	5.4	3.9	−1.6	1.8	−7.9	0.3	−9.8	−4.7
1976									
First	5.6	4.3	4.6	2.3	3.6	−9.2	3.2	4.9	3.2
Second	4.5	0.2	3.0	−14.2	6.5	−11.7	8.6	23.3	13.6
Third	5.0	5.9	6.6	17.1	3.8	−5.4	7.4	11.8	8.1
Fourth	5.2	4.6	4.5	−12.5	4.8	5.5	6.0	19.0	5.7
	6.3	3.4	5.1	5.7	8.3	−4.9	4.0	9.7	7.0
1977									
First	6.2	5.8	6.2	0.8	4.0	−0.7	8.5	21.4	8.1
Second	6.6	8.6	8.1	22.1	3.7	17.1	13.2	43.5	16.4
Third	7.3	8.4	7.5	−19.2	5.9	18.4	9.6	45.5	8.0
Fourth	4.6	2.7	3.2	−22.4	−2.3	−51.3	5.2	−21.1	1.1
	6.5	3.7	5.4	13.8	3.0	−10.2	0.9	−12.0	3.0

Sources: *Economic Report of the President, 1973–1979*; and information provided by Foreign Trade Section, Bureau of the Census, U.S. Department of Commerce, August 1979.
a. Based on unit value rather than actual prices.

ginning of the worldwide recession, and by 1975 the export and import price indexes of food products were falling, as was the index for imported industrial supplies. After a brief calm in 1976, inflation once again increased; this time the causes were mainly domestic. The Carter administration, which took office in January 1977 with a rather relaxed view of inflation, adopted a very stimulative economic policy for fiscal 1978. That proved to be a mistake, both because the economy had enough momentum to sustain itself and because the increase in the fiscal deficit complicated the problem of containing inflation. Failure to deal with the domestic roots of inflation—indeed many government policies, such as the sharp rise in the minimum wage, made it worse—permitted cost increases to become more general and widespread. The administration finally decided to take action when the inflation undermined confidence in the dollar.

Volume of International Trade

In the early 1970s U.S. imports grew faster than the gross national product in response to the weak competitive position of American producers (table 2-2). Similarly the U.S. share of world export markets was eroding because of weak competitiveness and also because productive capacity was growing faster in Japan and elsewhere than in the United States.

International trade was disrupted for a while following the adoption of the New Economic Policy in August of 1971. In the fourth quarter of 1971, both export and import volumes were sharply reduced, but both recovered in the first half of 1972. Until mid-1973, exports declined more than imports when trade was receding and grew slower than imports when trade was expanding. After the devaluation of the dollar, export volume grew rapidly (the fact that exports were not under the price control program may have contributed to the growth). With the recession, both exports and imports declined. In the subsequent recovery, import growth was very strong, faltering only when the rate of inventory accumulation decelerated. The high level of economic activity in the United States plus rising inflation made the United States an excellent market for other countries. But the weak state of economic activity in other industrial countries limited the market prospects for American exporters and forced foreign producers to sell even at concessional prices in order to sustain a minimum level of production capacity.[12]

---

12. Complaints against Japanese dumping of steel in the United States became so intense that the government instituted a "trigger price" mechanism to control it. Though the new mechanism gave less protection to American companies than authorized under

Thus the U.S. trade balance and current account deteriorated sharply and reached record deficits after 1975.

The divergent trends of export and import volume—exports of goods and services as a share of GNP (measured in 1972 prices) declined from a peak of 7.6 percent in 1974 to 7.4 percent in 1977 while imports rose from 6.3 percent to 6.7 percent—are another bit of evidence that the dollar had become overvalued and that a correction was necessary.

The relation of net exports of goods and services (exports minus imports) to gross national product is an important measure of an economy's link with other economies.[13] For many countries, net exports are a major determinant of gross national product. For the United States net exports have usually been below 1 percent of GNP and seldom above 1.5 percent, which lends support to the notion that the American economy is seldom moved by what happens abroad. Nevertheless, net exports can at times be important—in 1970 and 1974–77, changes in net exports were quite large in relation to changes in GNP (table 2-6). Furthermore, net exports have usually been a countercyclical or moderating force in the economy, weakening when the economy was growing stronger and strengthening when the economy was deteriorating. That relationship was sustained through the mid-1970s, alleviating fears that such moderating forces would be lost as the economic cycles of industrial countries became more synchronized. In 1977 the fact that the U.S. economy maintained its forward momentum was an important ingredient in heading off an incipient recession in Japan and moderating the stagnation in Europe. The decline of net exports was, however, a continual drag on the U.S. recovery—between 1975 and 1977 it reduced U.S. growth by 0.6 percent per year. It was directly responsible for the huge deficits in the U.S. current account in 1975–78. Those deficits were matched by record growth in Japan's surplus and the gigantic imbalance was an increasingly irritating point of conflict between the United States and Japan.[14]

---

existing law, it was accepted by the American industry because it was faster acting and more certain than the cumbersome dumping procedure.

13. An increase in net exports induces an even larger increase in domestic output. The increase, expressed by the foreign trade multiplier, is the link on which Keynesian economics focuses. See William H. Branson, "A Keynesian Approach to Worldwide Inflation," in Krause and Salant, *Worldwide Inflation*, pp. 63–92.

14. In the United States, Japan was seen as unwilling or unable to properly stimulate its economy to reach announced growth targets, unwilling to significantly liberalize its import restraints, and (until mid-1978) improperly interfering with the exchange-rate mechanism by holding down the value of the yen. In Japan, the United States was seen as unwilling or unable to restrain its imports of oil and control its domestic inflation. The problems of the dollar were not regarded as exclusively or particularly related to Japan.

Table 2-6. Value and Change in U.S. Gross National Product and Net Exports of Goods and Services, by Year and Quarter, 1970–77

Millions of dollars

Year and quarter	Current dollars				1972 dollars			
	GNP		Net exports		GNP		Net exports	
	Level	Change	Level	Change	Level	Change	Level	Change
1970	982.4	46.8	3.9	2.2	1,075.3	-3.6	1.4	2.7
First	964.2	10.9	3.9	1.6	1,073.6	-3.9	1.4	2.0
Second	976.5	12.3	4.4	0.5	1,074.1	0.5	1.4	0.0
Third	992.6	16.1	4.7	0.3	1,082.0	7.9	2.5	1.1
Fourth	996.3	3.7	2.7	-2.0	1,071.4	-10.6	0.3	-2.2
1971	1,063.4	81.0	1.6	-2.3	1,107.5	32.3	-0.6	-2.0
First	1,034.0	37.7	3.9	1.2	1,095.3	23.9	1.6	1.3
Second	1,096.2	22.2	1.4	-2.5	1,103.3	8.0	-1.4	-3.0
Third	1,072.4	16.2	1.9	0.5	1,111.0	7.7	-0.2	1.2
Fourth	1,091.2	18.8	-0.9	-2.8	1,120.5	9.5	-2.4	-2.2
1972	1,171.1	107.7	-3.3	-4.9	1,171.1	63.6	-3.3	-2.7
First	1,127.0	35.8	-4.6	-3.7	1,141.2	20.7	-5.7	-3.3
Second	1,156.7	29.7	-4.1	0.5	1,163.0	21.8	-4.4	1.3
Third	1,181.4	24.7	-2.3	1.8	1,178.0	15.0	-1.6	2.8
Fourth	1,219.4	38.0	-2.1	0.2	1,202.2	24.2	-1.4	0.2

Period								
1973	1,306.6	135.5	7.1	10.4	1,235.0	63.8	7.6	10.9
First	1,265.3	45.9	1.7	3.8	1,229.8	27.6	2.3	3.7
Second	1,288.4	23.1	4.3	2.6	1,231.1	1.3	5.7	3.4
Third	1,317.5	29.1	10.0	5.7	1,236.3	5.2	9.3	3.6
Fourth	1,355.1	37.6	12.7	2.7	1,242.6	6.3	12.9	3.6
1974	1,412.9	106.3	6.0	−1.1	1,217.8	−17.2	15.9	8.3
First	1,369.0	13.9	10.4	−2.3	1,230.2	−12.4	15.0	2.1
Second	1,400.1	31.1	3.2	−7.2	1,224.5	−5.7	15.4	0.4
Third	1,430.1	30.0	2.4	−0.8	1,216.9	−7.6	15.3	−0.1
Fourth	1,452.4	22.3	8.2	5.8	1,199.7	−17.2	17.9	2.6
1975	1,528.8	115.9	20.4	14.4	1,202.1	−15.7	22.5	6.6
First	1,453.0	0.6	15.4	7.2	1,169.8	−29.9	20.5	2.6
Second	1,496.6	43.6	24.3	9.1	1,188.2	18.4	24.5	4.0
Third	1,564.9	68.3	20.8	−3.5	1,220.7	32.5	22.8	−1.7
Fourth	1,600.0	35.1	20.8	0.0	1,229.8	9.1	22.3	0.5
1976	1,700.1	171.3	7.8	−12.6	1,274.7	68.9	16.0	−6.5
First	1,651.2	51.2	10.2	−10.6	1,256.0	26.2	16.8	−5.5
Second	1,691.9	40.7	10.2	0.0	1,271.5	15.5	16.4	−0.4
Third	1,727.3	35.4	7.9	−2.3	1,283.7	12.2	17.0	0.6
Fourth	1,755.4	28.1	3.0	−4.9	1,287.4	3.7	13.8	−3.2
1977	1,887.2	187.1	−11.2	−19.0	1,332.8	61.8	9.5	−6.5
First	1,806.8	51.4	−8.5	−11.5	1,306.7	19.3	11.2	−2.6
Second	1,867.0	60.2	−5.9	2.6	1,325.5	18.8	11.0	−0.2
Third	1,916.8	49.8	−7.0	−1.1	1,343.9	18.4	12.5	1.5
Fourth	1,958.1	41.3	−23.2	−16.2	1,354.5	10.6	3.1	−9.4

Sources: U.S. Department of Commerce, *Business Conditions Digest*, November 1977, and *Survey of Current Business*, vol. 58 (September 1978).

Capital Flows and Financial Intermediation

Financial links can be an important means of transmitting economic impulses, as the broad monetary consequences of the oil crisis for the United States revealed. The $15 billion rise in the value of U.S. oil imports contributed to a balance-of-trade deficit of over $5 billion in 1974. The American deficit was part of the world disequilibrium. The OPEC countries' current account surplus, which was $7.9 billion in 1973, ballooned to $67.4 billion in 1974 despite a 90 percent rise in the value of OPEC imports in that year.[15] The unprecedented surplus in the accounts of Saudi Arabia, Kuwait, and the United Arab Emirates was balanced by deficits in the accounts of oil-importing countries. Those deficits were financed, through financial intermediaries, by the OPEC countries themselves. A large portion of the OPEC investments was made in the United States or in dollar denominated assets.

Controls on U.S. foreign lending that had been maintained for balance-of-payments purposes ended in 1974. Tight money and high short-term interest rates attracted oil money to the United States, as seen in the $18 billion rise in U.S. liabilities ($12 billion greater than the previous year). American foreign short-term lending, however, expanded by an even greater amount—from $7 billion in 1973 to $21 billion in 1974 (table 2-7)—in response to both the developed and developing countries' need to pay higher oil bills. The deep recession in 1975 brought much lower interest rates to the United States. American short-term borrowing declined very sharply. American lending also declined but not nearly as much. Consequently net private lending was greater than in 1974 and much more of it went to developing countries. Also notable was the large increase in long-term lending as Americans bought a record number of new foreign bond issues.

The rapid rise in U.S. liabilities to foreign countries, particularly to OPEC countries, in 1974–78 and the similarly rapid increase in U.S. claims on foreigners, other than OPEC countries, are an indication of the important intermediary role that the United States and American financial institutions played in adjusting the international imbalance caused by the oil crisis. This intermediation function and the recycling of dollars through their overseas branches proved to be very profitable for American banks. The financial developments, however, contributed to the overexposure of the United States in the world financial system. The international role of the dollar increased just when it should have been reduced because of the declining importance of the United States in the world economy. The foreign exposure of Amer-

15. These figures, compiled by the U.S. Treasury, exclude official transfers; they differ in some respects from those reported by the IMF and the OECD.

ican banks, especially through loans to developing countries, continued to increase in 1976 and 1977, even after the U.S. current account went into deficit. Increases in private financial flows caused changes in the exchange rate, which led to further financial flows. Through most of 1977 this inter-action depended on interest-rate differentials, which could be managed through small adjustments in domestic monetary policy. With the United States in an overexposed position, however, foreign confidence in the dollar became an important factor in the behavior of U.S. financial markets. Their stability and that of the domestic economy were directly threatened when the dollar declined steeply in 1978. The United States was forced for the first time to make a large change in monetary policy toward restraint. It can no longer ignore the constraints that interdependent financial markets impose on domestic monetary policy.

The increasing interdependence of financial markets and complexity of financial management of the world economy has important implications for the Pacific basin.[16] As central banks increase the share of Japanese yen in their official reserves and private firms and individuals their use of yen for transactions, the role of the dollar and the overexposure of the U.S. financial system will be reduced. But the transition to a new equilibrium will be difficult.

A Change in Perspective

At the beginning of the 1970s the United States was enjoying the benefits of growing economic interdependence. To be sure, balance-of-payments deficits and the problems of certain import-competing industries caused concern from time to time, but in the main framers of American economic policy could ignore the rest of the world. By the mid-1970s the tensions of economic interdependence were all too visible. The energy crisis dramatized the change but was not the only element of it. Policymakers were forced to recognize the imported component of domestic inflation as well as the external drag on domestic efforts to stimulate real output.

Of course it was always recognized that the United States could not achieve its goal of a balance-of-payments equilibrium independent of events and policies of other countries. However, it was long believed that the United States could achieve its domestic goals related to growth (or employment)

16. In the Atlantic area the asset demand for German marks is beginning to have an impact on the dollar. The European Monetary System, if it is successful, should speed the process of portfolio diversification away from the dollar.

Table 2-7. Changes in the Flow of Capital into and out of the United States, by Year and Quarter, 1970–77
Millions of dollars

Year and quarter	Private capital		Public capital			
	U.S.-held foreign securities	Foreign-held U.S. securities	U.S. claims		U.S. liabilities	
			Long term	Short term	Long term	Short term
1970	−1,076	2,190	−431	−1,132	1,135	−5,419
First	−306	304	−367	−62	129	−1,711
Second	80	374	37	−375	385	−782
Third	−517	720	−117	−173	321	−870
Fourth	−333	792	16	−522	300	−2,056
1971	−1,113	2,289	−780	−3,429	134	−6,676
First	−408	559	−18	−583	51	−3,071
Second	−368	196	−152	−337	−16	−2,658
Third	−346	626	−284	−1,442	−160	−1,019
Fourth	9	908	−326	−1,067	259	72
1972	−619	4,507	−1,550	−210	743	4,826
First	−476	1,059	−263	−1,067	141	544
Second	−318	961	−410	415	291	1,632
Third	203	718	−340	−958	187	439
Fourth	−28	1,769	−537	1,400	124	2,211

1973						
First	−672	4,042	−1,329	−7,029	525	5,212
Second	55	1,718	−409	−3,388	397	−1,821
Third	−86	489	−376	−589	138	2,181
Fourth	−196	1,173	21	−224	210	1,223
	−445	662	−565	−2,828	−220	3,629
1974						
First	−1,853	377	−1,657	−21,058	−203	17,835
Second	−600	712	−306	−7,051	114	4,706
Third	−272	363	−913	−7,252	−357	4,923
Fourth	−282	227	−50	−1,621	−200	4,204
	−699	−925	−388	−5,134	240	4,002
1975						
First	−6,206	2,505	−2,814	−12,192	45	773
Second	−1,928	344	−419	−2,920	312	−2,449
Third	−979	385	−326	−3,435	−210	1,044
Fourth	−938	738	−747	−842	−213	1,711
	−2,361	1,038	−1,322	−4,995	156	467
1976						
First	−8,731	1,250	−2,114	−20,776	−96	11,138
Second	−2,460	1,030	−480	−3,888	338	1,171
Third	−1,357	131	−232	−5,526	−178	3,468
Fourth	−2,743	68	−912	−1,737	−166	1,643
	−2,171	21	−490	−9,625	−90	4,856
1977						
First	−5,398	2,869	−726	−12,401	−247	7,223
Second	−736	828	−273	3,189	−178	−5,472
Third	−1,766	725	84	−5,803	−72	5,900
Fourth	−2,165	513	−242	−148	212	3,018
	−731	803	−295	−9,639	−209	3,777

Source: U.S. Department of Commerce, *Survey of Current Business*, vols. 56 (June 1976), 57 (March and September 1977), 58 (September 1978).

and price stability without reference to foreign constraints. By the end of the 1970s, world rather than domestic economic developments had emerged as a focus for U.S. policymaking. The consequences of interdependence and the limitations it placed on domestic economic sovereignty were quite clear. The United States was no longer unique, but simply the largest of the industrial countries, more similar to than different from the others.

The clear implication of this is that the United States will follow and react to foreign developments in terms of their effects on the U.S. economy. This creates serious and practical problems for world economic policymaking. If the United States can no longer be counted on to ignore the rest of the world, then economic policy everywhere will be made with a greater degree of uncertainty and indeterminacy.

CHAPTER THREE

Japan's Emergence
as an Economic Force

THE LAST HALF of the 1960s witnessed the most rapid growth of real gross domestic product in Japan since World War II. With a rise in the average annual growth rate from 9.8 percent in the first half of the 1960s to 11.2 percent in the second half, Japanese foreign trade expanded rapidly.[1] Merchandise exports, which were valued at $4.1 billion in 1960 and accounted for only 5.6 percent of total exports by all industrial countries, had increased to $8.5 billion in value and 7.1 percent of exports by industrial countries by 1965 and to $19.3 billion and 9.3 percent by 1970. The growth of exports was naturally accompanied by an increase in imports. Thus Japan emerged from the 1960s as a major industrial country of great importance to other countries and particularly to those of the Pacific basin.

The expansion of Japanese trade, however, was unbalanced as exports grew much faster than imports (table 3-1). In 1964 Japan's merchandise trade showed a surplus which persisted until the oil crisis. Because of the deficit in the services account, the current account of the balance of payments recorded deficits until 1965. After that, the surplus in the current account expanded as did the outflow of long-term capital (there were brief

1. Growth rates and per capita income are based on Japan, Economic Planning Agency, *Annual Report on National Income Statistics, 1975,* and *Japanese Economic Indicators, 1978.* For an analysis of the transition from an economy with an unlimited supply of labor to one with a limited supply, see Ken-ichi Inada, Sueo Sekiguchi, and Yasutoyo Shoda, *Keizai hatten no mekanizumu: riron to jisho* [*Mechanism of economic development: a theory and empirical study*] (Tokyo: Sobunsha, 1972).

Table 3-1. *Japan's Growth Rate and Balance of Payments, 1961–70*

Item	1961	1962	1963	1964	1965	1966	1967	1968	1969	1970
						Percent				
Growth of GNP	14.4	7.0	10.5	13.2	5.1	9.8	12.9	13.4	10.8	10.9
Balance of payments						*Millions of dollars*				
Exports[a]	4,149	4,861	5,391	6,704	8,332	9,641	10,231	12,751	15,679	18,969
Imports[a]	4,707	4,460	5,557	6,327	6,431	7,366	9,071	10,222	11,980	15,006
Trade balance[a]	−558	401	−166	377	1,901	2,275	1,160	2,529	3,699	3,963
Services[a]	−383	−420	−569	−784	−884	−886	−1,172	−1,306	−1,399	−1,785
Net transfers	−41	−29	−45	−73	−85	−135	−178	−175	−181	−208
Current account	−982	−48	−780	−480	932	1,254	−190	1,048	2,119	1,970
Long-term capital flows	−11	172	467	107	−415	−808	−812	−239	−155	−1,591
Basic balance	−993	124	−313	−373	517	446	−1,002	809	1,964	379
Short-term capital flows	21	107	107	234	−61	−64	506	209	178	724
Errors and omissions	20	6	45	10	−51	−45	−75	84	141	271
Official settlements	−952	237	−161	−129	405	337	−571	1,102	2,283	1,374

Source: Bank of Japan, *Balance of Payments Monthly*, March 1970, pp. 1–2; May 1973, pp. 1–2; March 1974, pp. 1–2.
a. Valued free on board (f.o.b.).

deficits in the current and basic accounts in 1967). Meanwhile the economy achieved rapid growth in real terms—12.9 percent in 1967 and 13.4 percent in 1968. The simultaneous occurrence of rapid economic growth and a substantial surplus in the international payments in 1968 was evidence of a basic disequilibrium in the balance of payments. This imbalance had an impact on other countries—especially the United States, Japan's major trading partner —but most economists as well as the government did not recognize the problem.

Japan's domestic economy also showed signs of imbalance. In the latter half of 1969, real production began to stagnate because the economy was operating at full capacity. Excess demand caused wholesale prices, which had been fairly stable, to rise rapidly. The wholesale price index, which had gone up only 1.0 percent in 1968, rose 1.9 percent in 1969 and 3.7 percent in 1970. The rise spread to the labor market, where there was excess demand,[2] causing a wage-price spiral. Contract cash earnings of regular workers in manufacturing industries increased 15.0 percent in 1969 and 14.8 percent in 1970 but the increase in their productivity was 13.5 percent and 10.4 percent.

The Japanese economy in the late 1960s was suffering from imported inflation because of the undervaluation of the yen. Japan's rapid expansion of exports and its undervalued currency caused serious trade problems for importing countries. Furthermore Japan's rapidly growing imports of raw materials induced significant increases in the world prices of commodities. Not until much later, however, did the government realize Japan's impact on others.[3] Policymakers frequently discussed the impact of U.S. business cycles on the Japanese economy, but rarely considered the effects of the fluctuations in Japan's economy on the economies of the United States, Australia, and countries in the Far East and Southeast Asia.[4]

2. The unemployment rate was lowered to 1.12 percent in 1969 from 1.25 percent in 1967. The unemployment rate tends to be underestimated since temporarily laid-off workers are not counted as unemployed. It also reflects the practice of guaranteeing lifetime employment; firms tend to hold redundant workers rather than firing them.

3. In 1969 the Japan Economic Research Center suggested for the first time the necessity of revaluing the yen. (*Showa 50 nen no Nihonkeizai* [The Japanese economy in 1975] [December 1969].) For a review of the evolution of Japanese policy, see Lawrence B. Krause and Sueo Sekiguchi, "Japan and the World Economy," in Hugh Patrick and Henry Rosovsky, eds., *Asia's New Giant: How the Japanese Economy Works* (Brookings Institution, 1976).

4. Saburo Okita did warn the public to pay attention to Japan's impact on other countries in "Shigen yunyukoku Nippon wo jikakuseyo [Recognize Japan as large raw material importing country], *Chyuo Koron*, December 1967; reprinted in Hisao Kanamori, ed., *Boeki to kokusaihsyushi* [Trade and the balance of payments] (Tokyo: Nihon Keizai Shimbunsha, 1970).

The Breakdown of the Bretton Woods System

Under the Bretton Woods system, Japan successfully industrialized without devaluing the yen between 1949 and 1970, and the yen emerged as one of the strongest currencies in the late 1960s. Thus Japan had good reason to defend the fixed exchange rate. Because the value of the currency had not changed, domestic wages and prices had increased to adjust to the inflation abroad and domestic inflation had become the mechanism for correcting the external disequilibrium. However, elsewhere in the world the system of fixed exchange rates was collapsing. When debate on the value of the yen finally began in Japan, the economy was entering a recession. In response to inflation, the Bank of Japan had tightened money by raising the discount rate from 5.84 percent to 6.25 percent in September 1969.[5] Business activities had reached a peak in July 1970 and then declined. The government and some economists insisted that the balance-of-payments problem would be solved if business activity recovered. Even those who insisted on appreciating the yen rate were inclined to overestimate its demand-reducing effect and proposed that the government implement some demand-stimulating measures in conjunction with the yen revaluation.

If Japan had wanted to save the Bretton Woods system, it would have had to undertake a large appreciation of the yen in 1970 in order to simultaneously attain both external and internal equilibrium. The yen was not appreciated because manufacturers of internationally traded goods opposed it and because the government feared the deflationary consequences of such a move. Japan had not substantially liberalized its policies toward trade and capital transactions when it elected to adhere to article 8 obligations of the International Monetary Fund in 1964, and both government and industry were very cautious about doing so. In October 1969 Japan still had import quotas on a large number of items. Its tariff rates on industrial goods had been remarkably high just before the Kennedy Round of tariff reductions started in 1967, and the effective rates were even higher. Therefore, rather than appreciating the yen, the government chose to lower tariff rates and reduce quantitative import restrictions between 1969 and 1973—measures it should have taken much earlier.[6] It also eased restrictions on exchange trans-

5. For a summary of price movements in Japan, see Ryutaro Komiya and Yoshio Suzuki, "Inflation in Japan," in Lawrence B. Krause and Walter S. Salant, eds., *Worldwide Inflation: Theory and Recent Experience* (Brookings Institution, 1977), pp. 303–54.

6. Import restrictions were substantially reduced and tariff rates rapidly lowered in the Kennedy Round negotiations. Japan also unilaterally cut many of its tariff rates and adopted the general scheme of preferential tariffs for developing countries. See Krause and Sekiguchi, "Japan and the World Economy."

actions to increase capital outflow through economic cooperation and private investment abroad. But it was difficult to restore equilibrium to the balance of payments without revaluing the exchange rate of the yen, and without a yen appreciation the Bretton Woods system was doomed.

When many principal currencies in Europe were floated and revalued in the spring and summer of 1971, the Japanese government proposed a comprehensive program that it hoped would make a yen revaluation unnecessary. Therefore the yen was not revalued until after the U.S. measures of August 15, 1971. The Bank of Japan floated the yen in response to the U.S. measures but continued to intervene in the foreign-exchange market by buying dollars. Consequently, the yen rate rose from its old par value of 360 per U.S. dollar to 324 in the fourth quarter of 1971, the value that was formalized under the Smithsonian agreement.

As table 3-2 shows, the growth of real GNP slowed down in 1971.[7] The principal cause was a decline in plant and equipment investment because firms faced more uncertainty in their demand forecast as a result of the appreciation of the yen. The surplus in the current account decreased rapidly in the fourth quarter of 1971 (table 3-3), but for the full year it increased 194 percent over the previous year because of the delayed effect of the revaluation.[8] Wholesale prices fell 0.8 percent in 1971 reflecting the business recession and the effect of the currency appreciation. Employment expanded slightly, which kept the rise in the rate of unemployment negligibly small.

The Bank of Japan continued to buy dollars in the exchange market. Its purchase of dollars caused a rapid increase in domestic money supply. Moreover, government expenditures increased rapidly, partly in order to counter the overrated domestic recession and partly in accordance with the plan adopted by the Kakuei Tanaka cabinet for "remodeling the Japanese Archipelago." Thus both monetary and fiscal policy were expansionary on the eve of the world commodity boom.

The Commodity Boom in 1972–74

Because Japan imports all of its feed grains, industrial materials, energy supplies, and cereals (except for rice), the worldwide commodity boom in 1972–74 had a strong impact on the economy. Japan's stimulative domestic policies made it a major participant in the simultaneous expansion of industrial countries. Real GNP increased at an annual rate of 13–15 percent in the

7. Gross national product is identified as gross national expenditure in Japan's national account statistics.

8. The current account is identified as the current overseas account in Japan's statistics.

Table 3-2. *Value and Rate of Change of Main Items in Japan's Gross National Pro*

Year and quarter	Gross national product		Government fixed investment		Private plant and equipment investment	
	Billions of 1970 yen	Percent change	Billions of 1970 yen	Percent change	Billions of 1970 yen	Percent change
1970	70,613	10.9	5,790	10.6	14,195	14.7
First	68,009	2.6	5,316	−1.3	13,964	4.1
Second	70,078	3.0	5,829	9.7	14,012	0.3
Third	71,852	2.5	6,017	3.2	14,368	2.5
Fourth	72,460	0.8	6,173	2.6	14,430	0.4
1971	75,823	7.4	7,291	25.9	14,835	4.5
First	73,984	2.1	6,632	7.4	14,929	3.5
Second	74,901	1.2	7,156	7.9	14,900	−0.2
Third	76,688	2.4	7,743	8.2	14,843	−0.4
Fourth	77,766	1.4	7,922	2.3	14,637	−1.4
1972	82,708	9.1	8,447	15.8	15,670	5.6
First	80,066	3.0	8,119	2.5	15,359	4.9
Second	80,619	0.7	8,275	1.9	15,496	0.9
Third	83,475	3.5	8,658	4.6	15,484	−0.1
Fourth	86,270	3.3	9,012	4.1	16,196	4.6
1973	90,874	9.9	8,510	0.8	18,566	18.5
First	89,284	3.5	9,033	0.2	17,579	8.5
Second	91,173	2.1	8,842	−2.1	18,012	2.5
Third	91,068	−0.1	8,247	−6.7	18,891	4.9
Fourth	91,144	0.1	8,051	−2.4	19,440	2.9
1974	89,733	−1.3	7,944	−6.7	16,565	−10.8
First	88,247	−3.2	7,771	−3.5	17,544	−9.8
Second	89,240	1.1	7,715	−0.7	16,814	−4.2
Third	90,156	1.0	7,992	3.6	16,168	−3.8
Fourth	90,597	0.5	8,382	4.9	15,743	−2.6
1975	91,968	2.5	8,860	11.5	14,399	−13.1
First	90,326	−0.3	8,786	4.8	14,596	−7.3
Second	91,098	0.9	8,790	0.0	14,545	−0.4
Third	92,370	1.4	8,969	2.0	14,451	−0.6
Fourth	93,372	1.1	8,849	−1.3	13,997	−3.1
1976	97,499	6.0	9,007	1.7	14,893	3.4
First	96,056	2.9	9,038	2.1	14,463	3.3
Second	97,474	1.5	9,214	1.9	14,790	2.3
Third	97,862	0.4	9,090	−1.3	14,933	1.0
Fourth	98,693	0.8	8,820	−3.0	15,276	2.3
1977	102,482	5.1	9,921	10.1	15,294	2.7
First	100,804	2.1	9,136	3.6	15,479	1.3
Second	102,472	1.7	9,921	8.6	15,214	−1.7
Third	102,919	0.4	10,511	5.9	15,201	−0.1
Fourth	104,048	1.1	10,523	0.1	15,275	0.5

Sources: Japan, Economic Planning Agency, *Annual Report on National Income Statistics, 1977* for 1970–75, 197 for 1976 and first quarter of 1977; *Japanese Economic Indicators*, various issues for last three quarters of 1977.

duct, by Year and Quarter, 1970–77

Private housing construction		Inventory investment		Current account surplus		Export of goods and services		Import of goods and services	
Billions of 1970 yen	Percent change	Billions of 1970 yen	Percent change	Billions of 1970 yen	Percent change	Billions of 1970 yen	Percent change	Billions of 1970 yen	Percent change
4,761	13.2	3,031	74.0	781	−18.1	8,272	15.6	7,491	20.7
4,692	5.5	2,464	32.8	856	−4.7	7,852	3.9	6,996	5.0
4,711	0.4	3,268	32.7	767	−10.4	8,120	3.4	7,353	5.1
4,750	0.8	3,454	5.7	555	−27.6	8,353	2.9	7,797	6.0
4,818	1.4	2,935	−15.0	893	60.9	8,716	4.3	7,822	0.3
4,938	3.7	1,713	−43.5	1,947	149.3	9,736	17.7	7,789	4.0
4,852	0.7	2,254	−23.2	1,368	53.1	9,310	6.8	7,942	1.5
4,825	−0.5	1,153	−48.8	2,016	47.4	9,867	6.0	7,851	−1.2
4,877	1.1	1,389	20.5	2,470	22.5	10,028	1.6	7,557	−3.7
5,034	4.6	2,032	46.3	1,910	−22.7	9,715	−3.1	7,805	3.3
5,825	18.0	1,659	−3.1	1,949	0.1	10,380	6.6	8,431	8.2
5,355	5.0	1,728	−15.0	1,900	−0.5	9,967	2.6	8,067	3.4
5,878	9.8	631	−63.5	1,716	−9.7	9,772	−2.0	8,056	−0.1
6,097	3.7	1,762	179.4	1,902	10.8	10,598	8.5	8,696	8.0
5,863	−3.8	2,311	31.2	2,222	16.8	11,105	4.8	8,883	2.1
6,738	15.7	3,090	86.2	768	−60.6	11,136	7.3	10,368	23.0
6,228	6.2	2,496	8.0	1,804	−18.8	11,180	0.7	9,376	5.6
6,844	9.9	4,680	87.5	546	−69.8	10,880	−2.7	10,334	10.2
6,800	−0.6	3,430	−26.7	610	11.7	11,054	1.6	10,444	1.1
6,997	2.9	1,480	−56.8	144	−76.4	11,416	3.3	11,272	7.9
5,872	−12.9	3,302	6.9	1,841	139.8	13,500	21.2	11,657	12.4
6,361	−9.1	5,691	149.3	322	123.1	11,966	4.8	11,645	3.3
5,270	−17.2	3,809	3.2	1,700	428.4	13,486	12.7	11,786	1.2
5,356	11.1	3,041	−20.2	2,194	29.0	13,924	3.2	11,730	−0.5
6,022	2.8	2,372	−32.0	2,997	36.6	14,446	3.7	11,449	−2.4
6,299	7.3	1,375	−58.4	3,387	83.9	14,094	4.4	10,708	−8.1
5,998	−0.4	1,881	−46.0	3,160	5.4	14,021	−2.9	10,861	−5.1
6,334	6.4	933	−27.2	3,342	5.8	13,956	−0.5	10,614	−2.3
6,443	0.9	1,257	34.8	3,199	−4.3	13,947	−0.1	10,748	1.3
6,334	−0.9	1,857	47.7	3,868	20.9	14,484	3.9	10,616	−1.2
6,733	6.9	1,814	31.9	4,906	44.8	16,469	16.8	11,564	8.0
7,013	10.7	1,373	−26.1	4,625	19.6	15,672	8.2	11,047	4.1
6,849	−2.3	1,769	28.8	5,059	9.4	16,348	4.3	11,289	2.2
6,734	−1.7	1,829	3.4	4,817	−4.8	16,613	1.6	11,795	4.5
6,430	−4.5	2,146	17.3	5,146	6.8	17,210	3.6	12,065	2.3
6,710	−0.3	2,001	10.3	6,387	30.2	18,185	10.4	11,797	2.8
6,685	4.0	1,981	−7.7	6,207	20.6	18,038	4.8	11,831	−1.9
6,816	2.0	2,296	15.9	6,311	1.7	18,330	1.6	12,019	1.6
6,556	−3.8	1,684	−26.7	6,629	5.0	18,508	1.0	11,878	−1.2
6,816	4.0	1,974	17.2	6,459	−2.6	17,914	−3.2	11,455	−3.6

Table 3-3. *Japan's Balance of Payments, by Year and Quarter, 1970–77*
Millions of dollars

Year and quarter	Exports	Imports	Trade balance	Services balance	Transfers balance	Current account balance	Long-term capital balance	Basic balance	Short-term capital balance	Overall balance	Change in official reserves	Other changes
1970	18,969	15,006	3,963	−1,785	−208	1,970	−1,591	379	724	1,374	903	471
First	4,036	3,457	579	−465	−59	55	−438	−383	185	−16	372	−388
Second	4,586	3,741	845	−422	−50	373	−463	−90	149	23	−99	122
Third	4,939	3,834	1,105	−458	−48	599	−315	284	244	650	−213	863
Fourth	5,408	3,974	1,434	−440	−51	943	−375	568	146	717	843	−126
1971	23,566	15,779	7,787	−1,738	−252	5,797	−1,082	4,715	2,435	7,677	10,836	−3,159
First	4,922	3,867	1,055	−541	−80	434	−194	240	131	609	1,059	−450
Second	5,736	3,988	1,748	−433	−53	1,262	177	1,439	660	2,288	2,141	147
Third	6,236	3,747	2,489	−354	−35	2,100	−304	1,796	1,991	4,060	5,785	−1,725
Fourth	6,672	4,177	2,495	−410	−84	2,001	−761	1,240	−347	720	1,851	−1,131
1972	28,032	19,061	8,971	−1,883	−464	6,624	−4,487	2,137	1,966	4,741	3,130	1,611
First	6,009	4,321	1,688	−581	−149	958	−759	199	827	975	1,428	−453
Second	6,459	4,475	1,984	−556	−216	1,212	−738	474	−204	419	−818	1,237
Third	7,389	4,752	2,637	−491	−62	2,084	−1,158	926	434	1,538	644	894
Fourth	8,175	5,513	2,662	−255	−37	2,370	−1,832	538	909	1,809	1,876	−67
1973	36,264	32,576	3,688	−3,510	−314	−136	−9,750	−9,886	2,407	−10,074	−6,119	−3,955
First	7,414	6,364	1,050	−534	−22	494	−2,231	−1,737	996	−804	−240	−564
Second	8,513	7,920	593	−871	−138	−416	−2,230	−2,646	580	−3,307	−2,925	−382
Third	9,427	8,422	1,005	−842	−62	101	−2,392	−2,291	759	−2,110	−405	−1,705
Fourth	10,910	9,870	1,040	−1,263	−92	−315	−2,897	−3,212	72	−3,853	−2,549	−1,304

1974	54,480	53,044	1,436	−5,842	−287	−4,693	−3,881	−8,574	1,778	−6,839	1,272	−8,111
First	10,093	11,942	−1,849	−1,394	−45	−3,288	−1,591	−4,879	872	−4,137	180	−4,317
Second	13,473	14,321	−848	−1,418	−138	−2,404	−1,016	−3,420	137	−3,065	1,003	−4,068
Third	14,683	13,166	1,517	−1,595	−56	−134	−551	−685	467	−601	−260	−341
Fourth	16,231	13,615	2,616	−1,435	−48	1,133	−723	410	302	964	349	615
1975	54,734	49,706	5,028	−5,354	−356	−682	−272	−954	−1,138	−2,676	−703	−1,973
First	12,879	12,224	655	−1,512	−68	−925	207	−718	−5	−690	634	−1,324
Second	13,478	12,396	1,082	−1,226	−156	−300	215	−85	−953	−1,085	452	−1,537
Third	13,517	12,115	1,402	−1,357	−68	−23	−88	−111	−29	−315	−1,335	1,020
Fourth	14,860	12,971	1,889	−1,259	−64	566	−606	−40	−151	−586	−454	−132
1976	66,026	56,139	9,887	−5,867	−340	3,680	−984	2,696	111	2,924	3,789	−865
First	14,149	12,679	1,470	−1,522	−57	−109	219	110	−243	214	−1,367	−1,153
Second	16,070	13,687	2,383	−1,303	−139	941	49	990	78	808	1,215	−407
Third	17,088	14,373	2,715	−1,673	−59	983	−351	632	324	1,256	1,092	164
Fourth	18,719	15,400	3,319	−1,369	−85	1,865	−901	964	−48	646	115	531
1977	79,333	62,022	17,411	−6,004	−389	10,918	−3,184	7,784	−648	7,743	6,244	1,499
First	17,517	14,786	2,731	−1,751	−87	893	−403	490	48	542	393	149
Second	19,376	15,524	3,952	−1,520	−149	2,183	−528	1,655	−373	1,448	391	1,057
Third	20,197	15,480	4,717	−1,373	−83	3,261	−1,077	2,234	−452	1,740	480	1,260
Fourth	22,243	16,232	6,011	−1,360	−70	4,581	−1,176	3,405	129	4,013	4,980	−967

Sources: Bank of Japan, *Balance of Payments Monthly*, April 1978; Japan, Economic Planning Agency, *Japanese Economic Indicators*, June 1978.

latter half of 1972, while the surplus in the current account and inventory investment increased even more rapidly. Government investment also expanded substantially. Since plant and equipment investment did not increase as rapidly, however, some sectors, including electric power and chemicals, became a bottleneck in the flow of supplies in the succeeding quarters. Wholesale prices rose 5.6 percent per annum in the third quarter of 1972 and 11.6 percent in the fourth. The economy thus gradually entered into a period of general supply shortages and rapid inflation.

The steep rise in grain prices and the temporary U.S. export embargo of soybeans had an impact on Japan that lasted long after the commodity boom had ended. In 1972 Japan at the insistence of the United States had promised to increase its imports of agricultural products in order to reduce the imbalance in the two countries' trade and overall payments. But in June 1973 the United States imposed an embargo on soybean exports. Although the embargo lasted only a few months, it served to revive the argument that Japan should attain self-sufficiency to avoid a long-lasting shortage of food supplies.[9] Demands for agricultural protectionism gradually calmed down as the world supply of grain increased substantially in the following years.

The commodity boom also caused a rapid increase in the prices of industrial materials, which Japanese firms may have contributed to by their excessive accumulation of inventories. Before the boom in 1971, both inventories and the ratio of inventories to consumption of imported raw materials rose, primarily because of the moderate Japanese recession. With the subsequent strong recovery in Japan the inventory-consumption ratio tended to rise even further, probably because firms invested in raw materials as a hedge against the worldwide inflation and the rapid increase in the prices of raw materials. The higher raw material prices in dollars were offset to a certain extent by the rise of the yen's exchange rate in 1972–73. If the government had kept the money supply at a lower level in 1971–73, the purchase of raw materials would have been more moderate[10] and the large inventories of raw materials on hand would have been less disruptive during the 1974 recession.

9. See Tripartite Report, *Trade in Primary Commodities: Conflict or Cooperation?* (Brookings Institution, 1974); and Triangle Paper, *Seeking a New Accommodation in World Commodity Markets* (New York: Trilateral Commission, 1976). Raising the level of sufficiency is extraordinarily expensive for Japan. However, because of public support, the government raised substantially the producer's price of rice in 1974 even though the country was glutted with an excessive supply of rice.

10. Ryutaro Komiya, "Showa 48–49 nen no infureshon no gen-in" [Causes for the 1973–74 inflation in Japan], *Keizaigakuronshu*, vol. 42 (April 1976), argues that if the money supply had been restrained, the steep rise in the import prices of raw materials would have resulted in changes in relative prices and not in general inflation. As a practical matter, it seems difficult for a government to keep money supply constant

The Bank of Japan did take several steps in 1973 to limit the increase in money supply. It raised the discount rate from 4.25 percent to 5.00 percent in April and to 5.50 percent in May. It also raised reserve requirements and interest rates on deposits and strengthened administrative guidance. It did not, however, significantly retard the increase in money supply, principally because it allowed a substantial increase in high-powered money by increasing its lending to commercial banks. Fiscal policy was not tightened at the beginning of 1973 because of the government's commitment to expand social programs. The budget for fiscal 1973 was based on government plans to increase current expenditures 24.6 percent and government investments 28.3 percent over the previous year. However, in light of the high rate of inflation the government successively deferred the execution of public works contracts in April, June, and August. Government fixed investment in real terms began to decrease in the second quarter of 1973 as prices went up, and for the year it rose only 0.8 percent.

Because of the excessive money supply, plant and equipment investment by firms recovered, but only a little. Since the yen had risen and future appreciations were thought possible, firms preferred to buy real estate. They also built up their inventory of stocks in expectation of price rises rather than investing in plant and equipment. Supply shortages became conspicuous in some sectors because the increase in demand outstripped the expansion of productive capacity. Also a shortage of construction materials caused private housing construction to decline in real terms in the third quarter of 1973. Thus the growth rate of real GNP peaked after slowing down to 8.5 percent per annum in the second quarter of 1973. In the third quarter GNP declined by 0.5 percent at an annual rate and in the fourth quarter recovered slightly to 0.3 percent.

The Oil Crisis

The multifold increase in oil prices and the Arab embargo on oil exports in October 1973 had serious repercussions in Japan. The public, in a panic, bought up and hoarded oil and consumer goods from late 1973 until early 1974. The government responded immediately to the embargo by taking pro-Arab foreign policy positions, but its hasty reactions did not quiet the panic.

---

in order to confine the effect of import price increases to changes in relative prices. Increases in import prices force firms to drastically reduce production which may in turn lead to an increase in bankruptcy and unemployment (this was not the case in 1972–73, however).

It also adopted strict anti-inflation measures to counter the rise in oil prices. Labor unions in the spring wage negotiations in 1974 gained an approximate 30 percent increase in their money wage rates in response to the previous inflation and the large profits of business firms. Unless the government were able to cut the inflation rate and maintain labor's share in the income distribution, it seemed in danger of losing its political base.

In addition to increasing inflation, the oil crisis directly led to a balance-of-payments crisis. Because of dramatically higher prices for crude oil, even the trade account recorded a huge deficit ($1.8 billion in the first quarter of 1974 and $0.8 billion in the second quarter). The Bank of Japan in response stopped intervening in the foreign-exchange market except to smooth fluctuations. The yen rate immediately began to fall, reaching 300 yen per U.S. dollar in the fourth quarter of 1974.[11]

The import price index (based on 1970) went up to 210 in late 1974, whereas the export price index remained stable at 148. This lowered the terms of trade to 70. With costs rising, wholesale and consumer prices rose 31.4 percent and 24.4 percent, respectively, in 1974. In the face of this continuing inflation, the government became determined to fight it at all costs.

To limit the inflationary impact of the oil price rise, the prices of oil and related products and of various other goods were put under government control.[12] To offset the deterioration in the balance of payments, restrictions on the flow of foreign capital into the country were eased while those on the outflow of foreign exchange were strengthened in November 1973.[13] Taxes for fiscal 1974 were cut by 1.45 trillion yen to compensate for the automatic tax increase that came from inflation. A special corporate tax was imposed for two years, however, on windfall profits earned during 1973.

The government followed a strict demand-restraining policy to insure that

11. Since the exchange rates of other industrial countries also declined, the effective rate of the yen against fifteen major currencies did not fall as much. According to the Morgan Guaranty index, the effective exchange rate of the yen dropped from a 24.2 percent appreciation (compared to 1970) in the second quarter of 1973 to a 10.2 percent appreciation in the fourth quarter of 1974. Morgan Guaranty Trust Co. of New York, *World Financial Markets,* various issues.

12. Oil conservation was mandated under a crisis program in November 1973 (*Sekiyu kinkyu taisaku yoko*). A law for normalizing oil demand and supply (*Sekiyu jyukyu tekiseika ho*) and a law on emergency measures for stabilizing the nation's life (*Kokumin seikatsu antei kinkyushochi ho*) were enacted in December 1973. In July the Diet had passed a law on emergency measures to prevent the buying up and selling control of some consumption goods (*Seikatsu kanren bushi no kaisime urioshimi nitaisuru kinkyu shochi ho*).

13. In July 1974, when it was recognized that the balance-of-payments crisis had passed, the restrictions on borrowing from abroad were strengthened and those on the outflow of capital eased.

wage increases in the 1975 spring wage negotiations would be moderate. Nevertheless, it encouraged government financial agencies to extend loans to small firms. And the employment insurance system was revised to provide subsidies to firms that temporarily laid off workers instead of firing them.

The government also began efforts to cut down the use of petroleum, with some success. The volume of crude oil imports decreased by 4 percent in 1974 and by a further 5 percent in 1975, while real GNP scarcely increased (the reduction was in part a result of the recession); in 1976 real GNP grew 6.0 percent, yet crude oil imports increased by only 1.7 percent. In an effort to diversify the sources of Japan's oil, imports of crude oil from the People's Republic of China were increased and efforts to obtain oil from other sources were begun. Reserves of oil were built up to a sixty-six-day level by the end of fiscal 1974, and programs to increase the use of other sources of energy were reexamined.[14]

The steep rise in crude oil prices made it more difficult for Japan to reduce bilateral trade imbalances with various regions. The value of imports from the Middle East, where Japan already had a bilateral deficit, increased from 12.4 percent of Japan's total imports in 1970 to as much as 28.5 percent in 1975. In response to this increase, greater effort was made to increase exports to the Middle East; they grew from only 3.3 percent of Japan's total exports in 1970 to 10.8 percent in 1975. The argument for slower growth became increasingly popular given the energy constraint.[15] Thus the government set the growth target for 1975–80 at 6 percent in real GNP, much below the rate achieved in the 1960s.

With the oil crisis, Japan's energy-intensive industries began to face adjustment problems. (The textile industry was already having serious adjustment problems caused by increases in domestic wages and the rise in the exchange rate.) The rapid increase in energy prices caused a decline among industries engaged in refining nonferrous metals, particularly aluminum. The government's demand-restraining policies made the adjustment problem even more difficult. Thus the oil crisis caused long-lasting structural as well as macroeconomic problems for Japan.

14. The target for building a sixty-day reserve was the end of fiscal 1974. Inducements offered to oil refineries and local communities were not sufficient to achieve the ninety-day reserve suggested by the International Energy Agency. Japan's nuclear energy industry, which is dependent on enriched uranium purchased from the United States, provided less than 4 percent of Japan's total primary energy supplies in 1975. Japan's nuclear power development has been stymied by the same problems that have affected other countries. In addition a dispute between Japan and the United States surfaced in 1977 over the reprocessing of spent nuclear fuel.

15. Osamu Shimomura, an influential economist, argued that there should be no increases in wages or economic growth.

Table 3-4. Gap between Japan's Potential and Actual GNP and Manufacturing Production, 1969–76

Item	1969	1970	1971	1972	1973	1974	1975	1976
Gross national product								
Potential[a]								
Billions of 1970 yen	64,722	72,778	80,227	86,583	93,405	100,987	106,020	110,535
Percent growth	12.3	12.5	10.2	7.9	7.9	8.0	5.1	4.3
Actual								
Billions of 1970 yen	63,669	70,635	75,818	82,707	90,829	89,647	91,795	97,583
Percent growth	10.8	10.9	7.3	9.1	9.8	−1.3	2.4	6.3
Gap (percent)	1.6	2.9	5.5	4.5	2.8	11.2	13.4	11.7
Manufacturing production								
Potential[b]								
Index (based on 1970)	86.8	98.6	110.9	121.7	131.9	140.8	148.5	154.4
Percent growth	13.9	13.6	12.5	9.7	8.4	6.8	5.5	4.0
Actual								
Index (based on 1970)	87.8	100.0	102.7	110.3	127.8	123.8	110.1	125.3
Percent growth	16.3	13.9	2.7	7.4	15.9	−3.1	−11.1	13.8
Gap (percent)	−1.2	−1.4	7.4	9.4	3.1	12.1	25.9	18.8
Index of manufacturing production capacity (based on 1970)	86.7	100.0	108.7	114.6	125.6	135.3	142.0	149.7
Index of operating ratio (based on 1970)[c]	102.1	100.0	94.5	95.0	100.6	91.4	81.3	87.6

Source: Japan Economic Research Center, *18 Months Forecast*, March 1977.

Note: $Empe^*$ is the index of labor forces (all industries); $Enpem^*$, the index of labor forces (manufacturing); Ka, private productive capital stock; Km, manufacturing capital stock; Omm^*, manufacturing production index; ρ, ratio of capacity utilization; T, time trend; $V/^*$, real GNP; Va, variable for the vintage of capital stock (all industries); Vm, vintage for manufacturing capital; Wh^*, index of work hours (all industries); and Whm^*, index of work hours (manufacturing).

a. Derived from

$$\log V/^* = -2.18927 + 0.1709186 \log (\rho \cdot Ka) + 1.162890 \log (Wh^* \cdot Empe^*) + 0.06466608Va + 0.01574120T$$
$$(2.55) \qquad (5.45) \qquad (11.1) \qquad (8.37)$$

$R^2 = 0.998$; Durbin-Watson $= 0.905$; standard error $= 0.0127$.

b. Derived from

$$\log Omm^* = -8.992734 + 0.7248491 \log (\rho \cdot Km) + 0.8086603 \log (Whm^* \cdot Enpem^*) + 0.05580334Vm$$
$$(86.1) \qquad (11.7) \qquad (2.33)$$

$R^2 = 0.997$; Durbin-Watson $= 0.766$; standard error $= 0.0178$.

c. Ratio of the index of actual manufacturing production to the index of manufacturing production capacity.

Recession and Weak Recovery

The government's strict deflationary policies of 1973 caused real GNP to drop at a 13 percent annual rate in the first quarter of 1974. The rate did not show any substantial increase in the following quarters and registered a further drop in the first quarter of 1975, leading to a decline of 1.3 percent in 1974 and growth of only 2.4 percent in 1975. In April 1975 the Bank of Japan decided to take reflationary measures, lowering the discount rate from 9 percent to 8.5 percent. The rate was further lowered to 8 percent in June, to 7.5 percent in August, and to 6.5 percent in October.[16] The government should have given a large tax cut and expanded public investment to stimulate domestic demand and take advantage of a substantial excess supply capacity. Instead it continued its fight against inflation. Public investment was not increased very much. The government, adhering to its goal of a balanced budget, took only limited actions to speed up implementation of the public works program, increase the financing available for small enterprises, expand the eligibility and term of payment of employment adjustment subsidies for workers temporarily laid off, and offer tax incentives for housing loans and counterpollution investment.[17]

In 1975 the index of manufacturing production stood about 14 percent below the 1973 level. In contrast, the index of production capacity in manufacturing was 13 percent higher than in 1973 (table 3-4). Since the growth of real GNP was limited to 2.4 percent in 1975, GNP was 11.2 percent lower than its potential in 1974 and 13.4 percent in 1975. The economic outcome was somewhat better in 1976 in that growth reached 6.0 percent, but this was not adequate for the economy. The number of business bankruptcies and unemployment increased and permanent employment decreased although at a slower rate of decline than in 1975. Furthermore the economy's growth slowed substantially in the second half of 1976 which caused doubts toward the future.

The concern was heightened by the recognition that Japan's recovery was being propelled by the growth of exports (imports were decreasing because of weak domestic demand). In the fourth quarter of 1975 the current account registered a surplus of about $0.6 billion despite the fact that the terms

16. Although the substantial excess supply capacity made further reductions desirable, the rate was not reduced again until March 1977 (to 6 percent) because the Bank of Japan did not want to lower interest rates on deposits to adjust to it.

17. See Hisao Kanamori and Sueo Sekiguchi, *The 1974–75 Recession and Economic Stabilization Policy: The Japanese Experience,* Japan Economic Research Center Paper 30 (1977).

of trade were 35 percent less favorable than they had been in 1970. The surplus swelled to $3.7 billion in 1976 as exports continued to rise more sharply than imports.

Besides the fact that both the timing and scale of the reflationary policies were inappropriate, there was also a reluctance on the part of the government to stimulate the business recovery. This might have been a reaction against the expansionary policy of the Tanaka cabinet. The governing Liberal Democratic party was weakened by internal struggles and by allegations that its leaders were involved in the Lockheed scandal which was disclosed in February 1976 in the U.S. Congress. The government thus may simply have lacked the strength to take the actions that were needed. At any rate, in late 1976 Takeo Miki lost the support of the party and was replaced as prime minister by Takeo Fukuda.

Though there was still substantial redundancy in the supply capacity of the country, the rapid rise of 11.9 percent in the consumer price index in 1975 and 9.3 percent in 1976 apparently made the government unwilling to stimulate domestic demand. That reluctance was reinforced by the strong antigrowth atmosphere of the early 1970s and the growing uncertainty about future oil prices.

In order to better respond to foreign pressures as well as to solve domestic problems, the government decided to raise the growth target for fiscal 1977 to 6.7 percent, expecting that by doing so it could turn Japan's balance-of-payments surplus on current account into a modest deficit. The stimulative measures it took were not nearly strong enough, however, and the rate of growth for fiscal 1977 was only 5.4 percent—even lower than the 5.7 percent of the previous year. In fiscal 1978 the government again set a growth target (of 7.0 percent) that it did not pursue vigorously enough to realize.

Rather than being reduced, the balance-of-payments surplus on current account grew massively to reach $10.9 billion in 1977 and $16.5 billion in 1978. The surplus put great upward pressure on the yen and some of Japan's trading partners accused the Bank of Japan of intervening in the market to keep the yen undervalued (Japan's gold and foreign-exchange reserves rose $3.8 billion in 1976, $6.2 billion in 1977, and $10.2 billion in 1978). The yen rose over 20 percent in value (on a trade-weighted basis) in 1977 and a further 19 percent in 1978. The sharp appreciation helped to end Japan's inflation problem, for with a higher valued yen, import prices of raw materials were reduced, helping Japanese firms contain cost pressures. Also the fear of foreign competition combined with a generally weak labor market kept wage increases to very modest levels—only barely above cost-of-living increases. Thus wholesale prices began to fall at the end of 1977 and continued to decline in 1978. Despite this, profit margins in many Japanese industries were increased as some of the cost reductions were retained within firms.

By 1978, Japan's balance of payments had reached such a large surplus position that it had become one of the most destabilizing factors in international finance, surpassing even the OPEC surplus. However, Japan still did not appreciate the impact that it was having on other countries. It seemed not to comprehend the deflationary effects it was having on others by running massive balance-of-payments surpluses. Only when other countries threatened reprisals against the nation's trade did the Japanese government respond. This selective perception of the consequences of economic interdependence is a matter of international concern. It raises great resentment against Japan and reciprocally among Japanese who feel that other countries are discriminating against Japan.

The Transmission of Economic Impulses

During the four world crises, many economic impulses were transmitted to Japan. But Japan was also a transmitter of economic instability. As the largest importer of many commodities in the world, Japan dominated the trade of many of the commodity-exporting nations of the Pacific basin. Changes in its imports of raw materials had a profound effect on the economies of its trading partners. In 1974, Japan imported 92 percent of the Philippines' copper exports, 74 percent of its timber exports, and 24 percent of its sugar exports. In the same year it imported 25 percent of Thailand's exports of tin, 47 percent of its raw rubber, and 45 percent of its maize exports.[18] And in 1974 its share of Australian exports was 88 percent for iron ore, 89 percent for coal, 37 percent for wool, and 26 percent for sugar.[19] Fishery products, electrical machinery, and textile products occupied larger shares than raw materials in Japan's imports from the Republic of Korea. Clearly, changes in Japan's imports of raw materials would have had a strong impact on the Pacific basin economies.

The Exchange Rate and Overall Monetary Balance

One of the most important economic developments since World War II was the introduction of some flexibility in the movement of exchange rates

18. Based on JETRO (Japan External Trade Organization), *Overseas Markets,* June 1976.

19. John Crawford and Saburo Okita, *Australia, Japan and Western Pacific Economic Relations,* Report to the Governments of Australia and Japan (Canberra: Australian Government Publishing Service, 1976).

after 1970. Japan's delay in appreciating the yen in 1971 and failure to sterilize the flow of funds into the country (the money supply increased remarkably in 1971–72 with the rapid increase in official reserves) caused the inflation of 1972–73.

After the yen was floated in August of 1971, the Bank of Japan continued to buy dollars to minimize the rate of appreciation. In December, however, when the Smithsonian agreement took effect, the yen appreciated 16.88 percent against the dollar, but its effective rate against fifteen major currencies rose only 12.5 percent over the 1970 value. Throughout 1972 the Bank of Japan continued its intervention. In 1973, as part of its anti-inflation strategy, the Bank began to sell dollars in the foreign-exchange market in order to sustain a high-value yen. As a result the rate rose to 265 yen to the dollar after the movement to generalized floating in March 1973 (before August 1971 its par value had been 360 per dollar). The effective exchange rate of the yen rose 24 percent above the 1970 level. Since world trade prices, mainly those for raw materials, were then rising rapidly, this appreciation helped to hold down inflation in Japan. The Bank of Japan was at that time, however, increasing its lending to commercial banks to expand the money supply, thereby creating a serious inflationary problem. Consequently, in 1974 the government took a strong tight-money stance. Because it became difficult after the oil crisis to determine an equilibrium exchange rate, the government decided to let market forces play a larger role in fixing the yen's value. With market intervention by the Bank of Japan confined to smoothing drastic fluctuations, the yen rate fell to 300 per dollar in late 1974 (the effective rate dropped from a 24.2 percent appreciation in the second quarter of 1973 to a 10.2 percent appreciation in the fourth quarter of 1974). The overall balance of payments had deficits of $6.8 billion and $2.7 billion in 1974 and 1975, respectively, reflecting the higher costs of oil imports; by the end of 1975, however, the accounts were back in surplus. In 1976 the surplus expanded quarter by quarter because of the lack of demand in the economy and the exchange rate rose 6.8 percent as a consequence. Except during a relatively slight and temporary decline in the fourth quarter, the Bank of Japan bought dollars during 1976 to slow down the rate of the yen's appreciation.

The balance-of-payments surplus increased greatly during 1977, putting upward pressure on the yen despite extensive dollar purchases by the Bank of Japan. The weighted value of the yen appreciated by another 20 percent and the Bank of Japan made strenuous efforts to peg the dollar rate at 240 yen, but to no avail. The most immediate and possibly most significant consequence of the rapid appreciation of the yen was that it broke the back of the

Japanese inflation. Wholesale prices began to decline and retail prices to rise less slowly even than in previous good years. However, producers of tradable goods feared the loss of international competitiveness and hesitated to make new investments. Severe pessimism eased as exporters found their wares still competitive, but the private economy was greatly restrained. The government's principal demand-management problem was how vigorously it should pursue reflationary policies. The measures it took turned out to be too weak. While the rate of increase in outstanding high-powered money was only 11.1 percent in 1976, M_1 increased by 14.2 percent and M_2 by 15.2 percent; but both of the latter retreated in 1977 even as the overall surplus in the balance of payments was rising. Thus despite being pushed in an expansionary direction by the balance of payments, Japan's monetary developments were determined by excessive domestic restraint.

Export and Import Prices

The impact of fluctuations in the yen's exchange rate and Japan's domestic prices on its trade partners naturally varied depending on Japan's market share of their total foreign trade. (In 1970 Japan imported 26.2 percent of Australia's total exports, 28.2 percent of Korea's, 40.1 percent of the Philippines', and 25.5 percent of Thailand's.) All of them felt the effect of Japanese price fluctuations. From 1971 through the first half of 1973 while Japan's export prices in yen were stable, the rise in the yen's value meant that Japan's exports were becoming more expensive for its trading partners. From the latter half of 1973 to late 1974, export prices rose rapidly as costs increased following the rapid escalation of oil prices and the inflation in Japan. But the exchange rate of the yen fell, thus moderating the rise in import prices for trade partners. After 1975 Japan's export prices declined, but the rise in the yen relative to the currencies of Japan's trade partners left them at a disadvantage. Korea was particularly hard hit, but Japan's export prices were a factor causing some degree of inflation for all of its trading partners.

The appreciation of the yen and the slight recession in the Japanese economy insulated the Japanese market against the early rises in international prices of mineral fuels and primary commodities in 1971. Import prices for fuels rose only 15 percent compared to a world rise of 44.9 percent, and no increase was recorded for primary commodities while world prices rose 9.7 percent. When the worldwide boom and shortages of agricultural products caused world prices to go up drastically in 1972, the increases were not reflected in Japan's import prices until the fourth quarter. The time lag may have been a residual benefit of the yen revaluation in December 1971. Both import prices and wholesale prices eventually rose because of the excessive money supply within the country.

Even though the Bank of Japan intervened in the foreign-exchange market to raise the value of the yen, the import price index rose 21.0 percent in 1973, whereas export prices rose only 9.0 percent. Wholesale prices rose 15.8 percent and consumer prices 11.8 percent. In 1974 the prices of textile materials, timber, and other commodities began dropping, but the overwhelming increase in oil prices caused import prices to shoot up 66.3 percent. Export prices rose only 33.6 percent and the terms of trade deteriorated drastically. The import price increases (partly reflecting the effect of the yen devaluation) again led the domestic inflation, topping wholesale price rises of 31.4 percent (the highest rate since the Korean War) and consumer price rises of 24.4 percent. Even though the inflation was import-led, the government took strong demand-restraining policies and forced the economy into a serious stagflation.

One of the means developed by Japanese industries over a number of years to cope with price changes and security of supply was the long-term contract. In the 1972–74 commodity boom and the subsequent recession those contracts often caused conflicts between Japan and commodity-supplying countries. When prices rose rapidly, the sellers wanted to modify the contracts, and when they fell, the buyers tried to change them. During the 1972–73 boom, Japanese firms agreed to renegotiate the contract covering imports of iron ore from Australia. The agreement was important to both sides since nearly 90 percent of Australia's iron ore exports went to Japan and they accounted for an increasingly large share of Japan's imports of ore. An attempt by Japanese sugar refiners to reduce the contracted price of sugar imports from Australia was not so smooth. Within the first year of a five-year contract that went into effect in 1975, the world price of sugar fell to half the contracted price. Japanese manufacturers, suffering through the recession, initiated negotiations that finally ended in a revised contract in late 1977 after the Japanese government stepped in as mediator.

Trade Volume and the Current Account

Repeatedly between 1970 and 1977, changes in the volume of Japanese trade seem to have been an important factor in transmitting business fluctuations. The rapid increase in exports in 1970–71 gave rise to trade frictions with several countries. During the commodity boom and oil crisis, fluctuations in Japan's import demand had a strong impact on exporting countries.

And in 1976–77 both a rapid increase in exports and a stagnation in imports had repercussions for Japan's trading partners.

From 1970 through the third quarter of 1971 Japanese exports increased rapidly because of the undervalued exchange rate. The impact of Japanese imports on textile trade in the United States was so adverse that a so-called voluntary arrangement restraining Japan's exports was negotiated in 1972. A similar agreement was reached on the trade of steel between the two countries.

In 1973 Japanese imports increased rapidly under the stimulus of domestic inflation and the high value of the yen. Manufacturers, building their inventories of raw materials in anticipation of higher prices, caused such an extraordinary increase in imports that their elasticity with regard to GNP rose from 1.00 in 1972 to 1.54 in 1973 and then dropped to 0.33 in 1974. The recession in Japan and the rise in crude oil prices conspired to decrease import volume by 2.3 percent in 1974 and 12.7 percent in 1975.

Stagnation of Japan's imports had a recessionary impact on the countries that exported raw materials and industrial goods to Japan. Imports from the United States decreased in value from $12.7 billion in 1974 to $11.6 billion in 1975 and had risen only to $12.4 billion in 1977. The value of Japan's imports from Australia was $3.5 billion in 1973, having grown 58.5 percent in that year alone; it reached $4 billion in 1974, but after that, the imports stagnated. Japan's imports from Korea, which had increased rapidly in 1973–74, decreased even in absolute value in 1975, and imports from the Philippines showed a substantial decrease in 1976 after increasing rapidly in 1973–74.

Australia's trade in wool, about 40 percent of which went to Japan, was drastically upset by the inventory speculation of 1973. Japan's imports of textile materials from Australia soared to $820 million in 1973, moving up from $382 million in 1972 and only $235 million in 1971. They fell almost as steeply in 1974 to $426 million. Such fluctuations in demand must certainly have had a strong impact on prices in Australia.[20] Yet, despite the fluctuations, both the Australian and the Japanese governments left any necessary adjustments in this trade to the market.

Government intervention in the beef market was no more constructive than the laissez-faire system in the wool trade. In order to protect domestic producers of beef and stabilize prices, the Japanese government imposed

20. Imports of logs and lumber from the Philippines (representing 74 percent of Philippine lumber exports in 1974) also fluctuated widely. Lumber manufacturers in Japan established buffer stocks in 1974, but export regulations by the Philippine government seem to have caused trade to stagnate thereafter.

quotas on imports of beef. In 1971 Australia supplied 37 percent of Japan's total beef imports (accounting for about 14 percent of Australia's beef exports). During the 1972–73 period of inflation, imports were allowed to increase rapidly (from $76 million in value in 1971 to $140 million in 1972 and $343 million in 1973). But with the recession the Japanese government so limited imports that they fell in value to $154 million in 1974 and $134 million in 1975. Australian producers who relied on Japan as an export market thus had a difficult adjustment problem thrust on them. The Australian government was severely critical of Japanese policy, as were Japanese consumers who had to bear the burden in Japan.

In 1974, when excessive inventories became a heavy burden for Japanese firms, their solution was to try to reexport some of the raw materials to other countries.[21] Those exports caused the prices of the same goods in exporting countries to deteriorate. One of many requests for the Japanese government to limit primary exports in order to prevent a fall in prices was that of the copper-producing countries. The Japanese government responded by prohibiting the export of unwrought copper. While this may have helped support the price of copper, it made the inventory burden of Japanese firms even heavier.

The Japanese government was also forced to intervene on behalf of Japan's declining industries during the recession. Adjustment problems in the textile industry, for instance, prompted the government to seek from Korea voluntary restraint of Korean exports of textile products which it agreed to.

The volume of Japanese exports continued to grow during the worldwide recession, even rising almost 2 percent in 1975. The rise of 22 percent in 1976, occasioned mainly by the business recovery in the United States and the slow recovery in Japan intensified the trade disputes between Japan and the United States. One way or another Japan's large balance-of-payments surplus had to be corrected. The choice lay, in descending order of desirability, in Japan's increasing its domestic absorption through faster economic growth, encouraging imports and long-term capital outflow through further liberalizing its trade and payments restrictions, permitting the value of the yen to rise, using some nonmarket device to limit exports, or permitting other countries to raise import barriers against Japanese goods. Though among the least attractive in terms of economic welfare, the route followed

21. Some groups of private enterprises, with the help of government subsidies and preferential financing, began to establish buffer stocks of feed grains, timber, nonferrous metals, and other commodities. See Sueo Sekiguchi with the collaboration of Munemichi Inoue and Tadahisa Ooka, *Japanese Direct Foreign Investment*, Japanese Economic Research Center Paper 32 (1977), chap. 2.

was import restrictions and voluntary export restraints negotiated between Japan and its trading partners under pressure from the United States and Europe.

As Japan's export volume grew, the Japanese economy became more and more dependent on export markets. In 1973 exports of goods and services represented only 12.2 percent of GNP (in 1970 prices). The ratio jumped in 1974 to 15.0 percent and reached 17.7 percent in 1977. But the ratio of imports of goods and services to GNP was 11.4 percent in 1973, rose briefly to nearly 13 percent in 1974, and was back to 11.5 percent in 1977. Thus there was no rise of import penetration of Japan during the period of rapidly rising exports. The difference in these two trends was inevitably a cause of conflict. A rising export surplus can lead to domestic growth if there is excess capacity in an economy; otherwise it is likely to cause inflation, especially if the exchange rate is not appreciated. The rise in prices and wages—the so-called adjustment inflation—in Japan from the late 1960s through mid-1971 was the response of an economy that did not have much capacity to absorb an increase in exports. The ratio of Japan's current account surplus to GNP (in real terms) increased rapidly from 1.3 percent in the first quarter of 1970 to 3.2 percent in the third quarter of 1971. Throughout 1972 the excess foreign demand caused price increases rather than raising real production.

Imports increased rapidly in 1973 and the ratio of the current account surplus to GNP decreased to 0.6 percent in the second quarter of 1973. The enormous deficit that also developed in the overall balance of payments because of the deterioration in the terms of trade necessitated some increase in net exports. The real current account surplus thus increased to 3.3 percent of real GNP in the fourth quarter of 1974 and to 4.1 percent a year later.

Japan's excess supply capacity of about 15 percent in 1975 meant that foreign sales were an important source of demand to support domestic production in the following years. The current account surplus played an important role in the recovery of business activity throughout the 1974–77 period, reaching a remarkable 6 percent of GNP in 1977. However, the export-led recovery of an economy as large as Japan's inevitably made the adjustment process more difficult for other countries that were experiencing severe balance-of-payments deficits.

Japan's export multiplier—the degree of increase in real GNP that can be expected from a given increase in real exports—is estimated to be about 1.6 in the short run. Exports thus can act as a powerful stimulant to the economy: if they increase by $1 billion (1.8 percent of exports in 1975), GNP can be expected to increase by $1.6 billion (0.3 percent of nominal GNP in 1975) in the very short run. That assumes that only consumption and imports are affected by changes in export volume. But if the export surplus lasts long enough to induce changes in domestic fixed investment, the multiplier increases to an estimated 2.0–2.4, causing GNP to increase by $2.0 billion to $2.4 billion.[22] Simulations based on Japan's experience in 1975 and 1976 suggest that the average export multiplier is 1.5 in the first year and 3.0 in the second year.[23] Thus export growth appears to have been partially responsible for importing inflation in 1970–71 because the economy was operating near full capacity. On the other hand it appears to have promoted production to a great extent between 1974 and 1977.

Clearly Japan's recovery from the 1974 recession was too dependent on export trade. Growth in the current account explained 69 percent of the growth of Japan's total GNP in 1975, 27.5 percent in 1976, and 29.7 percent in 1977. While some external stimulation is to be expected at cyclical turning points, as in 1975, Japan's continued reliance on it was undesirable for its own economy and destabilizing for the world economy.

Financial Links and Direct Investment

A floating exchange rate is generally believed to insulate domestic employment from foreign monetary disturbances if capital movements respond to normal interest-rate differentials. However, speculation may cause capital flows to be disruptive. The monetary impact of short-term capital movements can be mitigated if the government moves to protect domestic capital from the flow of foreign funds into the country and to offset the flow of capital out of the country. On the whole it appears that for most of the 1970–77 period, capital movements were less disruptive to the Japanese economy than to the European economies, although the problem became more severe at the end of 1977 and in 1978.

It is difficult to determine to what extent market forces influenced portfolio investment in Japan during 1970–77. The institutional regulations governing foreign-exchange transactions were constantly eased and tightened

22. Estimated from econometric models of the Economic Planning Agency, based on quarterly data for fiscal 1960–73, and Kyoto University, based on quarterly data for 1956–74. In both models the variables explaining consumption include a time lag. The level of imports is calculated using the average propensity to import. Long-term multipliers incorporate the response to key domestic investment parameters such as average adjustment speed and desirable capital stock.

23. Analysis of the first quarter of 1975 through the fourth quarter of 1976. Japan, Economic Research Institute, Economic Planning Agency, *Keizai buneski* [Economic analyses], no. 60 (March 1976).

throughout the period to encourage the outflow of capital and restrict the inflow whenever the yen was under upward pressure and the reverse when downward pressure prevailed. The use of such controls could conceivably injure other countries, and it limits the yen's usefulness as an international currency.

Direct foreign investment was a relatively unimportant transmitter of economic impulses to Japan in the 1970s. By 1976 Japan had removed almost all restrictions on foreign investment in Japanese manufacturing industries, yet direct investment remained at a level of $30 million to $50 million in every quarter from 1970 through 1977. Sixty percent of the investment came from the United States and less than 20 percent from Europe. In 1974 the total cumulative amount of approved direct investment (some of which may never have been made) represented only 0.3 percent of the total domestic productive capital stock. It was not an important factor in the national economy, though in industries such as oil refining, chemicals, and machinery, foreign subsidiaries accounted for a high percentage of total capital and employment.[24]

Japan began to make direct investments in other countries in the 1970s, with some noticeable impact in Korea, the Philippines, and Thailand. Though the highest annual investments were only $200 million in Korea in 1973, $150 million in the Philippines in 1975, and $35 million in Thailand in 1973, the impact of direct investment was often substantial because of the local capital it mobilized. In a number of instances, Japanese investments designed to promote trade had favorable effects on both the Japanese and the host economy. In the early 1970s, for example, when Japan began to import more and more feed grains from Thailand, Japanese general trading companies invested in the manufacturing, storage, and distribution of mixed feed grains, and smaller companies engaged in the cultivation of feed grains directly. Such investments help mitigate the host country's export fluctuations as well as keeping Japanese imports steady since Japanese parent companies vary their purchases from nonaffiliated foreign suppliers to offset fluctuations in the operations of their foreign subsidiaries. Japan's imports of fishery products have developed in a similar way; direct Japanese investments have resulted in more and more Japanese imports of fishery products from Thailand, the Republic of Korea, and Australia.

Financial links and the trade in goods are far more important in the transmission of business fluctuations than is direct investment. But direct invest-

24. Sueo Sekiguchi, *The Future of Labor Problems in Japan* (Tokyo: Japan Economic Research Center, 1977). In 1974, employees in foreign subsidiaries were only 0.45 percent of total employees.

ment may have a serious social impact since it threatens the existence of self-employed workers and family-owned factories.[25]

A New Economic Role

Japan along with all other countries had many difficult economic lessons to learn in the 1970s, most of them arising from changes that growing international interdependence thrust on the economy. The widespread lack of understanding of how to manage the interdependent world economy was a significant inhibitor of good policy responses. Furthermore, Japanese policymakers were not quick to grasp the significance of Japan's new role as a major world economic power.

Not until the 1970s did it become clear how complex and important its links with other countries were for Japan. Of course the need to import raw materials and to export manufactured goods to pay for them was obvious, but the fact that Japan was enlarging its ties through direct investment and private financial markets of all sorts was not comprehended. Thus when Japan developed a fundamental balance-of-payments surplus late in the 1960s, there was no immediate policy reaction to it. It was believed that the surplus would be corrected by faster growth in Japan; besides, only deficits were viewed as a problem.

However, surpluses do constitute a problem because they signify an undervaluation of the currency which in time must be corrected. Much industrial investment was undertaken in Japan and misallocated because of the undervalued yen, and the misallocation created structurally depressed firms and industries which became visible when the yen was finally appreciated. Furthermore the efforts of the government to forestall the rise of the yen by buying dollars in the exchange market added significantly to the growth of the money supply, particularly in 1970 and 1971. Many policymakers believed that Japan's extensive foreign-exchange controls and guidance over the creation of domestic credit could solve any monetary disturbance. They found that the measures previously employed to control inflation were no longer successful.

For much of the postwar period, Japan was rather relaxed about inflation. In that respect it was not alone. Japan consistently had a high rate of consumer price increase, but it was ascribed to the dual nature of the economy, which included both very high and very low productivity industries; Japan's

25. This part of the society is thus likely to become a social force against direct investment. Ibid.

international competitiveness depended on wholesale prices which were well behaved. With rapid economic growth, households continued to save a relatively large portion of their income even though they were getting a negative rate on interest on their savings accounts. Furthermore, every time inflation started to get out of hand, which occurred simultaneously with a weakening of the balance of payments, the Japanese government had only to slow down the rate of growth of the economy to cause prices to fall. A real recession was unknown in Japan. This relaxed attitude toward inflation was largely responsible for the failure to move to contain domestic inflationary impulses in 1972–73.

The Japanese inflation rate in 1972–73 was one of the highest among industrial countries and the worst in Japan since the immediate postwar episode. The consequences for Japan were serious because the economy was becoming much wealthier and more mature. Householders responded to the inflation by increasing savings, thus inhibiting the government's ability to run the economy. Businesses responded by becoming more speculative; land prices in particular became so distorted as to disrupt the economy. Also because structural underemployment was low, labor-market pressures perpetuated the inflation. And as a consequence of greater economic interdependence, Japanese efforts to restrain the inflation, which was worldwide, were less successful than in the past. Japan, as the world's largest importer of raw materials, contributed greatly to the commodity boom and, through it, exported its inflation.

Japan's delay in switching back to reflationary policies following the 1974–75 recession and the lack of vigor in the policies it finally adopted had very serious consequences for other countries, although Japan's economy also suffered. In the latter half of 1975 there was evidence that prices were stabilizing and that Japan's balance-of-payments crisis had passed. However, many countries were experiencing serious stagflations and balance-of-payments crises. Japan could have afforded to stimulate its domestic demand, and it should have done so in the interest not only of itself but of the world economy. The virulence of the previous inflation, however, made the government extremely cautious for fear of rekindling it. And the government's adherence to the ideology of an annual balanced budget meant that a rise in the fiscal deficit, which was needed to cure the domestic financial imbalance, was itself treated as a distortion; it was strongly resisted, particularly by the Ministry of Finance, and was financed in the least stimulative way possible, through issue of long-term bonds. Moreover, the government's monetary and fiscal policies were restricted because they were designed to reduce wage demands by the labor unions. Finally, the split within the governing party over the Lockheed scandal in 1976 created a void in political leadership.

If the Japanese government had been willing to take strong domestic reflationary measures—for instance, to reduce personal taxes sufficiently to generate domestic-led growth—Japan could have recovered with reasonably balanced relations with the rest of the world. As it was, Japan's reliance on export-led growth resulted in a balance-of-payments surplus that forced up the value of the yen. The rising yen weakened business firms' willingness to invest, and with inadequate domestic demand firms were under even greater pressure to increase exports and reduce imports which exacerbated the original imbalance. The rise in the exchange rate added to pressures to restrict imports. And difficulties of domestic adjustment, which routinely are converted in the political process into demands for import restrictions, particularly on manufactured goods from Pacific basin countries, compounded the trade problems.

The impact on Pacific basin economies of Japan's export-led balance-of-payments surplus is apparent in their bilateral trade balances for 1977 (though it is a country's overall balance that matters, its surplus is reflected as a deficit in other countries' accounts, which makes bilateral balances interesting). In 1977 Japan had a huge overall trade surplus of $9.7 billion. It had a bilateral surplus with the United States of $7.3 billion which was 24 percent of the U.S. trade deficit (almost 50 percent of its current account deficit).[26] Its surplus with Korea was $2.0 billion or four times the total Korean trade deficit and with Thailand over $600 million or 77 percent of its total deficit. Japan's surplus with the Philippines was over $200 million or 24 percent of the total Philippine deficit, but until 1976 the Philippines had a surplus in its trade with Japan. Only with Australia did Japan have a deficit, which was close to $3.0 billion. The sum of Japan's trade with the five countries in 1977 was a surplus of $7.1 billion, nearly three-quarters of Japan's total surplus.

In the 1970s Japan's economy became so deeply interrelated with other economies, and particularly those in the Pacific basin, that these links cannot be ignored in any of Japan's economic policies. Japan can no longer ignore the impact it is having on others because it is so important to them that a reaction is inevitable. Either exchange rates will be destabilized, or trade restrictions will be enforced, or some other undesirable consequence will occur. The health of the Japanese economy depends on these things not happening.

26. Japanese bilateral balances are from Japan Tariff Association, *Summary Report, Trade of Japan*, 2:1978; other countries' overall trade balances are from IMF, *International Financial Statistics*, vol. 31 (December 1978).

CHAPTER FOUR

Australia's Shrinking Markets

ROSS GARNAUT

THE MACROECONOMIC PROBLEMS that came to preoccupy the governments of most industrial countries after 1970 were late to arrive in Australia. But they were well established by 1973 and became more severe than in most countries. In 1977, Australia was still experiencing high and rising unemployment, stagnation of total output, and high inflation. Economic instability was both cause and effect of the most intense polarization in Australian political life since the 1930s. It was also an important cause of a widespread distrust of outward-looking economic policies and of structural change that seemed likely to prolong the country's economic difficulties and to reduce long-run growth prospects.

There were many major changes in Australia's domestic and external economic environment in the early 1970s. On the normal difficulties of stabilization policy (including considerable rigidity in Australian factor markets) were heaped three exceptional external influences: the worldwide monetary expansion, the commodity boom and slump, and then the transition to lower growth in the advanced industrial countries. The coincidence of these external shocks with the domestic political polarization was very important in limiting the range of policy responses that governments judged to be open to them.

Australian Experience in the 1970s

Australia's economy was relatively stable from the time of the commodities boom associated with the Korean War until the early 1970s. Inflation averaged about 3 percent per year, a lower rate than that of most other rich industrial countries. Unemployment rates were exceptionally low, rising above 2 percent only between 1960 and 1962. The only other members of the Organization for Economic Cooperation and Development with lower average unemployment rates were West Germany and Japan. Growth in industrial production (a little over 5 percent a year through the 1960s) and in real product was about average by OECD standards and relatively stable. Growth in real gross domestic product was positive in all financial years between 1952–53 and 1974–75 and was rapid from the early 1960s.

Australia's levels of growth, unemployment, and inflation did not deteriorate as rapidly in the 1970s as most other OECD countries'. Inflation rates remained low until 1973, but they did not moderate as much as other OECD countries' in 1975 and 1976; unemployment held down relatively well until 1974, but labor market conditions deteriorated sharply in 1974 and 1975, and the proportion of unemployed continued to rise in 1976 and 1977 after the downward trend had been arrested in several countries. Real output held up better than in other OECD countries in 1974 and early 1975 but failed to recover as rapidly after mid-1975.

Australia's stabilization problems were compounded by poor management of two important changes in the economic environment—the very rapid growth of a large, high-productivity mining sector in Australia, and world monetary expansion, which originated in the United States. It was inevitable that the minerals growth would force large-scale structural change in the economy. This change could have occurred either in an inflationary manner, as increased demand for labor associated with the monetary effects of balance-of-payments surpluses found its way into increases in money wages and the general price level, or in a noninflationary way, through successive currency revaluations (or reductions in barriers to imports). Whatever the process of adjustment, some increase in frictional and structural unemployment was likely. Sooner or later the international monetary expansion would find its way into increases in the general price level through the monetary effects of balance-of-payments surpluses, unless it was undercut by revaluation of the Australian dollar.

The Australian authorities maintained tight fiscal and monetary policies in 1970 and 1971, holding monetary growth down to modest levels despite the large balance-of-payments surplus and thus postponing adjustment to the growth in minerals production and to the international inflation. It is doubtful whether tight monetary policies could have worked after late 1971, as the undervaluation of the Australian dollar combined with relatively high domestic interest rates began to attract foreign capital. At any rate, relaxed fiscal and monetary policies in 1972 had gotten Australia well on its way to inflationary adjustment to the recent experience of strong export growth and overseas inflation when a Labor government took office in December 1972.

The postponed adjustment became tangled with a further destabilizing influence from overseas: the commodities boom of 1972–74 and the subsequent collapse of international markets for most industrial raw materials and some foodstuffs in 1974. Australia's terms of trade, which tend to rise in times of buoyant world economic conditions and fall in times of world recession, showed a huge improvement in early 1972, and Australia felt very rich by early 1973. The cyclical deterioration in the terms of trade in 1974 was compounded by the increase in the price of oil imports, but rising prices of coal exports soon offset the petroleum costs.

In the first half of 1974, domestic expenditure and wages rose to very high levels, at the time that the terms of trade were falling (they reached historically low levels by the end of the year). Aggregate real expenditure in 1972 and 1973 had risen beyond levels that were consistent with the balance in external payments, and real wages beyond levels consistent with low levels of unemployment, at normal terms of trade. The deterioration in the terms of trade coincided with a range of policy initiatives that turned the balance of payments around into large deficit. The resulting monetary contraction was the proximate cause of recession and a sudden increase in unemployment.

One factor made the onset of world recession especially virulent in Australia. The high inflation, oil crisis, and recession in early 1974 marked the end of the period of high growth in Japan. With Japan's transition to more moderate growth, there was a sharp reduction in demand for minerals and metals, which for a decade had accounted for a large part of the growth in total Australian exports. The loss of this opportunity for export expansion and the effects of international recession in 1974 and 1975 left Australia with stagnation in total output, high and rising unemployment, and high and slowly diminishing inflation. Whether these problems are mainly a legacy of the early 1970s or the result of domestic policy mistakes is a focus of dispute in Australian economic analysis and politics.

Major External Sources of Instability

The exchange rate is a crucial factor in the transmission of international instability to the Australian economy. Government management of fluctuations in the exchange rate affects the impact of other international influences —prices of exports and imports, variations in their volumes and in the current account balance, international financial links, and the overall balance of payments.

The Exchange Rate

In the 1950s and 1960s the Australian dollar was formally pegged against sterling, but its exchange rate with the U.S. dollar remained constant, even after the British devaluation of 1967. The effective trade-weighted average exchange rate with fifteen major currencies fell about 1 percent in 1970 and a further 1 percent in 1971.[1] Following the international monetary agreement of December 1971, the foreign-exchange value of the Australian dollar was depreciated slightly against sterling (which amounted to a small depreciation of the effective rate and an appreciation of about 6 percent against the U.S. dollar). At the same time the Australian dollar was formally pegged against the U.S. dollar. By December 1972 the effective rate was about 3 percent below the mid-1970 level, despite Australia's extremely strong balance of payments and the high priority accorded to the control of inflation in 1970 and 1971.

The Labor government appreciated the dollar shortly after taking office in December 1972 (by 7 percent) and twice more in 1973. By January 1974 the effective rate was 20 percent above that of mid-1970. In September the process of appreciation was reversed with a devaluation by 12 percent to an effective rate about 4 percent above the 1970 level and the peg was shifted to a trade-weighted basket of currencies. Because two weak currencies—the pound sterling and the New Zealand dollar—had substantial weights in the new basket, the Australian dollar depreciated considerably against the stronger currencies in 1975–76 (7 percent against the U.S. dollar).

A huge devaluation of 17.5 percent was effected in November 1976, and the government announced a new exchange-rate regime—"something in the manner of a managed float." The rate of the dollar against the trade-weighted basket was adjusted upward about a dozen times before the new year, reducing the November change to a net depreciation of about 12.5 percent. The rate was kept almost constant against the basket during the first half of 1977, with the effective rate a little less than 10 percent below the 1970 level. In reality, the new exchange-rate regime had none of the characteristics of a floating rate. It was simply the old adjustable peg, reworked on the principle that adjustments should be small and should come more frequently than in earlier times.

1. Effective exchange rates are from Morgan Guaranty Trust Co. of New York, *World Financial Markets,* August 1976.

Export and Import Prices

The rate of increase in international wholesale prices was very high in 1971 (in comparison with historical experience). It accelerated in the next three years and eased in early 1975.[2] The combined effects of these trends and Australian exchange-rate policy are reflected in the changes in the Australian export and import price indexes (tables 4-1 and 4-2). Import prices began to rise rapidly in financial 1968–69, the rate of increase accelerating until the revaluations of 1972–73. In 1973–74, despite a further revaluation, the rate of increase (45 percent) was almost twice as high as in any previous year; it fell by half but remained very high (24 percent) through 1974–75. From mid-1975 the rate of increase of import prices remained well below Australian inflation rates until a sharp increase in the March quarter of 1976–77 was precipitated by devaluation of the Australian dollar.

In financial years 1967–71, while import prices were accelerating, export prices were unusually stable. But in 1972–73 the export price index exploded with a one-third increase despite revaluations, and it continued to rise thereafter. Prices of all major export commodities rose, reflecting the very broad impact of the boom in international commodity markets, whereas in earlier booms, increases had been concentrated in one or two commodities, such as wool and metals in the Korean War boom.[3]

In the early stages of the acceleration of world prices the terms of trade moved against Australia, then strongly toward Australia in 1973, and as strongly against it in 1974. These changes involved huge variations in Australian real incomes, adding perhaps 7–9 percent in one year and withdrawing a similar amount the next.

The variations in the domestic price of imports and exports appear even more dramatic in quarterly than in annual data (table 4-2). Over half the improvement in the terms of trade that occurred through the export boom was concentrated in the March quarter of 1973 (which happened to be the first quarter of the new Labor government's period in office). In that quarter, export prices rose by 21 percent and import prices fell by 6 percent in the wake of the December revaluation. The subsequent decline in the terms of trade, which took place almost wholly in 1974, was concentrated in the first half of the year.

2. Wolfgang Kasper, "The Exchange Rate—A New Instrument of Economic Policy," *Australian Economic Review,* Fourth Quarter 1975, chart C.

3. See John D. Pitchford, "Inflation in Australia," in Lawrence B. Krause and Walter S. Salant, eds., *Worldwide Inflation: Theory and Recent Experience* (Brookings Institution, 1977), pp. 379–80.

Table 4-1. Australian Macroeconomic Performance, by Financial Year, 1946–69

Percent

Financial year	Un-employ-ment	Job vacancies	Change in export price index	Change in import price index	Change in money supply		Change in award (minimum) wages	Change in award wage estimate	Change in consumer price index	Change in gross domestic product deflator	Change in real gross domestic product
					M_1	M_3					
1946–47	1.1	2.80	n.a.	n.a.	5.29	n.a.	...	n.a.	n.a.	n.a.	n.a.
1947–48	0.6	4.20	43.49	11.75	10.26	5.68	11.86	n.a.	8.86	n.a.	n.a.
1948–49	0.6	4.30	2.61	1.14	13.93	9.37	8.79	13.45	11.33	n.a.	n.a.
1949–50	0.5	4.10	43.22	12.22	20.12	14.32	7.84	9.60	8.43	9.06	8.03
1950–51	0.4	4.50	41.96	28.79	27.94	18.90	24.71	19.59	13.03	25.54	5.86
1951–52	1.2	1.70	−28.63	0.97	3.30	−1.03	18.90	22.41	22.49	4.29	2.83
1952–53	2.1	0.88	11.52	−5.29	12.28	10.23	6.79	9.13	9.41	14.45	−0.85
1953–54	0.8	1.70	7.02	−0.31	5.60	7.21	1.52	5.48	1.94	2.67	6.46
1954–55	0.7	2.10	−10.27	1.84	0.96	2.89	3.74	4.89	0.68	1.20	5.91
1955–56	1.1	1.30	−4.21	2.20	2.18	0.88	4.84	7.00	4.05	2.57	5.05
1956–57	1.7	0.70	15.85	1.96	4.82	6.72	3.63	4.63	5.34	6.17	1.89
1957–58	2.2	0.60	−25.26	1.92	1.85	2.34	1.55	2.86	0.98	0.73	2.21
1958–59	1.6	0.70	7.04	0.19	2.99	5.08	3.48	3.04	1.58	−1.35	7.38
1959–60	1.1	1.00	2.63	1.41	7.54	7.73	5.44	7.86	2.51	4.47	5.37
1960–61	2.6	0.50	0	1.11	−6.48	1.52	2.00	4.78	4.00	3.10	3.19
1961–62	2.1	0.60	−1.28	−1.01	2.58	7.45	2.24	3.70	0.45	1.26	1.02
1962–63	1.8	0.60	8.57	0.93	2.55	8.57	1.80	2.72	0.22	1.44	6.23
1963–64	1.1	0.79	4.79	1.38	7.74	12.20	4.86	5.31	0.89	3.31	7.41
1964–65	0.9	0.96	−9.82	2.00	1.55	8.17	2.51	7.56	3.75	2.19	6.92
1965–66	1.2	0.69	10.51	2.31	0.71	5.81	2.67	4.50	3.62	3.76	1.75
1966–67	1.4	0.59	−6.76	−0.78	6.73	8.10	6.71	6.72	2.67	2.93	6.39
1967–68	1.3	0.57	2.33	−1.75	8.35	8.30	5.77	5.82	3.30	2.80	3.75
1968–69	1.1	0.68	1.76	3.83	7.61	9.13	7.03	7.48	2.61	3.31	8.84

Sources: Australian Department of Labour, *Monthly Review of the Employment Situation,* various issues; Australian Bureau of Statistics, *Monthly Review of the Employment Situation and Employment and Unemployment,* various issues, and *Quarterly Estimates of National Income and Expenditure,* various issues; Reserve Bank of Australia, *Statistical Bulletin.*

n.a. Not available.

The immediate impact of the commodity boom on Australia's domestic price level was less severe than on many countries' because of various domestic price stabilization and support schemes. Over the longer term, domestic prices tend to be adjusted upward toward world prices, but there is no tendency for them to fall when world prices go down. Price support schemes introduced to protect producers insulated domestic prices of flour, sugar, and dairy products (all important consumer goods) from the major part of the increase in world prices. But domestic prices of some exportable foodstuffs did rise with the international market. The rising price of meat, the single most important Australian wage good, became a symbol of the inflation problem, contributing more than one-quarter of the increase in the consumer price index in 1973, the first year of very high inflation. Among the institutional devices that cushioned exportable industrial raw materials against fluctuations in world market prices was a prices justification tribunal established in 1973 to hear arguments on price increases sought by large corporations. The maximum domestic price that it set for copper kept Australian prices well below world prices until the collapse of the international copper price in mid-1974.

Crude petroleum from Australian sources, which accounted for almost two-thirds of Australia's requirements, was sold domestically at prices near the pre-1974 world parity until late 1977, when a gradual rise to world parity was approved. In the intervening years the average price of all crude petroleum used by refiners roughly doubled, and the domestic price of petroleum products rose by a much smaller amount. For these reasons and because Australia is a large exporter of coal, prices for which rose in sympathy with the increase in oil prices, the world oil crisis was not seen by Australians as a major problem in itself.

It is a common view that a uniform 10 percent increase in the Australian domestic currency price of exports and imports has the immediate effect of raising the average price level by 1.0–2.5 percent.[4] Thus the increase in export and import prices between financial years 1971–72 and 1974–75 would have raised the domestic price level 7–18 percent (accounting for something between one-sixth and one-third of the total increase). But the inflationary impact of the price increases does not stop there, for powerful institutional mechanisms tend to transmit the increases to other domestic prices. Wage-setting institutions tend to maintain historical wage relativities, and large

4. See J. W. Nevile, "The Exchange Rate, Inflation and Unemployment," in *Exchange Rate Changes and the Australian Economy,* University of New South Wales, Centre for Applied Economic Research, Occasional Paper 2 (May 1977), pp. 26–27. Recent estimates are in the top of the range.

Table 4-2. *Australian Macroeconomic Performance, by Quarter, 1969–77*
Percent

Financial year and quarter	Unemployment	Job vacancies	Change in export price index	Change in import price index	Change in money supply		Change in award (minimum) wages	Change in award wage estimate	Change in consumer price index	Change in gross domestic product deflator	Change in real gross domestic product
					M_1	M_3					
1969–70											
September	1.0	0.91	1.02	0	0.83	1.68	0.58	2.35	0.56	1.48	1.66
December	1.1	0.95	−2.02	1.96	2.64	2.18	3.82	1.62	0.84	0.27	1.53
March	1.0	1.05	0	0.58	3.35	1.85	0.29	2.26	1.01	0.82	−0.75
June	1.0	0.93	0	0.86	−2.05	0.25	0.75	2.60	1.28	2.53	3.23
1970–71											
September	1.1	0.89	−2.06	0.38	1.67	0.96	1.37	2.02	0.63	0.79	0.49
December	1.1	0.92	−1.05	1.61	1.53	1.92	2.03	2.36	1.88	0.52	0.34
March	1.2	0.76	2.13	1.58	0.97	1.77	6.92	4.73	1.05	1.04	2.41
June	1.3	0.71	1.04	2.48	2.08	2.64	0.93	2.78	1.74	4.55	0.30
1971–72											
September	1.5	0.67	−2.06	2.42	2.26	2.31	3.20	1.58	1.88	1.07	3.06
December	1.6	0.72	0	−0.35	0.09	1.76	1.99	1.77	2.35	−0.33	−0.03
March	1.1	0.53	8.42	1.40	1.97	2.45	1.02	0.98	0.98	2.04	−0.59
June	1.9	0.53	5.83	1.73	4.74	3.71	4.13	3.13	0.89	3.20	1.37
1972–73											
September	2.0	0.60	2.75	−0.26	5.15	5.99	1.90	2.62	1.37	2.48	0.84
December	1.7	0.69	10.71	−1.28	7.28	6.48	2.61	2.04	1.19	1.13	2.16
March	1.5	0.88	20.97	−6.04	3.72	4.63	1.70	1.70	2.11	2.24	2.41
June	1.6	1.12	−3.33	3.03	7.83	6.48	8.15	4.72	3.30	3.66	0.41

1973–74											
September	1.4	1.44	0	5.17	3.66	5.52	1.96	4.78	3.64	4.87	2.64
December	1.4	1.28	0.69	2.03	−0.16	3.02	2.11	3.31	3.58	3.70	0.89
March	1.4	1.46	9.59	19.27	−0.25	2.65	2.32	2.86	2.42	2.01	1.33
June	1.5	1.22	1.88	13.65	2.37	2.08	20.06	7.08	4.05	4.45	−2.06
1974–75											
September	2.5	0.74	3.68	4.72	−1.57	−1.29	7.13	10.23	5.13	6.82	−1.18
December	3.8	0.65	5.92	15.33	3.21	1.59	3.17	5.35	3.77	4.17	1.54
March	4.4	0.56	−1.68	1.98	6.20	6.07	1.78	2.37	3.57	1.31	−0.25
June	4.5	0.48	−3.41	1.00	4.51	4.43	5.06	2.85	3.50	3.19	2.97
1975–76											
September	5.1[a]	0.46	0.59	1.48	4.97	5.42	3.98	2.64	0.78	4.29	−2.39
December	4.6[a]	0.46	4.09	4.27	5.81	3.36	0.79	4.51	5.56	5.82	−0.99
March	4.4[a]	0.36	2.81	1.49	4.25	1.43	6.43	2.28	2.97	4.0	2.83
June	4.9[a]	…	2.73	1.56	−1.17	2.87	2.96	4.46	2.53	3.1	2.11
1976–77											
September	4.4[a]	0.39	2.81	4.66	2.84	4.49	2.01	4.01	2.22	1.6	2.6
December	4.2[a]	0.56	10.92	4.09	2.81	2.84	2.16	1.27	5.99	2.9	−0.6
March	5.4	0.50	14.18	2.33	3.36	3.36	4.23	2.48	2.28	3.2	−1.5
June	5.1	0.40	0.49	1.94	−0.62	−0.62	1.96	3.13	2.36	0.6	0.9

Sources: Same as table 4-1.
a. Australian Bureau of Statistics, *Household Survey*, reported unemployment percentages in 1975–76 as 4.2 in September, 5.3 in December, 4.6 in March, and 4.1 in June, and in 1976–77 as 4.3 in September and 5.4 in December.

wage settlements in relatively profitable industries producing tradable goods sometimes flow readily to other industries.[5] They also tend to maintain real wages, even when formal wage indexation arrangements are not in force.[6] The long-standing rigidities in the wage structure were reinforced when formal, quarterly wage adjustments, by all or part of the percentage increase in the consumer price index, were instituted in 1975.

But despite wage rigidity, the speed with which and the extent to which changes in export and import prices are transmitted into wages and the prices of other goods and services depend on domestic economic conditions. This was apparent in 1977, when the general price level rose by little more than the export and import price rises after the large devaluation of November 1976. Rising export and import prices seem to have had a much wider effect when easy monetary conditions prevailed in 1972 and 1973 than in the more taut monetary environment of later years.[7]

Trade Volume and the Current Account Balance

The ratios of exports and imports to gross domestic product averaged about 15 percent in the 1970s. This is not high for an economy as small as Australia's (it reflects, in part, Australia's geographic isolation and protectionist trade policies), but it is high enough for fluctuations in the trade balance to have an important impact on total domestic incomes. Exports tended to increase a little more rapidly than GDP, and imports to grow a little less rapidly than GDP, as the ratio of net capital inflow to GDP declined.

The emergence of a large petroleum-mining industry, producing about two-thirds of domestic petroleum requirements, tended to reduce the foreign-trade orientation of the Australian economy in the late 1960s. But this tendency was offset by strong growth in several export industries, especially minerals and metals, which rose as a share of total exports from 25 percent in financial 1967–68 to 30 percent in 1971–72 and 36 percent in 1975–76.

5. This is not a uniquely Australian phenomenon. See, for example, Odd Aukrust, "Inflation in the Open Economy: A Norwegian Model," in Krause and Salant, *Worldwide Inflation*, pp. 107–67.

6. The tendency to real wage rigidity in Australia was noted by John Maynard Keynes in *The General Theory of Employment, Interest and Money* (London: Macmillan, 1936), pp. 269–70.

7. Kasper argues, in "The Exchange Rate," that because of the rigidity of the wage structure and the power of organized labor to maintain wage relativities, increases in the domestic price of tradable goods are likely to be fully transmitted into the general domestic price level in a relatively short time. Increased prices of tradable goods lead to high profits and high wage settlements in export and import-competing industries, and the wage increases are spread throughout the economy. Kasper's case depends on the existence of accommodating domestic monetary conditions.

The composition of imports changed considerably in the 1970s. The share of petroleum in total imports declined with the increase in world prices in 1973 and 1974. Labor-intensive manufactured goods became more important in total imports after 1973.

The reorientation in the pattern of trade specialization was closely linked to rapid world economic growth in the 1960s (especially in Japan) and to high levels of direct foreign investment in Australia. The associated strengthening of the Australian economy meant that it could support higher real domestic incomes and expenditure and finance the considerable restructuring of domestic industry that was required.[8]

Australia's major exports are industrial raw materials, which are very much affected in both volume and price by the external business cycle. Fluctuations in world market conditions directly affect the Australian economy by changing export income and indirectly through the monetary impact of variations in the balance of payments. Worldwide fluctuations also provide grounds for reassessing long-term market prospects for major exports and thus affect the level of investment in Australia's export industries. In the 1960s Australian exports typically reached a peak in response to world demand for industrial raw materials slightly in advance of the peak of the external business cycle. This relationship was not apparent in the early 1970s.[9] Export values continued to increase even during the external contraction from the second quarter of 1970 to the first quarter of 1972, in response to earlier minerals investment and to the undervaluation of the Australian dollar (which promoted rapid growth in manufactured exports) as seen in table 4-3. In 1973 the Australian dollar value of exports rose by a huge 25 percent despite the successive revaluations, in response to extraordinarily buoyant world market conditions. There was a small fall in the real value of total exports in 1974, although the usual decline in exports with the downturn in activity overseas was broken somewhat by the increase in energy (most importantly, coal) prices in early 1974. The old relationships seem to have been restored in 1975. The real value of exports again grew strongly as some major foreign economies entered the early stages of recovery. After that, the real value of exports roughly held its ground. With the growth of Australian economic nationalism, and after 1974 the loss of optimism about growth in the Japanese and world economies, the impetus to strong secular growth in exports seems to have disappeared.

8. For a controversial discussion of the domestic structural implications of the minerals export growth, see R. G. Gregory, "Some Implications of the Growth of the Mining Sector," *Australian Journal of Agricultural Economics*, vol. 20 (August 1976).

9. P. F. Barry and C. W. Guile, "The Australian Business Cycle and International Cyclical Linkages, 1959–1974," *Economic Record*, June 1976.

Table 4-3. *Value of Australia's Exports and Imports, by Quarter, 1970–77*

Year and quarter	Exports		Imports	
	Millions of dollars	Percent change on previous quarter	Millions of dollars	Percent change on previous quarter
1970				
First	1,049	3.76	943	−3.29
Second	1,058	0.86	986	4.56
Third	1,085	2.55	1,089	10.45
Fourth	1,063	−2.03	1,037	−5.69
1971				
First	1,032	−2.92	978	−6.03
Second	1,195	15.79	1,046	6.95
Third	1,229	2.85	1,044	−0.19
Fourth	1,150	−6.43	1,028	−1.53
1972				
First	1,190	3.48	979	−4.77
Second	1,333	12.02	914	−6.44
Third	1,358	1.88	939	2.74
Fourth	1,539	13.33	1,044	11.18
1973				
First	1,667	8.32	1,053	0.86
Second	1,657	−0.60	1,087	3.23
Third	1,649	−0.49	1,265	16.38
Fourth	1,754	6.38	1,436	13.52
1974				
First	1,688	−3.76	1,546	7.66
Second	1,823	8.00	1,837	18.82
Third	2,009	10.20	2,205	20.03
Fourth	2,169	7.96	2,181	−1.10
1975				
First	2,160	−0.42	1,847	−15.31
Second	2,351	8.84	1,847	0.00
Third	2,278	−3.11	1,959	6.06
Fourth	2,286	0.35	1,979	1.02
1976				
First	2,331	1.97	2,121	7.18
Second	2,684	15.14	2,181	2.83
Third	2,983	11.14	2,415	10.73
Fourth	2,778	−6.87	2,418	0.12
1977				
First	2,855	2.77	2,777	14.85
Second	3,032	6.20	2,801	0.86
Third	3,076	1.45	2,828	0.96
Fourth	3,064	−0.39	2,626	−7.14

Source: Reserve Bank of Australia, *Statistical Bulletin*, various issues.

Variations in the level of Australian imports have typically followed the domestic business cycle with a lag of one or two quarters.[10] But the value of imports grew very slowly in 1971 and 1972 despite moderately high growth in domestic product, and held very steady in 1973 despite the extremely buoyant domestic conditions, possibly in response to the earlier undervaluation of the dollar. Imports then jumped sharply by 43 percent in 1974, as domestic demand exceeded domestic capacity and spilled over into imports, and as the economy responded to the changes in relative prices associated with the revaluations and the 25 percent across-the-board tariff cut of July 1973. Imports grew at the high rate of 30 percent in 1975, but the usual effects of recession, helped along by reversals of exchange-rate and protection policy, took over and the real value of imports fell from mid-1975.

In the 1960s variations in the overall trade balance helped to stabilize domestic activity.[11] Low imports in times of domestic recession and rising exports in response to improved external conditions moved the balance of trade into surplus and commonly led the way to recovery. The subsequent downturn in exports and increase in imports late in the expansionary phase of the domestic cycle moderated the growth in domestic activity. This pattern was not apparent in the early 1970s (table 4-4). The Australian business cycle tended to move into phase with the international business cycle— at the time that cycles of the major industrial countries were tending to synchronize. The trade balance did not turn down during the strong expansion of late 1972 and 1973. The largest-ever surplus in the current account was recorded in 1973. When the trade account did turn around in 1974, the current account moved over $2.5 billion into deficit. This reversal was so large that it was very likely to send the economy into recession, especially as its late arrival meant that it coincided with a marked slackening in the growth of domestic inventories.[12]

The trade balance seems to have returned to a moderate, countercyclical role from mid-1975. Its unusual behavior in 1972 and 1973 seems to have been due to the undervaluation of the Australian dollar in combination with an unusually long external expansion. It is possible that import growth was frustrated in 1973 by commodity scarcities in the worldwide boom conditions (and that Australian imports were encouraged excessively as overseas exporters responded to incipient recession in their home countries in 1974). The unusually severe reversal of the trade balance in 1974 can be attributed

10. Ibid.
11. Ibid.
12. Fred Gruen, "What Went Wrong? Some Personal Reflections on Economic Policies under Labor," *Australian Quarterly,* vol. 48 (December 1976), pp. 24–25.

Table 4-4. *Australia's Balance of Payments, by Quarter, 1970–77*

Millions of dollars

Year and quarter	Exports	Imports	Trade balance	Current account balance	Foreign capital flow To government	Foreign capital flow To private sector	Overall balance
1970							
First	1,013	855	158	−136	−34	188	176
Second	1,021	906	115	−214	−45	508	364
Third	1,038	962	76	−204	−17	151	6
Fourth	1,033	938	95	−239	−49	313	120
1971							
First	933	909	24	−235	26	471	286
Second	1,153	981	172	−165	−23	569	553
Third	1,185	1,047	138	−167	7	426	404
Fourth	1,112	987	125	−231	−11	504	387
1972							
First	1,154	912	242	−53	−1	415	603
Second	1,278	844	434	56	−52	551	989
Third	1,327	895	432	135	39	470	1,076
Fourth	1,500	939	561	205	−22	444	1,188
1973							
First	1,629	960	669	264	−58	−505	370
Second	1,505	1,016	489	57	−63	78	561
Third	1,601	1,235	366	−23	78	−59	362
Fourth	1,730	1,302	428	44	−10	−36	426
1974							
First	1,626	1,473	153	−267	−14	33	−95
Second	1,737	1,743	−6	−537	−62	283	−322
Third	1,926	2,103	−177	−625	−40	80	−762
Fourth	2,167	2,087	80	−438	−6	300	−64
1975							
First	2,139	1,766	373	−43	−33	101	398
Second	2,299	1,711	588	49	18	161	816
Third	2,157	1,858	299	−268	−91	72	12
Fourth	2,293	1,905	388	−246	−101	−376	−335
1976							
First	2,324	2,037	287	−341	−44	370	272
Second	2,636	2,124	512	−242	99	148	517
Third	2,858	2,398	460	−290	156	−133	193
Fourth	2,804	2,408	396	−262	122	131	387
1977							
First	2,799	2,794	5	−662	−35	832	140
Second	2,939	2,746	193	−652	−126	428	−157
Third	3,013	2,826	187	−605	411	−539	−546
Fourth	3,086	2,641	445	−301	340	−105	379

Source: Reserve Bank of Australia, *Statistical Bulletin*, various issues. Trade figures are adjusted for balance-of-payments purposes and thus may differ from figures in table 4-3.

to the very large increase in imports, which was due to a rapid increase in domestic expansion, appreciations of the exchange rate, shortages of Australian supplies, and to a lesser extent the tariff cuts.[13]

The increase in the general level of export and import prices in the early 1970s and the boom in commodities prices in 1972 and 1973 were worldwide phenomena. Their effect on Pacific basin countries was more or less similar to that in other parts of the world. But since a considerable part of the worldwide instability was caused by the United States and Japan, the smaller Pacific basin countries were at times affected by their proximity to and close ties with these economies. The worldwide inflation probably posed no greater problems for Pacific basin countries than for others. But the commodities boom did have wider repercussions for them since a disproportionate share of the growth in industrial countries' demand for raw materials came from Japan. Japan contributed 13 percent of the growth in the real value of world imports in 1970. By 1973 it contributed 16.3 percent and was by far the world's largest importer of foodstuffs and industrial raw materials. Japan accounted for more than one-quarter of the expansion in world imports of petroleum in the late 1960s and early 1970s and over one-half for timber and nonferrous metals and ores.[14]

Australia, because of its close trade ties with Japan, was particularly vulnerable to instability in Japanese demand. Japan purchased about half of Australian minerals and metals exports in the early 1970s and three-quarters or more of the major commodities iron ore, coal, and aluminum.[15] Japanese metals consumption declined much further than total economic activity in 1974 and did not recover with the economy as a whole from 1975; it remained well below 1973 levels in 1977. This was an inevitable but poorly foreseen consequence of the adjustment to lower growth in Japan with its associated decline in Japanese investment (and hence demand for metals-intensive capital goods) and in the relative size of the Japanese (metals-intensive) manufacturing sector.

A large part of the minerals trade between Australia and Japan was conducted within long-term contracts. When exchange-rate changes and then inflation distorted contract prices, Australian exporters called for the renegotiation of contracts. Next, the slump in Japanese metals demand caused

13. R. G. Gregory and L. D. Martin, "An Analysis of Relationships Between Import Flows to Australia and Recent Exchange Rate and Tariff Changes," *Economic Record*, March 1976.

14. See Jenny Corbett and Ross Garnaut, "Japan and the Resource-Rich Developing Countries," Australia-Japan Economic Relations Research Paper (Canberra, 1975), pp. 6–7.

15. See Ben Smith, "The Japanese Connection," in P. Hastings and R. Farran, eds., *Australia's Resources Future* (Melbourne: Thomas Nelson, 1978).

Japanese importers to insist on purchasing less than the minimum contract tonnages. Thus the pressures of the marketplace challenged the stable framework of long-term contracts, both in the boom years of 1972 and 1973 and in the recession of 1975.

Similar problems arose in agricultural trade, especially sugar. About half of the tonnage in Australian sugar contracts negotiated in 1975 was covered by a fixed-price contract to supply the Japanese market (the contract covered about one-third of Japanese import demand). The contract price, which was much lower than the world price when negotiated, was higher by the time deliveries began and by mid-1977 about twice the spot world price. The Japanese contractors (but not their domestic competitors) claimed that the contract was unfair and insisted on its renegotiation. The Japanese government, like the Australian government in the minerals case, exerted pressure for renegotiation of the contract. Such interventions were resented by the private parties who stood to lose from renegotiation and they contributed to uncertainty in the trade.

Direct government intervention was even more important in contributing to instability and uncertainty. Sudden changes in the protection policies of foreign governments were felt especially in Australia's beef trade. Australian producers invested heavily around 1970 to expand production in response to strong growth in Japanese and world import demand. Sales to Japan represented over one-quarter of Australia's total beef exports by value in 1973, and beef was one of the country's leading exports, valued in U.S. dollars at $1.4 billion, compared with only $0.8 billion in 1972, and $0.4 billion in 1970. Suddenly, in 1974 Japan placed a complete embargo on beef imports. Closure of the Japanese market was the largest single factor behind a reduction of almost 60 percent to $0.6 billion in total Australian beef exports. But exports fell also to the United States, Europe, and other markets as protectionist measures grew.

The rapid expansion in demand for beef in 1972 and 1973 was partly brought on by other governments liberalizing their import trade measures in an attempt to moderate increases in domestic consumer prices. Not only did Australian exports expand in response, but Australian food prices increased. When major consuming countries shifted to protection of domestic producers in recession conditions, the sudden reduction in Australian exports contributed to major local economic problems as well as to general recession in Australia.

Just as the opening and closing of markets by the large Pacific economies damaged Australian economic interests, so Australia's moves to protect domestic production of labor-intensive manufactured goods damaged Southeast Asian economies. The tariff cut of July 1973 was implemented to increase the supply of goods to Australian markets, and so to alleviate inflationary pressures. It was an important factor behind the rapid increase in Australian imports of manufactured goods in 1974 and 1975, along with the earlier appreciations of the Australian dollar, the monetary expansion, and the increase in Australian wages. The dollar value of Australian imports of labor-intensive manufactured goods (including textiles, clothing, and footwear) in 1974 was double that of 1973. Australia's share of world imports of these goods, which had always been important, rose to 2.7 percent in 1974 from 1.9 percent in 1971. Some new investment in Southeast Asian countries was premised on that growth. When growth stopped, Australia applied severe import restrictions to a wider and wider range of manufactured commodities between late 1974 and late 1977. The new restrictions were most damaging to Malaysia and the Philippines, whose manufacturing industries were strongly oriented toward the Australian market.

Those are countries that may provide Australia with a large market in the future. Several East Asian and Southeast Asian countries in the latter 1960s and 1970s experienced a growth in incomes and imports reminiscent of Japan's growth in the 1950s.[16] It is likely that seven of these developing countries (including Korea, the Philippines, and Thailand) with a total population a little larger than that of Japan will see very rapid growth in industrial production, foreign trade, and incomes over the next decade. Australia may have to look to these countries for markets since it is unlikely that the growth in Japanese import demand will return to the high rates of earlier decades. As in the early stages of the expansion in Japanese-Australian trade, new institutions must be developed to handle the trade if its full potential is to be realized.

Financial Links and the Payments Balance

Through most of the 1950s and 1960s the flow of capital into Australia was very high, often amounting to 20–25 percent of the value of imports. This surplus on capital account roughly balanced the usual goods and services deficit. With it went high levels of direct investment and the expansion of domestic productive capacity. As links between Australian and international financial markets grew in the early 1970s, speculative capital movements became important for the first time and greatly complicated domestic

16. See Ross Garnaut, "Industrialisation in East and Southeast Asia and Some Implications for Australia," in W. Kasper and T. Parry, eds., *Growth, Trade and Structural Change in an Open Australian Economy* (University of New South Wales, Centre for Applied Economic Research, 1977).

Table 4-5. *Australian Monetary Data, by Quarter, 1970–77*

Year and quarter	Money supply (millions of dollars)[a]		Official reserve assets (millions of dollars)[b]		Interest on Treasury notes (percent)	
	M_1	M_2	Total	Change	Three-month notes	Six-month notes
1970						
First	5,337	8,112	1,232	106	4.90	5.04
Second	4,985	7,747	1,538	306	5.41	5.48
Third	5,035	7,757	1,504	−34	5.57	5.69
Fourth	5,446	8,280	1,511	7	5.65	5.80
1971						
First	5,415	8,440	1,855	343	5.65	5.80
Second	5,312	5,233	2,280	426	5.45	5.62
Third	5,467	8,444	2,536	256	5.37	5.57
Fourth	5,541	8,784	2,726	251	5.18	5.36
1972						
First	5,640	9,036	3,179	453	4.70	4.85
Second	5,900	9,482	3,764	585	4.59	4.74
Third	6,189	10,087	4,401	637	4.09	4.30
Fourth	6,667	10,880	4,816	662	3.90	4.11
1973						
First	6,920	11,359	4,250	−327	3.89	4.09
Second	7,441	12,280	4,331	95	4.53	4.74
Third	7,693	12,945	3,932	−16[c]	5.05[d]	5.23[d]
Fourth	7,711	13,529	3,871	12	7.35	7.49
1974						
First	7,708	14,016	3,750	−121	7.81	8.01
Second	7,498	14,401	3,560	−206[c]	7.81	8.01
Third	7,361	13,982	3,348	−586	7.23	7.51
Fourth	7,625	14,822	3,217	−141	7.19	7.47
1975						
First	8,066	15,986	3,220	26	7.42	7.58
Second	8,527	16,784	3,010	242[c]	9.35	9.41
Third	8,950	17,753	3,318	−271	10.75	10.76
Fourth	9,335	18,052	2,588	−738[c]	8.68	8.84
1976						
First	9,650	18,132	2,571	−37	6.98	7.25
Second	9,688	18,742	2,576	−7	6.98	7.25
Third	9,953	19,694	2,632	42	7.48	7.74
Fourth	10,185	20,227	3,550	−7	8.61	8.90
1977						
First	10,448	20,648	3,731	181	8.60	9.12
Second	10,522	20,737	3,312	−425	8.60	9.12
Third	10,810	20,873	2,820	−492	8.52	8.99
Fourth	10,967	21,053	2,879	59	8.38	8.78

Source: Reserve Bank of Australia, *Statistical Bulletin*, various issues.
a. Average of weekly figures; until February 1973, includes Papua New Guinea.
b. Amount at end of period; official parities are used until February 1973, after that market rates.
c. Net movements of assets differed from the official change in four quarters, decreasing an estimated $12 million in the third quarter of 1973, $205 million in the second quarter of 1974, and $737 million in the fourth quarter of 1975, and increasing an estimated $241 million in the second quarter of 1975.
d. Issue temporarily suspended, September 14–October 4, 1973.

management (table 4-5). Fluctuations in short-term capital movements obscured for a time the transition to lower normal levels in the net inflow of private capital as investors reassessed the growth capacity of the Australian economy.

Tight Australian domestic monetary policies in 1970 and 1971 coincided with a considerable easing of world monetary conditions. In the United States, monetary aggregates were allowed to rise and short-term interest rates to fall in 1970. In response, comparable interest rates began to decline in the Eurodollar and Asiandollar markets. The rapid expansion in the U.S. monetary aggregates continued until late 1971, when it was interrupted briefly before being resumed in 1972. The divergence between Australian and international monetary conditions induced an unprecedented flow of capital into the country. The flow intensified in 1971 as the crisis in the Bretton Woods system drew attention to the undervaluation of the Australian dollar. Long-standing restrictions on capital outflow were removed (in September 1971) and an embargo placed on short-term foreign borrowing. Capital inflow eased slightly as domestic monetary policy was relaxed in 1972 but remained very high. Expensive conditions in the form of a variable deposit ratio were placed on long-term foreign borrowings at the time of the 1972 revaluation and tightened in September 1973.[17] The various initiatives in external policy and the substantial easing of domestic monetary policy in 1972–73 saw the capital account turn around in 1973 to an unusual deficit position.[18]

Capital inflow remained well below historical levels after 1972, except during a brief period of tight domestic monetary conditions in 1974. Speculation against possible devaluation on the return to Liberal-Country party government late in 1975 led to high levels of capital outflow. Speculation resumed in mid-1976 and survived a tightening of domestic monetary policy in early November; within the month the government devalued the dollar.

The official external settlements balance was the most volatile element affecting Australia's money supply in 1970–77.[19] The high levels of capital inflow combined with a strengthening current account to produce large surpluses in external payments in 1970–71 and 1971–72. The monetary authorities set upon a remarkable exercise in sterilization of the monetary

17. In December 1972, domestic borrowers were required to deposit with the Reserve Bank, without interest, 25 percent of long-term borrowings, and in September 1973, 33.3 percent.

18. See M. G. Porter, "The Interdependence of Monetary Policy and Capital Flows in Australia," *Economic Record,* March 1974.

19. See I. G. Sharpe, "Sources of Growth of the Australian Money Supply," *Australian Journal of Management,* vol. 1 (April 1976).

impact of the surplus by calling up cash from the commercial banks, restricting bank lending, and selling government securities on the market. The effort was, on the whole, successful, although it did not prevent an historically high growth in money supply in financial 1971–72 (11 percent for M_3, virtually all accounted for by the external payments surplus) or the rapid expansion of bank lending the following year.

Despite the turnaround in the capital account, the strong current account led to a further large (although much reduced) balance-of-payments surplus in financial 1972–73. Coming at a time of strong domestic credit expansion, it contributed to the extraordinarily rapid monetary growth that year (26 percent growth in M_3). There were payments deficits in each of the next four financial years, partly in response to such policy interventions as the revaluations and the tariff cut. The deficits imposed a brake on monetary expansion and were the major reason that the monetary growth rate dropped to little more than half that of financial 1972–73. The flow of speculative capital out of Australia was especially useful in complementing official monetary policy which was directed heavily at the limitation of monetary expansion.

For a brief period, beginning in December 1976, there was a large-scale flow of capital into the country as speculators took their profits at the new exchange rate. The reintroduction of the embargo on short-term borrowings and of the variable deposit ratio for certain purposes, together with the series of small revaluations, stemmed the inflow, and external payments were roughly in balance during the first few months of 1977, although reserves began falling in mid-1977.

Direct Foreign Investment and Immigration

In the early 1970s there was a sharp break from long-standing patterns of overseas investment in Australian companies. Overseas investment, of which direct investment is the main component, rose from about one-sixth of the national value of gross fixed capital formation plus changes in value of stocks between 1959–60 and 1969–70 to about one-quarter in 1970–71 and 1971–72, before falling to 7.4 percent in 1972–73 and 4.9 percent in 1973–74.[20] The level of direct investment grew fairly steadily, in Australian dollars, from less than $200 million in the mid-1950s to about $600 million per year at the end of the 1960s.

The level of direct investment had no obvious relation to the level of

20. G. J. Crough, "A Compendium of Official Statistics on Foreign Investment Flows to and from Australia," Transnational Corporations Research Project (University of Sydney, 1976), p. 37.

domestic economic activity; its fluctuations were at times stabilizing and at other times destabilizing. The upward climb was broken by low levels in 1961–62, a year of severe recession, and 1966–67, a year of very buoyant domestic conditions.

There was a sharp increase in direct investment to a peak of $928 million in 1971–72, followed by an equally sharp fall in 1972–73 and subsequent years to levels below those common in the late 1960s. No doubt there was a speculative element in this cycle, which paralleled the cycle in other capital flows into Australia. But the domestic political environment was distinctly less favorable for foreign investment. From 1972, investment controls, especially in relation to mining, became more restrictive. Some of these restrictions survived the change of government in 1975. Exchange-rate and commodity-price fluctuations together with economic difficulties in investors' home countries probably encouraged the decline. Reductions in investment were most marked in mining, where loss of confidence in the long-term growth prospects of the Japanese economy was a very important factor.

About half the value added in the Australian mining industry in the early 1970s was produced within overseas-owned corporations. When investment in mining (including oil exploration and production) fell from $352 million in financial 1971–72 to $71 million in 1972–73 and lower levels in subsequent years, the contraction in foreign funds was much greater than in domestic investment.[21] The loss in investment had important consequences since mining had contributed about 9 percent of Australian gross fixed capital formation in financial 1970–71 and 1971–72 (compared to about 2 percent in the early 1960s).

The decline in direct investment seems to have reduced the trend growth in the productive capacity of the Australian economy and to have been one factor behind the slow adjustment to the large wage increases of 1974 and the failure to climb from the recession that commenced in that year. The lower expectations of growth themselves contributed to lower levels of private foreign investment.

The wage explosion of 1974, it has been remarked, was led by trades to which there had been a large reduction in migrant arrivals.[22] Immigrants, mainly from Europe, had added about 1 percent a year (or one-half of the national increase) to the population in the 1950s and 1960s, providing the Australian work force with considerable occupational and geographic mobility. The level of net migration fell rapidly between 1969 and 1972, rose a little through the commodities boom, and fell to very low levels subse-

21. Ibid.
22. *Bulletin of Australian Labour Studies,* March 1975, p. 71.

quently. Rising European prosperity reduced the supply of migrants at the same time that attitudes to migration were undergoing radical reevaluation in Australia.

Both the economy and Australian economic policy were affected by fluctuations in the level of migration. While the absolute number of migrants in professional categories was substantially maintained, the size of the immigration program was reduced and the proportion of craftsmen and production and process workers fell considerably. With a migrant flow less complementary to the native additions to the labor force,[23] matching the characteristics of the workforce with those of labor demand—an important factor in combating structural unemployment—became very difficult.

Policy Response to External Instability

Worldwide inflation, the commodities boom and slump, and then the weak international recovery, all had very important consequences for Australia. To insulate the economy from the impact of the first two of these disturbances would have required actions outside the normal range of policy responses. Successive governments took bold steps in the required directions, but the range of their responses was never sufficiently wide for their policies to be successful.

In 1970 and 1971, the first half of the period of high inflation, fiscal and monetary policy were both operated strongly to limit monetary growth. The authorities were very successful in the short term, despite the large payments surpluses generated by the combination of strong export growth (and direct foreign investment in export industries) and monetary conditions that were more restrictive than those of the rest of the world. The short-term success was marked by low inflation in 1972, when the consumer price index rose by a little more than 4 percent. The higher rate of increase in the previous year seems to have had as its major proximate cause an unusually large increase in award wages in December 1970[24]—the strong balance of payments was influential in convincing the wages authorities that economic conditions could support the increase.

The restrictive fiscal and monetary policies served not only to insulate the economy from the effects of worldwide inflation, but to protect established export and import-competing industries against increases in costs that would

23. Ibid., December 1976, p. 9.
24. See Pitchford, "Inflation in Australia," pp. 374–79, for a description of the Australian system of award wages.

otherwise have flowed from the growth in mining investment and exports. Australian real incomes and expenditures were being maintained below the maximum levels that could be supported by the economy's productive capacity. By financial 1971–72 it was clear that the economy would have to accept either an exchange-rate appreciation or an inflation adjustment.[25] Monetary growth was historically high in that year, in part deriving from high capital inflow, despite exceptionally strong measures to sterilize the payments surplus.

An early appreciation of the Australian dollar, say, in 1971, would have allowed monetary growth to be maintained at low levels and would have allowed Australia to avoid the importation of the worldwide inflation. A substantial revaluation would have insulated the economy against the inflationary effects of export and import price increases and would also have reduced greatly the speculative capital inflow that began in late 1971. But revaluation would not have allowed Australia to avoid the structural adjustment that was required by the growth of the minerals industries. It is possible that the short-term effects of early currency revaluation would have worsened unemployment in 1972, at a politically difficult time for the government. Any employment effects would have been less important if the appreciation had been secured in a number of small steps. In any case, such deflationary effects could have been offset by increases in real domestic expenditure, without balance-of-payments difficulties.

Domestic policy in 1970 and 1971 was stabilizing in its short-term effects,[26] but it sowed the seeds of acute problems in later years. It temporarily avoided some of the effects of international inflation, but it postponed some monetary adjustments, and important real structural adjustments, to a later time. When the adjustment got under way, it was complicated greatly by entanglement with the commodity boom.

The long, successful, but ultimately self-defeating attempt to sterilize the

25. For an analysis of the protective effects of an undervalued exchange rate, see W. M. Corden, "Exchange Rate Protection" (forthcoming).

26. A simulation exercise by P. D. Jonson ("Our Current Inflationary Experience," *Australian Economic Review,* Second Quarter, 1973) suggests that the general thrust of domestic policy in 1972 tended to moderate domestic inflation. Jonson superimposed both the major external shocks of 1969–72 (represented by growth in export and import prices and changes in capital inflow) and the major changes in domestic economic policy (the large award wage increase in 1970–71 and the increased social service payments and reduced taxation in the 1972 budget) on the Reserve Bank of Australia's model of the economy in the mid-1960s. The simulated inflation for the 1960s was substantially higher than actual rates in 1969–72; external influences (principally export and import price increases) appeared to be responsible for the greater part of the increase in inflation.

monetary effects of expanding payments surpluses ceased in 1972. The conservative government, fighting for its political life, eased fiscal and monetary policy and signaled the commencement of the inflation adjustment. The very large increase in outlays included in its budget submitted in August eventually generated the largest deficit recorded to that time. On the monetary side there was an extremely large expansion of bank advances which in company with the payments surplus, the budget deficit, and large sales of government securities to the banks caused the money supply to grow by 26 percent in financial 1972–73.

This was the inheritance of the Labor government elected in December 1972, committed to a large increase in public expenditure and to the rapid elimination of any remaining unemployment, and soon to be blessed by a huge improvement in the terms of trade. The new government allowed the high rate of expansion of bank advances to continue until late in 1973. Its budget for financial 1973–74 provided for an even larger increase in outlays, and an even larger deficit, than in the previous year (revenue growth so greatly exceeded the budget estimates—partly because of the effects of inflation on progressive personal income tax scales—that the final deficit was small). Revaluations and the across-the-board cut in tariffs to offset the direct price effects of worldwide inflation and the commodity boom, in combination with the large increases in domestic expenditure, contributed to the elimination of the payments surplus.

The new government's policies were, on the whole, stabilizing in relation to inflation,[27] but they were disastrously destabilizing in relation to the level of economic activity and, as a result, to unemployment. The crucial error of stabilization policy through the commodities boom was to allow real domestic expenditures to rise excessively, to levels that could not be sustained at normal terms of trade. The tariff cuts and the currency appreciations did little to avert this error—and possibly contributed to higher real expenditures, since they contributed to the moderation of the rate of increase in the domestic price level at a time when very little effort was being made to moderate

27. Simulations by V. Argy and J. Carmichael ("Models of Imported Inflation for a Small Country—with Particular Reference to Australia," in W. Kasper, ed., *International Money—Experiments and Experience, Papers and Proceedings of the Port Stephens Conference* [Department of Economics, Research School of Social Sciences, Australian National University, 1976]) suggest that the increase in Australian inflation through 1972 and 1973 was attributable to the increase in the prices of exports and imports; the net effect of domestic monetary and exchange-rate policy was deflationary. In their simulations, based on the Reserve Bank of Australia's model of the economy, external inflationary impulses were removed by setting growth in export and import prices, speculative capital inflow, and Eurodollar interest rates at their trends for the 1960s.

the rate of nominal expenditure on exports. Scarcities of labor and of some goods developed, and by the end of 1973 wages were moving up in response to the high levels of domestic expenditure.[28]

The large increases in real wages through this period were to be an enduring cause of labor-market problems. Whether they were the result primarily of the autonomous decisions of the wages-setting authorities or of excess demand in the labor market is a matter of heated debate. The two explanations are, in fact, closely intertwined. The wages authorities take heed of labor-market conditions and in times of strong demand probably follow wage increases in the market. Their decisions clearly have an autonomous effect on the timing of wage increases. They are also effective in determining minimum wages for persons who, on account of their skills, industrial experience, or sex, would otherwise be able to command only low wages in the unconstrained marketplace.

It seems unlikely that major shifts would occur in the structure of real wages established under awards, as in early 1974, unless they were led by high wage settlements in the market. The special contribution of the wage-setting authorities, encouraged by the government, was to compress wage differentials, raising the relative wages of relatively unskilled workers, young people, and especially women. Once real wages had risen to excessive levels, it was extremely difficult to reduce them.

Measures adopted in late 1973 to limit domestic sources of monetary expansion were not effective in restraining domestic expenditure until well into 1974. Their effects thus coincided with the deflationary impact of the sharp deterioration in the terms of trade and of the huge deterioration in the balance of payments. The latter factor was helped along by the lagged effects of the tariff cuts and the later currency appreciations. It was clearly destabilizing to act so strongly to reduce the relative prices of tradable commodities, and to reduce a surplus in external payments, so late in such a strong boom in domestic economic activity.

A successful stabilization strategy would have required strong action to keep real domestic demand within something like the normal bounds of growth. The monetary authorities' net holdings of foreign financial assets

28. J. W. Nevile ("Australian Inflation: Made at Home or Imported?" in Kasper, *International Money*), employing a model based on experience in 1950–73 which gave a major role to exogenous decisions of the wage-setting authorities, found that foreign impulses were important but not so important as domestic factors in Australian inflation. This and other models based on earlier periods do not have good simulation properties for the mid-1970s because of structural changes in the labor market. Nevile emphasized this point in "The Exchange Rate, Inflation and Unemployment," in W. M. Corden and others, *Exchange Rate Changes and the Australian Economy* (University of New South Wales, Centre for Applied Economic Research, 1977), p. 25.

would have risen very considerably and could have been run down later, when world recession turned the terms of trade against Australia. Implementing such a strategy through the commodities boom would have been difficult. Use of those macroeconomic instruments that have a general effect across all sectors of the economy would have caused a major short-term redistribution of incomes and access to credit within the Australian community. For example, to balance the greatly increased farm incomes and expenditures would have called for reducing government expenditure or disposable income or access to credit (through increased taxation or more restrictive monetary policy) thus injuring nonfarm households and businesses. Such measures would have been unpopular at any time and especially difficult for a new government committed to an expansion of expenditure.

It might have been more acceptable for the authorities to deny exporters immediate access to part of the proceeds of the overseas sales through the boom, pending the return of prices to normal levels. This tactic was discussed seriously during the commodity boom of 1950–51 but does not seem to have been contemplated in the early 1970s.

A substantial accumulation of foreign exchange would of course show up on the capital account of the balance of payments, encouraging an inflow of foreign capital, which might possibly have swamped the stabilization strategy. The experience of 1970 and 1971 suggests that tight domestic monetary policies and rising foreign-exchange reserves could be maintained for about two years without being overwhelmed by speculative capital inflow. Restrictive monetary policies directed at allowing the accumulation of foreign-exchange reserves would, in principle, be easier to maintain during a temporary commodity boom, as in 1972–74, than in a period when real domestic expenditure was well below levels consistent with balance in external payments, as in 1970–72. However, the commodity boom began to affect Australia at a time when the currency was already clearly undervalued, foreign-exchange reserves were at an unprecedentedly high level, and there was an established flow of speculative capital into the country. It would have been very difficult to avoid a further rush of speculative capital if the current account of the balance of payments had been in surplus to the extent required to insulate domestic economic activity from the commodities boom. At any rate, the government was not interested in maintaining moderate expenditure growth and building foreign-exchange reserves through this period.

Domestic policy was locked in by past mistakes by the last quarter of financial 1973–74. Real domestic expenditure had risen so far that it was not possible to avoid a large reduction in expenditure, except perhaps temporarily. Wages were going up rapidly in response to the strong demand for labor at the new, very high expenditure levels. Given the high degree of downward rigidity in real wages, there was no way of avoiding the emergence of historically high rates of unemployment.

The government did have to choose between rapid downward adjustment of domestic expenditure and more gradual adjustment over a longer period. Policy was set on the former course with a tightening of domestic monetary policy in the first quarters of financial 1973–74. This seemed at first to have little effect (although the money supply began to contract during the second quarter). As the lags worked themselves out, however, monetary policy intensified the tendency for the deteriorating terms of trade, balance of trade, and balance of payments to precipitate a recession. Inflation was a major issue in the May 1974 election, and the government planned to maintain tight fiscal and monetary policies through financial 1974–75.

By mid-1974 the contraction in the money supply was being reflected in reduced activity in some industries that were heavily dependent on bank credit, and also in rapidly rising unemployment. The government, unprepared to accept the short-term consequences of such rapid adjustment, changed the setting of several policy instruments to secure a more gradual reduction in expenditure. The budget for the 1974–75 financial year was framed to produce a small domestic surplus. However, only two months after it was presented to parliament, the stance of fiscal policy (and other policies as well) was turned around. Further outlays were authorized by the government. Midyear policy adjustments and overexpenditure (due in part to cost increases in excess of those estimated in framing the budget) raised government outlays 11 percent above the levels specified in the budget. Revenues were reduced below expectations by recession, and the estimated domestic surplus was transformed into a domestic deficit of almost $2 billion. Domestic monetary policy was relaxed over this same period, and there was a large devaluation of the Australian dollar in September 1974. A number of manufacturing industries were granted increased protection against import competition in the course of financial 1974–75.

The overall effect of domestic policy from the second half of 1974 was to offset the strong deflationary pressures through the balance of payments. Monetary growth fluctuated widely in financial 1974–75, the money supply (M_3) expanding by 15 percent, about half the rate of the previous year. In retrospect, it seems that the easing of monetary and related policies late in 1974 entrenched a relatively high rate of inflation, for relatively little gain in the moderation of the increase of unemployment. The retreat to a gradualist strategy may have prolonged the period of recession and high unemployment. The industrial countries in which aggregate activity held up fairly well through 1974 (Sweden, Canada, and the United Kingdom, in addition to Australia) took longer than other OECD countries to return to moderate growth.[29] In Australia's case, the policy reversals in mid-1974 probably induced the worst consequences of both strategies.[30] The sharp monetary contraction led to a large, sudden increase in unemployment, and the reversion to a moderately high rate of monetary expansion entrenched fairly high inflation without removing the unemployment.[31]

The dividing line between the periods of worldwide recession and slow and abnormal international recovery is not clearcut. By the end of 1975 the rate of deterioration in Australia's terms of trade had lessened, and an increase in exports provided a mild boost to domestic economic activity from mid-1975. There was a widespread expectation in Australia in late 1975 that higher commodity prices, export volumes, and direct foreign investment, associated with world recovery, would help to lift the economy out of recession. Fiscal and monetary policy remained geared to achieving gradual reduction in the rate of domestic inflation, and the combination of the completion of domestic inventory reductions and the buoyant international conditions was expected to produce mild recovery in output and slow reduction in unemployment.

29. See Wynne A. H. Godley, "Inflation in the United Kingdom," and Lars Calmfors, "Inflation in Sweden," in Krause and Salant, *Worldwide Inflation.*

30. It seems likely that the effects of high levels of demand on real wages are more deeply entrenched the longer the high demand is maintained.

31. P. D. Jonson and J. C. Taylor ("Inflation and Economic Stability in a Small, Open Economy: A Systems Approach," *Journal of Monetary Economics,* 1978 Supplement) suggest that had a managed float been substituted for historical exchange-rate policy from 1971, so that the rate responded automatically to relative-price, balance-of-payments, and monetary variables, the fluctuations in real product would have been lower. The rate of inflation would have been lower throughout the period, but high and accelerating in 1975. Tightening of money in 1972 and 1973, in addition to the managed float, would have produced even steadier growth in output and lower inflation, but prices would still have been high and accelerating in 1975. If there had also been a more steady expansion in government outlays (higher than historical rates in 1970–71 and 1971–72 and lower in 1972–73 and succeeding years), the rate of price increases would have been even lower (but still about 13 percent per year and accelerating in 1975) and growth in output more even, but lower. Finally, if in addition the large increases in award wages from 1970–71, 1973–74, and 1974–75 had been removed, growth in real product would have been steady (and there would have been no recession in 1974 or 1975), total output higher, and the rate of price increases low throughout the period and heading downward in 1975. Jonson and Taylor's conclusions are based on simulations using a Reserve Bank of Australia model whose wage and labor relationships look better than those of earlier models. However, because of structural change in the labor market, it is not possible to be confident about the estimation of relationships between the exogenous (wages awards) and endogenous (prices, demand) variables.

The rate of increase in government outlays fell by half in financial 1975–76 but remained very high. Again, revenue fell below estimate—mainly because of the deceleration in the growth of money incomes—adding about $1 billion to a deficit that had been planned at about the level of the previous year. There was some resumption of economic growth from the first quarter of 1976 and there were signs of moderation in the rate of inflation, but there was no reduction in unemployment.

The conservative government that came to power late in 1975 maintained the basic thrust of fiscal and monetary policy, emphasizing reduction in government expenditure as a means of lowering the rate of monetary expansion. Its first budget, for financial 1976–77, was designed to generate a lower rate of growth of government outlays and a deficit similar to the previous year's. The budget made substantial taxation concessions to the manufacturing and mining sectors. In an innovation in monetary policy, the government announced with the budget that growth in the money supply was to be held to 10–12 percent, compared with 14 percent in the previous year.

The new government's most important change was its intention to reduce real wages, as a means of reducing inflation and unemployment. But it had no means of implementing the policy directly. The government placed submissions calling for real wage reductions (at first at the upper end of the wage and salary structure) before the arbitration commission at its quarterly hearings. By mid-1977 the commission had effected small reductions at the upper end of the wages scale, where there was relatively little unemployment and thus no important contribution to the alleviation of unemployment.

As part of its anti-inflationary strategy, the new government announced that it was committed strongly to maintaining the trade-weighted average foreign-exchange value of the Australian dollar. This commitment was challenged in 1976 by the weak capital account of the balance of payments and by the government's deviation in the second half of the year from its stated monetary policies in allowing the postponement of quarterly company tax payments. The brief period of rapid monetary expansion facilitated increased capital outflow and contributed to the pressures that led to the November 1976 devaluation. The monetary authorities did not move to relieve this devaluation as they had in September 1974 and the target rate of monetary expansion was maintained over the year as a whole. This reduced greatly the inflationary effect of the devaluation. However, the maintenance of tight monetary policy meant that the devaluation was accompanied by a further reduction in economic activity and increase in unemployment. By mid-1977 it was apparent that important changes in the domestic and international environment made the simultaneous pursuit of low levels of unemployment, low inflation, and balance in external payments more difficult than in earlier times.

Why Stabilization Policy Failed

Australian governments' failure to respond adequately to external disturbances was due sometimes to a problem of identifying optimal policies, sometimes to political difficulties in implementing policies, and sometimes to institutional barriers to the implementation of policy. The failure of stabilization policy in the early period of worldwide inflation can be attributed mainly to political problems. The failure of the domestic response to the commodities boom derived mainly from identification problems, although political and institutional factors were also important. Political problems were the main cause of the erratic management of the domestic response to the worldwide recession of 1974 and 1975. After that, identification and institutional problems both constrained stabilization policy.

In each of the critical periods of external instability, structural changes in the labor market contributed to identification problems. Unemployment and inflation had long been seen as opposite sides of the one coin, aggregate demand. Virtually all of the econometric models that sought to explain Australian inflation included simple and stable trade-offs between unemployment and inflation. In the 1950s and 1960s the models revealed reasonable simulation properties, and stabilization policy based on them was remarkably successful. When relationships changed, monetary expansion continued to be accepted as the appropriate response to the historically high unemployment of 1972 and the higher unemployment of late 1974.

But frictional and structural factors have become very much more important in Australian unemployment. Variations in the rates of unemployment by age, sex, geographic location, and industry are exceptionally wide. In some recent periods of high unemployment (for example, in late 1976), unemployment of men twenty-five years old and over in two major cities, Melbourne and Adelaide, was not unusually high, and increases were heavily concentrated among women and young people. The extremely large increases in unemployment benefits that were granted in 1972 and subsequent years, especially for single, young people but also for others, undoubtedly have made it worthwhile for workers to spend more time in the search for better jobs than before, thus contributing to frictional unemployment.

Decline in the rate of growth in demand for Australian mineral exports, the cycle in the terms of trade, and increase in the relative price of energy have contributed to secular change and fluctuations in the profitability of particular industries in Australia and in the structure of demand for labor. Within Australia the failure of stabilization policy caused frequent change in the composition of demand for labor, and this was compounded by the extraordinary slumps (financial years 1970–71, 1971–72, 1976–77, and 1977–78) and booms (1972–75) in public expenditure growth. In these changing conditions, it was very difficult to match the characteristics of jobs and workers. There have been major changes in minimum wages that have changed the relationship between aggregate demand and the structure of demand for labor. Women won very large increases in minimum wages from 1971 until equal pay was achieved in 1975, with strong government encouragement from December 1972. Among men, as minimum wages were lifted and the growth of incomes high in the wage and salary scale slowed, wage differentials contracted.

These changes in the labor market caused the authorities to underestimate the dangers of demand pressure in 1972 and 1973, and throughout the period to the end of 1976.[32] In the earlier years they were very important in causing governments to underestimate the inflationary effects of monetary expansion. After 1975 the failure to recognize the structural nature of modern unemployment led to efforts to reduce real wages that emphasized average levels rather than the real wages of labor groups in excess supply.

The failure to recognize the cyclical nature of the improvement in Australia's terms of trade through the commodity boom was a second major identification problem. With hindsight, it is difficult to imagine that the huge increase in the terms of trade in 1972 and 1973 could have been viewed as permanent. But the prevalent view was that the world was entering an era of resource and food shortages that would lift permanently the terms of trade of countries like Australia. This contributed to the difficulty of enforcing restraint in expenditure through the boom period.

Fashions in exchange-rate and monetary policy exacerbated the problem. An effective stabilization strategy would have held real expenditure in 1973 at a level that would have allowed the authorities to accumulate foreign-exchange reserves at a high rate. But in those early post-Smithsonian days, market-determined exchange rates were held in very high regard, even in countries whose institutional environment made it impossible to float the

32. The natural rate of unemployment has been estimated at 1.5–2.0 percent up to 1972 (M. Parkin, "The Short Run and Long Run Trade-offs Between Inflation and Unemployment in Australia," *Australian Economic Papers,* December 1973). It probably was 2.5 percent and possibly 3.5 percent through 1974 and 1975 (M. Parkin, "The Short Run and Long Run Trade-offs Between Inflation and Unemployment in Australia: A Reply to John Nevile," *Australian Economic Papers,* June 1975).

exchange rate. In Australia the exchange rate (and other policy instruments) were thought to be moving in the right direction so long as their movement was contributing to the removal of short-term excess supply of foreign exchange. Thus from December 1972 the government sought to reduce inflationary pressure through measures that operated mainly on the relative prices of domestic and foreign goods, rather than measures that would have restricted directly the real level of aggregate domestic expenditure.

In the later phase, of adjustment to slow world recovery, the tendencies for levels of export growth and direct foreign investment to remain low were seen for a very long time as temporary phenomena that would depart with the end of the world recession. That resulted in a strong tendency to underestimate the extent of the downward reduction in aggregate expenditure, and in some real wages, needed to restore low unemployment and, simultaneously, balance in external payments. The deceleration of growth in the world badly damaged the medium-term growth prospects of the Australian economy. Failure to recognize this reality, and the reality that very large adjustments must be made within the Australian economy, helped to prolong the period of high unemployment.

Throughout the period from 1970 to 1975, political problems hampered the implementation of stabilization policies. In the early years of worldwide inflation it was simply impossible politically for the conservative government to take the unusual step of raising unilaterally the foreign-exchange value of the Australian dollar. By late 1971 the need for an appreciation of the dollar was widely recognized in government, university, and press circles and among the parliamentary leaders of the Liberal party, the senior party in the conservative coalition. But the Country party, with a strong representation in the coalition, would not agree to an appreciation because of its supposed adverse effects on the income of rural producers who relied heavily on export markets. (In reality, the loss of real farm incomes associated with an early appreciation would have been balanced by a lower rate of increase in the domestic price level; it might even have raised farm incomes if it had helped to avoid the extreme inflationary pressures of 1973 and 1974.) The Country party's perceptions of the interests of its constituency nearly caused it at one stage to break the conservative coalition over exchange-rate policy.

The intense electoral competition in 1972 between the Liberal-Country coalition and the Labor opposition was not conducive to the maintenance of the policies that were necessary to insulate Australia from accelerating worldwide inflation. The government's adoption of strongly expansionary fiscal and monetary policy in 1972 made it inevitable that a major part of Australia's adjustment to the earlier growth in minerals investment, and to the inflationary situation overseas, would be made through domestic inflation.

The Labor government that took office in December 1972 was constrained politically in different ways. It was committed to a considerable expansion in public expenditure and was under internal pressure to expand budget outlays up to the most generous assessments of the economy's capacity to support government spending. It was also more sensitive than its predecessor to unemployment, and more ready to respond to any appearance of unemployment with monetary expansion. The natural inclinations of the party were reinforced by its precarious hold on power throughout its two successive eighteen-month terms in office. It lacked a majority in the senate, which blocked a major revenue bill in financial 1974–75 and threatened on several occasions to block appropriations bills (despite the fact that the constitutional propriety of such a move was in dispute). The senate threats led to general elections in May 1974 and December 1975, each halfway through a normal three-year term. The government was thus campaigning electorally more or less continuously and had always to judge economic policies by the short-term criteria of politicians facing early elections.

The period immediately following the election of the Labor government certainly held more economic policy traps than usual for a government committed to raising the level of public expenditure.[33] But the prospects for a considerable expansion of real domestic expenditure, based on minerals growth, seem to have been better then than at any time in postwar years. The Labor government squandered its opportunity in a more or less indiscriminate expansion of expenditure, in its first year especially. If it had moved quickly to moderate the private sector boom set in train by the monetary expansion of 1972, it could have implemented new public sector programs at the same time as it allowed foreign-exchange reserves to accumulate through the commodities boom. The intense competition with its political opponents was an important cause of the government's inclination to react to short-term adversity with measures designed to produce a large, immediate response.

The most important institutional constraint on stabilization policy was the complex system through which wages are established in Australia. This system prevented the implementation of government policy on wages. Had wage indexation been adopted in early 1974, it is possible that it would have moderated the wages explosion in that year. And implementation of the conservative government's policy to reduce real wages might have slowed

33. Gruen, "What Went Wrong?" has commented that the Labor government possibly came to power at the worst possible time for two decades.

the increase in unemployment in 1977. Wage-setting arrangements have interfered with the implementation of government economic policy, but they probably also helped to reduce industrial disputation.[34]

Lessons of the 1970s

The experience of international instability contains many lessons for Australian macroeconomic policy. Australia's domestic policy responses to externally induced instabilities were probably stabilizing in their overall effect, but weakly so. In retrospect, it is possible to specify alternative approaches to macroeconomic policymaking that would have been more effective in insulating the Australian economy from international instability. Some of the lessons that have been learned may assist stabilization policy in future. But some of the lessons of the 1970s, and especially the retreat from intense participation in foreign trade, will make it more difficult to achieve both growth and stability in the Australian economy.

The general awareness of the dangers of excessive rates of monetary expansion and wage increase will help to avoid a repetition of some of the policy mistakes that were made in the period from 1972 to 1974. The less common awareness of the economic costs of restrictive policies on foreign investment, and in particular on mining investment, may also be of help in future disturbances.

But the folklore carries important fallacies. The association of the Australian dollar revaluations between December 1972 and September 1973 with the rapid expansion of imports which precipitated the recession in 1974 will make it more difficult in future to use the exchange rate as an instrument of anti-inflationary policy. Similarly, the association of large budget deficits with recession in the 1970s will make it more difficult to use variations in the budget as an instrument of stabilization policy.

A widespread disillusionment about the usefulness of an active stabilization policy has grown out of the poor record of the main conventional indicator of the extent of excess demand, the proportion of unemployed persons in the work force. To be successful in the new economic environment, stabilization policy will depend on close monitoring of the structural characteristics of labor supply and labor demand as well as the aggregates. Employment policy must be formulated within an explicit, long-term framework. Structural change, which was an important cause of the rise in unemployment in

34. For an assessment of the institutional arrangements, see J. Isaacs, "Wage Determination and Economic Policy," Giblin Memorial Lecture, Melbourne, 1977.

the 1970s, seems likely to remain so unless measures are taken to adjust the structural characteristics of the supply of and demand for labor. The Australian government must attempt to identify imbalances well in advance of their emergence if it wishes to combat unemployment effectively.[35]

Expenditure policy needs to be considered in a medium-term framework, as Australian experience through the commodity boom and slump demonstrated. The downward rigidity of real wages and real public expenditure in Australia raises the cost of allowing excessive expansion when terms of trade or capital inflow are high. Stabilization policy can be effective only if aggregate expenditure is maintained on a trend that is sustainable in average or normal conditions.

Maintaining real public expenditure on a steady trend poses problems for exchange-rate policy for which neither recent experience in exchange-rate management nor a freely floating rate offers a satisfactory solution. Pegging against a single foreign currency in the early 1970s caused Australia to import the worldwide inflation. The large managed movements in the Australian dollar exchange rate from December 1972 increased business uncertainty and provided opportunities for destabilizing speculation (based on second-guessing the government). The smaller managed movements after November 1976 were not as disruptive but they did not remove any of the underlying dilemmas of exchange-rate policy.

Within a freely floating exchange-rate regime, the Australian dollar would tend to appreciate in times of buoyant external demand and, through its effect on the domestic price level, cause real domestic expenditure to rise to unsustainable levels (as the managed appreciations did). Perverse cyclical movements in the foreign-exchange value of the dollar would be less destructive to the extent that speculators could foresee the changes (however, private markets have an unimpressive record on the anticipation of commodity prices).

If the Australian domestic expenditure is to be kept on a steady course through the external business cycle, the authorities must decide what the average levels of commodity prices and probably of net capital inflow are likely to be. Exchange-rate and expenditure policies must be developed together, within the framework of medium-term projections of macroeconomic conditions. These two instruments could be coordinated by pegging the ex-

---

35. Some Labor party spokesmen have noted the structural aspects of the unemployment problem and the need for an explicit medium- and long-term framework for economic policy. See in particular W. Hayden, "Longer-term Economic Policy," paper presented to the Economics Society of Australia and New Zealand, Sydney, November 1977.

change rate against a basket of currencies and moving against that basket from time to time so as to keep the direct price effects of external inflation at an acceptable and manageable level. The trade-weighted average exchange rate would be raised in times of worldwide inflation. Nominal domestic expenditure would then be maintained on a path that was consistent with external viability under the selected exchange-rate regime, through the use of the normal instruments of fiscal and monetary policy. Exchange-rate and expenditure policy would be coordinated so as to achieve a low rate of inflation and a steady expansion in real domestic expenditure. The authorities would accumulate reserves of foreign exchange when the terms of trade were high and run them down when the terms of trade were low.

Another approach, diverging further from past Australian practice, would be to allow a freely floating exchange rate, constrained only by the authorities' intervention to remove the effects of variations in the terms of trade and perhaps net capital inflow. The basis of official intervention, and information on official transactions, would be made public, to facilitate the efficient operation of the foreign-exchange market. The authorities would set nominal expenditure growth at a low and steady level and rely on the appreciation of the currency to offset the direct price effects of abnormally high inflation overseas.

The steady trend in real domestic expenditure that should emerge from either of these approaches to exchange-rate policy would facilitate implementation of the longer term approach to employment policy and would provide fewer opportunities for error in wage-setting agreements and for dispute over wages. Under either approach, however, assessing sustainable trends in real domestic expenditure and manipulating fiscal and monetary policy to maintain expenditure growth on the desired trend would be difficult. In any recurrence of the conditions of the commodity boom, the burden of restrictive fiscal and monetary policy on the nonexport sectors would be lessened to the extent that part of the abnormally high export incomes was frozen temporarily by the fiscal authorities.

Errors in the assessment of sustainable trends could be corrected relatively quickly, and at low cost, in times of higher general economic growth. But Australia's prospects for growth are poorer and less certain than in the two decades after World War II. The cessation in the growth of Japanese import demand for minerals and metals and the associated reduction in normal levels of private capital inflow have removed one powerful source of growth in the decade to 1973. An even more important impediment to Australian stabilization is the loss of tolerance among policymakers and the public toward foreign trade and structural adjustment, partly as a consequence of the recent experience of unstable international economic conditions. One curious attitude is an opposition to rapid growth in minerals exports on the grounds that it reduces profitability and output and forces structural change in the established rural and manufacturing industries.[36] If the external environment should become conducive to large increases in minerals exports, this resistance to structural change could act as a brake on Australian economic growth.

The recent instability has weakened one of the institutional pillars of growth in Australian minerals exports. Many large investments in minerals and metals were financed on the security of long-term contracts to supply the Japanese market. These contracts almost certainly worked in the direction of stabilizing the volume and price of exports of minerals, metals, and agricultural commodities from Australia to Japan. But when there are large unforeseen shortfalls in demand, the long-term contract is very much less valuable as security for borrowings to finance mining investments. Though the deceleration of Japanese growth has removed the immediate possibility of rapid Australian growth on the pattern of the decade to 1973, rapid industrialization in a number of smaller East and Southeast Asian countries could in the 1980s provide the kind of impetus that Japan generated in earlier years. This is very likely if recent growth trends continue in Korea, Taiwan, Hong Kong, and the five countries of the Association of Southeast Asian Nations. But new institutions will be required to take full advantage of these opportunities. The huge scale of incremental demand for particular commodities in Japan allowed new mines to be opened in Australia on the basis of contracts signed with importers in one country. Future growth in demand for Australian minerals and metals exports will be much more dispersed, and this will complicate the coordination of financing and marketing in new mining investments.

One of the clear lessons of the 1970s experience is that countercyclical variation in the level of protection is a poor instrument of stabilization policy for a single country, and that it is likely to be destabilizing for the country's trading partners. Australian economic problems were intensified by the sudden expansion and contraction as levels of protection in Japanese and U.S. beef markets changed. Australia likewise transmitted part of its instability to neighboring Asian countries in the countercyclical variation in levels of protection for labor-intensive manufactured products. Stable economic conditions in each country are likely to be stabilizing for its trading partners if they are achieved through the use of macroeconomic policy instruments, but

36. This opposition was encouraged by the publication of what has become known as the Gregory thesis. See Gregory, "Some Implications."

destabilizing if they are achieved (or, more likely, attempted unsuccessfully) through intervention in trade in particular commodities.

Recent instability, and especially the rise in unemployment, has greatly increased protectionist pressures in Australia, as in many other countries. This weakens the prospects for economic growth in Australia. It is likely to be the most costly consequence of the 1970s instability. Not only are its direct effects on domestic resource allocation and growth likely to be limiting for Australia, but its indirect effects on trade-oriented growth in developing Asian countries are likely to reduce their export opportunities and contribute to a climate of opinion in OECD countries antipathetic to imports of manufactured goods from developing countries. Most important of all, it raises doubts about the viability of export-oriented strategies in the Asian developing countries themselves.

CHAPTER FIVE

Economic Miracles in Korea

HEE-YHON SONG

LIKE OTHER small trade-oriented countries, the Republic of Korea is very sensitive to economic impulses from abroad. Because of its early stage of industrial development, Korea is much more susceptible to these impulses than are its major trading partners. Although Korea's share of world exports has risen remarkably from 0.34 percent in 1971 to about 0.80 percent in 1976, Korea is likely to remain primarily an impulse taker rather than an impulse maker in the world for some time to come.

Between 1970 and 1976, international involvement of the Korean econ-omy—as reflected in the ratio of exports to gross national product—rose very rapidly: total exports of goods and services increased from 16.5 percent of GNP to 37.7 percent. Korea's most extensive trade was with the Pacific basin countries, which in 1976 purchased approximately two-thirds of its total exports. The United States and Japan were by far the most important trade partners, accounting, respectively, for 32.3 percent and 23.4 percent of Korea's total exports and 22.4 percent and 35.3 percent of its total imports. Japan in the early 1970s became a vital source of capital equipment and semifinished raw materials for Korean industries.

The Korean Economy, 1970–76

Instability generated abroad tended to affect the Korean economy much more severely in the early 1970s than it had during the 1960s. Until 1970, when world demand became very weak, Korea was unaware of how vulner-able its economy was to changing conditions of its trading partners. The

117

favorable world economic conditions of the 1960s were perhaps taken for granted; and at any rate Korea's international involvement was limited. However, in 1970–71 when recession hit the United States and Japan, the situation changed rather drastically, and the high degree of economic interdependence showed up in the form of imported inflation in Korea; the effect on trade, finance, and the overall monetary situation was readily recognizable. Korean policymakers were forced to begin studying economic situations abroad to better deal with economic policy issues at home.

In the second half of the 1960s, after the successful completion of its first five-year plan, Korea enjoyed strong foreign demand and moderate price increases for its exports and had little difficulty in financing its capital investment with foreign borrowing. Korean industries increased their investment in plant and equipment very rapidly, without much concern for the effects of an economic recession abroad. In 1966–69, GNP grew at an average annual rate of nearly 12 percent and the money supply (M_1) at an annual rate of 36 percent. The economy was overheated, in the sense that the payments deficit was somewhat more than it could handle. Ambitious development expenditures and growing demand for its exports had put strong demand pressures on the economy. Price increases were relatively moderate, however, because of controls on the price of rice and on public utility rates and the slow adjustment of foreign-exchange rates. An increase in imports and deterioration of the net goods and services balance also helped to keep prices from rising excessively.

In the first half of the 1970s Korea could not help but feel the substantial effect of external instability. Between 1970 and 1972 the growth rate dropped to an average of 8 percent, as U.S. and Japanese demand for Korea's exports weakened. The government, beginning in late 1969, used both monetary and fiscal policy in its efforts to improve the balance of payments. Growth in the money supply was held to 22 percent in 1970 and 16 percent in 1971. Other elements of the economy that had grown at a rapid rate over the previous four years were abruptly cut back: government budget expenditures, public investment and loans, and gross fixed capital investment. The restrictive policies reduced the growth of output and imports in 1970, but they did not succeed in stabilizing prices since utility rates were allowed to go up and the overvalued won was devalued.

Thus the government in 1971 eased fiscal policy and increased its expenditures by an impressive 25.8 percent. Private consumption also rose, and imports were permitted to rise somewhat. In spite of the various stabilization measures, inflationary pressures continued into 1972 while the real growth rate declined substantially. In the first half of 1972, real GNP rose at an annual rate of only 5.5 percent, the lowest growth rate since 1965; investment declined very sharply, most seriously in construction.

Economic policymakers faced a serious dilemma: the economy needed some stimulus but the stimulus would aggravate inflation and create serious balance-of-payments problems. The solution was an emergency economic decree, issued on August 3, 1972. To check inflation, extensive price control measures were introduced. The foreign-exchange rate and public utility prices were frozen. Interest rates were lowered, and repayment and credit terms eased. Both productivity and investment incentives were offered to bolster industry.

The expansionary measures and stable prices, which helped to maintain the competitiveness of goods, combined with an increase in foreign demand, were responsible for Korea's recovery. In 1973 real output expanded by 16.0 percent, matching the highest growth rate recorded during the 1960s. As a result, the problem of excess capacity vanished gradually. With a large increase in the value of commodity exports, and only a modest increase in import values, the balance-of-payments deficit fell to its lowest level since 1967. Despite the expansionary monetary policy introduced late in 1972 and the rapid growth of income, the price rise in 1973 was modest, mainly because of a strict price control program. Inflation, however, was not cured; it was simply restrained by the wage-price freeze. Soaring prices of imported raw materials and grains, rapid expansion of the money supply, appreciation of the Japanese yen, all contributed to the inflationary pressure.

Policymakers, perceiving a serious misallocation of resources, loosened the price control measures at the end of the year. But by that time the oil crisis had added insistent, new inflationary pressures. Prices shot up in 1974, and export demand slowed down with the worldwide recession. Restrictive monetary policies were introduced early in the year to restrain aggregate demand and limit the balance-of-payments deficit. Aggregate demand continued to be strong in the first half of 1974 and real output grew at the high rate of 13.6 percent, but in the second half the growth rate declined very sharply.

Because of a rapid rise in import prices, nominal imports rose by 68.1 percent while nominal exports increased by 38 percent. The current account deficit of more than $2 billion was the largest ever. Special presidential measures, promulgated on January 14, 1974, reduced income taxes substantially in an effort to reduce the burden of inflation on low-income families, postponed the initiation of contributions to a welfare pension program, and created a large public works program to provide employment. On December 7 another special measure was adopted to correct the worsening payments deficit; it devalued the won and provided substantial amounts of money to stimulate business. In a very sensible move, the measure stipulated that more than 60 percent of the government investment and loan projects it funded were to be implemented during the first half of 1975, when weak foreign demand was expected to hit bottom.

The Korean economy began to recover under the stimulus of the special me asures, reinforced by a sharp increase in exports in the second half of 1975. The nominal value of exports did not increase, however, because of a decline in prices, and the deficit as a consequence was little better than in 1974. The rate of inflation fell but remained high, thus raising critical questions of how to keep inflation at the one-digit level, maintain a high rate of export growth, and maintain the competitive position of Korean manufactured goods without devaluing the won. Policymakers were most concerned about the stabilization of prices and the reduction in balance-of-payments deficits.

The 1976 targets for growth in real output, money supply, and price stability were very conservative, as were the government's monetary and fiscal measures. Real output, however, grew by 15.5 percent because of very strong export demand. Exports, particularly to the Middle East, increased in volume and value, while imports rose at a much more moderate rate. Receipts widely outpaced payments in invisible trade, with tourism, construction services, and insurance primarily responsible for the positive balance. The payments deficit recorded the lowest level since 1967 and foreign reserve holdings were double those at the end of the previous year. The debt service ratio had declined considerably from 21 percent in 1970 to 11 percent in 1976. At the end of the year the principal threat to price stability in Korea was the increase in money supply stemming from the foreign sector. The economy's ability to absorb such large foreign-exchange earnings was limited, and sensible management was needed if stability was to be maintained over the long term.

Changes in the Exchange Rate

The introduction of flexible exchange rates following the breakdown in the international monetary system and subsequent exchange-rate instability was one of the most important causes of price fluctuations in Korea in 1970–77. Changes in the exchange rate altered the prices of both imports (in terms of domestic currency) and exports (in terms of foreign currency). Import and export prices had a profound influence on the wholesale price index, nearly 40 percent of which was represented by internationally traded goods. The relation of the wholesale price index to that of Korea's major trade partners

—defined as the purchasing power of the won—and the level of foreign-exchange holdings were the principal bases for determining government decisions regarding the exchange rate.

Throughout 1970–77 the won was pegged to the dollar. The effective value of the exchange rate was altered substantially, however, by the won's rate of exchange with the yen, since a major share of Korea's trade was with Japan. The yen rate, export subsidies, and changes in relative prices between the domestic and foreign markets are the determinants of the real effective exchange rate (table 5-1). The ultimate impact of changes in the exchange rate on trade depends largely on price elasticities. Korea's export competitiveness could be undermined if domestic prices rise rapidly, but if the exchange rate is devalued and the response is large and prompt, then little loss of export volume will occur. Korea's export price elasticity reflects the competitive position of Korean goods in the international marketplace, while its import price elasticity reflects the economy's ability to absorb price changes. Between 1967 and 1976, Korean exports had an elasticity with respect to relative prices of a little over 1.0.[1] The elasticity of manufactured imports between 1964 and 1976 was 0.6.[2] The larger the price elasticity of the exchange rate, the smaller is the net impact of changes in the rate on trade because of the effect of changes in the exchange rate on domestic prices. Since the price elasticity of the official exchange rate in the early 1970s was rather large, the net effect of changes in the rate on the real effective exchange rate was relatively small.

Generally speaking, during the early 1970s, and particularly from 1970 to 1972, the won which was overvalued in the late 1960s was adjusted to close to an equilibrium level.[3] The index of the won's purchasing power (the wholesale price index ratio in table 5-1) deteriorated by 15 percent in 1970–72, while the official exchange rate depreciated by 28.0 percent. Between 1972 and 1974 the official exchange rate was relatively stable, but the adjusted rate, reflecting changes in the exchange rate per Japanese yen, depreciated by 5.5 percent because of the yen's appreciation. After the oil crisis the Korean won was devalued by 20 percent, to 483 won per dollar in

1. Export price elasticity was determined by regression analysis of data on commodity exports, exchange rate, wholesale price indexes of Korea and its major trading partners, and GNP growth in Japan and the United States. Hee-yhon Song, "Growth, Money and Inflation in Korea," Korea International Development Institute, Internal Seminar Series, no. 21 (November 30, 1977).

2. Import price elasticity was determined by regression analysis of data on imports, exchange rate, tariff rate, and major trading partners' wholesale price index. Ibid.

3. In 1965–69 the index of the won's purchasing power declined by 18.6 percent, while the official exchange rate per U.S. dollar depreciated only by 13.0 percent.

Table 5-1. *Estimated Real Effective Export Exchange Rate of Korea, 1969–77*

Item	1969	1970	1971	1972	1973	1974	1975	1976	1977
Exchange rate (won per dollar)	288.2	310.4	350.1	393.1	397.5	405.0	483.0	484.0	484.0
Effective exchange rate (won per dollar)[a]	370.2	399.5	456.6	522.0	538.6	523.8	611.1	607.8	634.5
Change in rate of won per yen (percent)	...	1.000	0.974	0.860	0.760	0.814	0.825	0.828	0.726
Exchange rate adjusted by change in yen rate (won per dollar)	288.2	310.4	353.1	414.3	439.3	435.7	516.8	517.8	544.5
Subsidy per dollar of export (won)	82.0	89.1	103.5	107.7	99.3	88.1	94.3	90.0	90.0
Wholesale price index ratio[b]	1.05	1.00	0.94	0.85	0.90	0.79	0.66	0.63	0.60
Major trade partners' index	96.5	100.0	101.9	105.1	118.7	148.5	157.7	168.9	177.3
Republic of Korea's index	91.6	100.0	108.6	123.8	132.4	188.2	238.0	266.7	293.4
Real effective exchange rate (won per dollar)[c]	388.7	399.5	429.2	443.7	484.7	413.8	403.3	382.9	380.7
Change from previous year (percent)	...	2.8	7.4	3.4	9.2	-14.6	-2.5	-5.1	-0.6

a. Sum of actual rate adjusted for change in yen rate and subsidy per dollar of export.
b. Ratio of index of foreign goods to index of domestic goods (based on 1970 prices); represents the purchasing power of the won.
c. Product of effective exchange rate and wholesale price index ratio.

December 1974. As a result, the index of the won's purchasing power declined by 26.6 percent from 0.90 in 1973 to 0.66 in 1975. In 1976 the purchasing power index deteriorated nearly 5 percent more, but the exchange rate remained unchanged. After 1974, Korea's balance-of-payments surplus made it possible to maintain a fixed exchange rate.

Import and Export Prices

After several years of increasing excess demand, inflation in the early 1970s was high enough to make price stabilization one of the major economic concerns of Korean policymakers. The price control program outlined in the emergency decree of August 1972 did suppress inflation, particularly in 1973, as can be seen in the changes in the consumer and wholesale price indexes (table 5-2). When price controls were eased somewhat in late 1973 and 1974, the suppressed inflation exploded. Of course, the situation was aggravated by the rise of oil prices.

Import prices began to increase at double-digit rates in early 1973, reaching a peak in the first half of 1974. The largest increases were in prices of primary products and commodities that required the use of petroleum inputs. The import prices of capital goods, in which the ratio of primary to total inputs is relatively low, increased at a moderate rate. At first the increases in the prices of imported raw materials showed up only in the wholesale index but later they were reflected in the consumer index and the GNP deflator.

In 1975, import price increases, as measured by changes in the unit value index, decelerated rather dramatically, as did domestic inflation. These trends continued into 1976. During 1972–76, import prices for all commodities (measured on a contract basis) increased by 85 percent while export prices increased by 42 percent. The primary channel of inflation was the importation of raw materials—prices of mineral fuels increased by 388 percent, of logs and wood products by 65 percent, of metal and metal products by 77 percent, and of chemical products by 72 percent.[4] The substantial devaluation of the U.S. dollar against the Japanese yen—11.7 percent on average in 1972 and 11.6 percent in 1973—also contributed to the increase in prices, particularly of imports from Japan.

The major determinants of Korea's medium- and long-term price fluctuations appear to be changes in excess money supply and import prices.[5]

4. Bank of Korea, *Monthly Economic Statistics*, vol. 32 (April 1978), pp. 82–83.

5. Hee-yhon Song, "Growth, Money and Inflation in Korea," and "An Econometric Forecasting Model of the Korean Economy," in Chuk Kyo Kim, ed., *Planning Model and Macroeconomic Policy Issues* (Korea Development Institute, 1977).

Table 5-2. *Change in Various Korean Price Indexes, by Year and Quarter, 1970–76*

Percent change over twelve-month period

Year and quarter	GNP deflator	Price index			
		Consumer	Wholesale	Export[a]	Import[a]
1970	15.3	16.0	9.1	4.4	3.7
First	16.0	16.5	8.7	−1.0	2.5
Second	10.7	17.7	9.4	4.7	3.5
Third	17.0	15.8	9.2	5.1	1.9
Fourth	16.9	14.0	9.2	7.8	8.5
1971	11.5	13.5	8.6	−1.2	−0.4
First	7.1	15.7	6.6	2.7	2.8
Second	10.4	12.8	6.4	1.0	1.8
Third	9.2	15.0	8.7	3.0	1.2
Fourth	15.6	10.7	12.8	−2.4	−4.3
1972	14.5	11.7	14.0	1.1	1.7
First	12.7	9.1	15.4	−0.1	1.9
Second	14.6	13.3	16.9	0.8	0.3
Third	13.4	13.8	15.0	4.3	3.2
Fourth	15.7	10.6	8.9	1.7	3.1
1973	9.6	3.2	7.0	26.6	33.5
First	11.2	4.8	6.2	8.5	10.3
Second	8.8	1.9	4.2	20.5	27.3
Third	8.8	0.7	6.2	25.0	34.9
Fourth	10.3	5.5	11.2	39.5	53.0
1974	26.7	24.3	42.2	26.6	55.5
First	23.0	18.0	32.7	46.2	66.9
Second	22.5	23.9	46.0	36.5	66.6
Third	23.1	27.7	45.2	25.7	58.9
Fourth	33.1	27.4	44.1	11.8	40.9
1975	24.1	25.3	26.5	−7.4	2.9
First	26.6	21.9	32.3	−0.2	24.3
Second	27.7	25.1	25.3	−10.1	4.0
Third	25.9	26.4	25.6	−10.8	−4.4
Fourth	19.8	27.3	23.7	−4.5	−8.5
1976	15.7	14.4	11.2	11.7	−2.0
First	17.1	21.6	15.5	−0.1	−11.0
Second	15.6	15.5	11.0	10.6	−5.8
Third	15.9	11.4	9.3	16.9	2.0
Fourth	15.5	10.2	9.3	15.0	7.0

Source: Bank of Korea, *Monthly Economic Statistics,* various issues.
a. Based on dollar value of merchandise trade.

Table 5-3. *Contribution of Excess Money Supply and Import Prices to Korean Inflation, 1970–77*
Percent

		Estimated value of components of wholesale price index			
Year	Wholesale price index	Excess money supply[a]	Import prices[b]	Total	Difference from index
1970–72	10.6	11.5	0.7	12.2	1.6
1973–76	21.7	13.2	9.0	22.2	0.5
1973	7.0	15.1	13.4	28.5	−21.5
1974	42.2	17.2	22.2	39.4	2.8
1975	26.5	10.8	1.2	12.0	14.5
1976	11.2	9.6	−0.8	8.8	2.4
1977	9.0	12.4	0.8	13.2	−4.2

Source: Hee-yhon Song, "Growth, Money and Inflation in Korea," Korea International Development Institute, Internal Seminar Series, no. 21 (November 30, 1977). Based on nominal values.
a. Difference between changes in weighted averages of money supply and GNP at price elasticity of 0.6.
b. Change in unit price of imports at price elasticity of 0.4.

Short-term variations in wholesale prices are explained not only by those two factors, but also by changes in the foreign exchange rate, public utility prices, and the price of rice. The latter three factors are significant because they are highly dependent on policy adjustments that have a life span of less than a year or two. In the long run, changes in these factors, which are really components of the overall price structure, are reflected in the price index. Changes in excess money supply (the nominal money supply divided by real GNP) and import prices between 1966 and 1976 suggest that the price elasticity of excess money is about 0.6 and that of import prices nearly 0.4.[6] When these results are applied to 1970–72 data, the rise in the wholesale price index can be attributed almost entirely to excess money supply (table 5-3).[7] Thus, during this period Korea's inflation was mainly caused by two domestic factors: the nominal money supply and the availability of goods and services.

Between 1973 and 1976 the rise in the wholesale price index was more than double the 1970–72 increase. Excess money supply was still responsible

6. Price equations used in the analysis of both short-run and long-run changes in Korean economic indicators are developed in ibid.
7. In 1970–72 the actual change in the wholesale price index was not as great as the estimated value of the change (table 5-3). The potential price rise was held down by a decline in interest rates and stable price expectations, the two factors that represent the income velocity of money.

for part of the increase, but import prices contributed significantly to the inflation. During these years, which included the commodity and oil crises, about 40 percent of Korea's inflation originated from international pressures, while the remainder was caused by domestic factors. The decisive domestic cause of inflation was a 51 percent increase in the money supply in 1973. The rate of increase in the money supply in 1974 and 1975 was a more modest 26 percent. In 1976 a relatively tight monetary stance was taken considering the exceptionally rapid growth of GNP. Specifically, money supply expanded 30.4 percent per year, while GNP grew 15.5 percent.

In 1973 the estimated price rise was 28.5 percent but the realized rise was only 7.1 percent. Thus 21.5 percent of the potential rise in prices was suppressed. In a small country such as Korea, where the number of enterprises in a particular industry is not large and where growth is very rapid, it is entirely possible that individual firms would choose to increase output to capture larger shares of both domestic and foreign markets rather than raise prices and hope to recover cost increases through productivity gains. If the inflationary pressures are very virulent, however, cost pressures must eventually be passed on in higher prices. Most of the potential price increase of 1973 was postponed and showed up in the following three years, when estimated increases in excess money supply and import prices indicated potential increases in the wholesale price index that were lower than the actual increases.

Volume of Trade

International trade is the major determinant of growth in the Korean economy, as the high correlation of variances in the volumes of exports and imports with variances in GNP indicates (table 5-4). Korea's international trade was greatly disrupted in 1970 and in the first half of 1972, mainly because of weak foreign demand. The recessions in the U.S. economy during 1970–71 and in the Japanese economy during 1971–72 lowered the import demands of Korea's major customers and Korea's real exports recorded very low growth rates of less than 20 percent. There were no significant lags between changes in Korea's exports and its trade partners' variations in GNP and imports (table 5-4). However, there was a six-month lag between changes in either Korea's exports or its trade partners' GNP and the resulting change in Korea's GNP.

During the second half of 1972 and throughout 1973, Korea's exports recorded their highest average annual growth rate of more than 55 percent in real terms because of exceptionally strong foreign demand and the de-

Table 5-4. *Change in Value of GNP and Commodity Trade in Korea, the United States, and Japan, by Half-Year, 1970–76*

Percent change over twelve-month period[a]

Year and half-year	Korea			United States		Japan	
	GNP	Exports	Imports	GNP	Imports	GNP	Imports
1970							
First	10.8	20.6	8.4	−0.3	6.1	11.2	22.2
Second	6.1	10.4	7.0	−0.3	1.1	10.9	16.3
1971							
First	14.2	19.5	26.4	2.4	2.6	7.9	4.6
Second	6.0	17.6	15.7	3.6	7.8	7.0	−5.2
1972							
First	5.5	23.8	−0.8	4.8	13.0	7.9	4.1
Second	8.0	45.4	6.1	6.7	13.9	10.0	21.0
1973							
First	17.8	56.0	35.2	6.6	7.9	12.2	27.6
Second	15.6	43.5	19.7	4.1	2.9	7.4	27.9
1974							
First	13.6	13.4	6.5	−0.4	−2.2	−1.5	8.5
Second	5.1	−7.7	3.2	−3.2	0.3	−0.7	−8.7
1975							
First	3.2	−2.6	0.6	−4.9	−15.5	2.2	−18.8
Second	11.1	38.3	3.7	−0.9	−8.9	2.1	−0.8
1976							
First	16.9	55.3	16.4	7.3	20.1	6.1	10.4
Second	14.3	36.3	37.5	5.2	22.7	5.8	12.4

Sources: Bank of Korea, *Economic Statistics Yearbook, 1978;* U.S. Department of Commerce, *Business Conditions Digest,* November 1978; Japan, Bureau of Statistics, *Monthly Statistics of Japan,* various issues.
a. Based on 1970 prices.

preciation of the Korean won (resulting from its being pegged to the U.S. dollar). After a six-month lag, Korea's GNP started to recover in the first half of 1973 and the boom ended in the first half of 1974. The world economy sharply decelerated in the second half of 1973 when the oil crisis occurred, and so did Korea's exports. Korea's growth rate of exports reached its low point in the second half of 1974 and in the first half of 1975.

As a result of very active exploration for export markets in Europe, the Middle East, and Africa, Korea's exports began to pick up in the second half of 1975 when both the U.S. and Japanese economies were just beginning to recover from their recessions. The recoveries in the United States and Japan gathered speed in the first half of 1976, stimulating demand for Korea's exports that eventually led to a remarkably high GNP growth rate of 15.5 percent. However, the strong foreign demand was temporary—starting in the fourth quarter of 1976, export volume decelerated as foreign demand weakened. By 1976 the Korean economy had become less sensitive to economic fluctuations in the United States and Japan. Their share of total Korean exports had declined from 70 percent in 1973 to 56 percent. Over the same period the share of exports to the Middle East had increased from 1.4 percent to 9.1 percent, and the share to Europe from 11.8 percent to 17.5 percent.

Five major determinants of Korea's export volume are foreign demand, competitiveness of exports (reflected in the real effective export exchange rate), export market exploration, the expansion of producing capacity, and the pressure of domestic demand (a negative factor). Foreign demand can be represented by income elasticity of Korean exports, which is estimated to be 2.4.[8] In other words, Korea's commodity exports are highly sensitive to changes in the real incomes of the major countries it exports to. Not only are most Korean exports still unfamiliar to foreign consumers, but they have not penetrated deeply enough into the major foreign markets to occupy more than a marginal share of importing countries' markets. Korea's exports are less sensitive to relative prices—their price elasticity is a little over 1.0—because most Korean export items are less expensive than comparable, well-known products that they compete against. Thus the success of Korea's trade promotion may very well be determined by effective marketing of Korea's export commodities.

Market factors are likely to be overlooked as important determinants of Korea's exports because they involve neither foreign demand nor relative price elements. Private business and government are, so to speak, jointly involved in a continuous effort to explore new export markets and encourage the active promotion of Korean merchandise, the development of new export items, the penetration of new geographical markets, improvement in the quality of established exports, the development of infrastructure, and the expansion of production capacity. The government's aggressive trade drive policy, which has the vigorous support of the president, has been extremely important in realizing these goals. Econometric analysis suggests that in 1967–73 Korea's exports in real terms increased at an annual rate of about 38 percent, of which 16.3 percentage points were explained by foreign demand and 2.4 percentage points by the real effective exchange rate. The

8. Song, "Growth, Money and Inflation." Foreign income elasticity was determined by regression analysis of semiannual data for 1966–74 on Korea's commodity exports and exchange rate, on GNP growth in the United States and Japan, and on wholesale price indexes in the three countries.

Table 5-5. *Contributors to Growth of Korean Exports, 1967–77*
Percent

Commodity exports excluding ship and steel	Average rate of increase				
	1967–73	1974	1975	1976	1977
Nominal value	43.7	29.7	16.1	54.7	27.3
Real value	37.3	3.0	25.4	36.1	14.9
Real effective exchange rate[a]	2.4	−15.7	−2.7	−5.0	−0.6
Foreign GNP[b]	16.3	−4.8	0.2	14.6	...
Trade promotion[c]	18.6	23.5	27.9	26.5	...

Source: Song, "Growth, Money and Inflation." Real values based on 1970 prices.
a. Elasticity of 1.0; based on real effective exchange rates in table 5-1.
b. Elasticity of 2.4; based on changes in U.S. and Japanese GNP.
c. All other contributors to export value, such as marketing, quality improvement, production capacity, management ability, government export drive policy, general economic development.

remaining 18.6 percentage points were explained by residual factors, that is, market exploration, capacity expansion, and domestic demand.

With the deterioration of Korea's export markets, the role of market exploration and trade promotion became increasingly important and was a major factor in insulating the Korean economy from the external shocks of 1974–76 (table 5-5). Immediately after the oil crisis, in 1974–75, the U.S. and Japanese GNPs fell sharply and their weighted averages declined at an average annual rate of about 1.5 percent. As a consequence, Korea's commodity exports declined by about 3.6 percent (assuming a foreign income elasticity of 2.4). Korea's real effective export exchange rate (which is the product of the effective exchange rate adjusted for export subsidy and the ratio of foreign price change to domestic price change) also deteriorated substantially, by an estimated 9 percent annually, because Korea's inflation rate was higher than the rates of its major trade partners. Under normal economic conditions these two factors plus the market exploration factor would have caused exports to expand at an annual rate of about 6 percent during the worldwide recession of 1974–75. However, the increase in Korea's commodity exports in real terms averaged nearly 15 percent a year in 1974–75. To a large extent the active export expansion drive, reflected in an increase in the market exploration factor of about 25 percent, insulated Korea from the severe recession of its major trading partners and enabled the economy to grow at a respectable rate of 8 percent over the two-year period. Middle East ventures and continued export expansion in European countries together with the gradual movement from light to heavy manufactured export products contributed greatly to this reasonably high rate of export growth during the recession period.

Table 5-6. Relation of Korea's Imports to GNP, 1970–77

Item	1970	1971	1972	1973	1974	1975	1976	1977
Total imports								
Millions of dollars	1,804.2	2,178.2	2,250.4	3,837.3	6,451.9	6,674.4	8,405.1	10,810.5
Percent annual increase	9.3	20.7	3.3	70.5	68.1	3.4	25.9	28.6
Millions of 1970 dollars	1,804.2	2,186.9	2,221.5	2,838.2	3,068.0	3,085.5	3,966.5	4,989.9
Percent annual increase	5.4	21.2	1.6	27.8	8.1	0.6	28.6	25.8
GNP								
Millions of dollars	7,558	8,747	9,824	12,306	16,680	18,761	25,090	31,488
Percent annual increase	18.1	15.7	12.3	25.3	35.5	12.5	33.7	25.5
Millions of 1970 dollars	7,558	8,251	8,825	10,238	11,125	12,053	13,917	15,322
Percent annual increase	7.9	9.2	7.0	16.0	8.7	8.3	15.4	10.1
Elasticity of imports								
Nominal value	0.52	1.32	0.27	2.79	1.92	0.27	0.77	1.12
Real value	0.68	2.30	0.23	1.74	0.93	0.07	1.86	2.55
Imports as a share of GNP								
Nominal (percent)	23.9	24.9	22.9	31.2	38.7	35.6	33.5	34.3
Real (percent)	23.9	26.5	25.2	27.7	27.6	25.6	28.5	32.6

Source: Korea, Economic Planning Board, *Handbook of Korean Economy*, 1978.

In 1970, food-based products and raw materials accounted for 21.5 percent of Korea's total commodity exports, manufactured materials and articles for 68.6 percent, and machinery and transportation equipment for only 7.4 percent. By 1976 the composition of Korea's export commodities had changed significantly. Manufactured materials and articles maintained their level of nearly 70 percent, but food-based products and raw materials declined to 10.1 percent, and machinery and transportation equipment alone rose to 16.6 percent.

The rate of increase in imports was remarkably high during 1973 and then dropped sharply in the first quarter of 1974. It recovered, however, in the fourth quarter of 1976. As export volume declined in the fourth quarter of 1974, growth of import volume also fell substantially. During six consecutive quarters of low GNP growth rates starting in the second quarter of 1974, the import volume fell.

In 1970–71, imports in real terms increased at the relatively high rate of 13.3 percent, and income elasticity of imports was 1.5 (see table 5-6). The primary reason was the adoption of a less restrictive import policy in 1971. In 1972, however, a very restrictive import policy was adopted because of the deterioration in the balance of payments in 1971, and commodity imports rose only slightly. Real imports rose again, by 28 percent in 1973, but then weakened in 1974–75 when economic activity slowed down.

The phenomenal increase in the prices of import commodities in 1974 and the won devaluation of December 1974 also discouraged imports in 1974–75. In 1976 the combination of weak import prices, exports recovery, and high GNP growth brought about the very sharp increase of 28.6 percent in imports; the import elasticity was 1.86 in real terms and 0.77 in nominal terms.

Imports of industrial raw materials (which are highly cyclical) were less sensitive than capital goods imports to changes in import prices. Those raw materials used in the production of export commodities were very inelastic with respect to prices as long as the additional cost could be passed on to foreign buyers. While the elasticity of capital goods imports in 1964–73 with respect to the real effective import exchange rate is estimated to be 1.68, that of intermediate commodities is 0.33.[9]

The sources of Korea's imports did not change during the 1970s as much as the markets for its exports. But the share of total imports that came from Japan declined from 38 percent in 1974 to 35 percent in 1976, and the share from the United States from 25 percent to 22 percent. At the same time the

9. Ibid.

Table 5-7. *Korean Gross National Product and Net Exports of Goods and Services, 1970–76*

Billions of 1970 won

Year	GNP	Net exports
1970	2,589.3	−249.3
1971	2,826.8	−316.2
1972	3,023.6	−170.0
1973	3,507.5	−79.4
1974	3,811.3	−142.6
1975	4,129.3	−13.7
1976	4,767.9	168.6

Source: *Handbook of Korean Economy, 1978.*

share of imports from Europe increased significantly from 6.7 percent to 9.0 percent.

The Goods and Services Balance

The balance of Korean trade in goods and services (exports minus imports) was negative from 1970 through 1975 (table 5-7). In the second half of 1975, net exports became positive. As a percentage of GNP they fluctuated widely, depending on the external economic situation, from a negative 9.6 percent to a positive 3.5 percent in 1976. When the economies of major trade partners were in a boom period, net exports increased and the GNP grew quickly, and when the external economies deteriorated, net exports declined. Indeed, changes in net exports are a direct and decisive cause of changes in Korea's GNP.

A particularly large portion of the change in GNP can be attributed to changes in net exports in the second half of 1972 through 1973 and in the second half of 1975 through 1976 (table 5-8). External economies were then in boom periods and Korea's GNP grew at the very high rate of about 15 percent a year. The exception to this relationship was the first half of 1971 when Korea adopted an expansionary fiscal policy. This expansionary policy was a countercyclical or moderating force when the external demand deteriorated. This countercyclical force, however, could not last long because of limitations in the government's policy.

In the first place rapid domestic expansion leads to greater imports, and without a rise in exports, to a balance-of-payments deficit too large to be tolerated. Secondly, industrial capacity geared for the export market may not be usable to meet rising domestic demand if the product structure of that demand differs from that of the export market. The annual GNP growth rate declined from 14.2 percent in the first half of 1971 to 6.0 percent in

Table 5-8. *Change in Korean Gross National Product and Net Exports of Goods and Services, by Quarter, 1970–76*

Billions of 1970 won; change over twelve-month period

Quarter	GNP	Net exports
1970		
First	40.2	−2.3
Second	58.3	14.1
Third	49.1	7.0
Fourth	41.2	−6.3
1971		
First	72.4	−11.2
Second	71.0	−39.9
Third	58.8	−22.6
Fourth	35.4	20.7
1972		
First	34.6	13.2
Second	28.4	51.4
Third	49.5	56.0
Fourth	84.3	35.8
1973		
First	100.8	21.8
Second	100.7	−2.3
Third	139.9	30.5
Fourth	142.5	55.1
1974		
First	102.5	1.3
Second	93.9	26.0
Third	46.5	−21.0
Fourth	60.9	−63.2
1975		
First	23.2	−24.4
Second	42.9	−0.7
Third	83.1	101.4
Fourth	168.8	73.5
1976		
First	123.6	64.3
Second	166.7	70.6
Third	153.8	−13.6
Fourth	194.5	48.7

Source: *Economic Statistics Yearbook, 1978.*

the second half of the year (table 5-4). This trend continued until late in 1972 when other countries began to recover and net exports started to increase.

Late in 1972 when both the U.S. and Japanese economies were fully recovered, Korea's exports increased very rapidly. Imports also increased

Table 5-9. *Korean Balance of Payments and Foreign Reserve Holdings, 1970–77*

Millions of dollars

Item	1970	1971	1972	1973	1974	1975	1976	1977
Current account	−623	−848	−371	−309	−2,023	−1,887	−314	15
Trade balance	−922	−1,046	−575	−567	−1,937	−1,671	−590	−439
Exports (f.o.b.)	882	1,132	1,676	3,271	4,515	5,003	7,815	10,046
Imports (f.o.b.)	1,804	2,178	2,250	3,837	6,452	6,674	8,405	10,485
Services balance	119	28	33	67	−309	−442	−72	231
Receipts	497	484	550	849	838	881	1,643	2,998
Payments	378	456	517	782	1,146	1,323	1,715	2,767
Transfers (net)	180	171	170	190	222	226	349	223
Long-term capital (net)	449	528	496	597	1,052	1,287	1,371	1,334
Loans and investment	536	557	730	856	1,057	1,467	1,639	1,972
Amortization	−107	−135	−202	−261	−338	−306	−407	−536
Other	20	106	−32	2	333	126	139	−102
Basic balance	−174	−320	125	288	−971	−600	1,057	1,349
Short-term capital (net)	122	135	−16	83	−45	680	357	21
Errors and omissions	16	13	41	19	28	−218	−241	−57
Bank borrowings (net)	70	123	9	−50	1,003	631	349	36
Foreign reserve holdings, annual level	584	535	694	1,034	1,049	1,542	2,961	4,306

Source: *Handbook of Korean Economy, 1978*, p. 37.

substantially beginning in early 1973. Since there was excess capacity in the manufacturing sector of the Korean economy until late 1972, the effect of real income expansion was extremely beneficial. As a result the economy recorded its highest growth rate since the 1960s and this trend continued until the first half of 1974.

In the second half of 1974, net exports actually declined from their level a year earlier and the economy grew at the low annual rate of about 5.1 percent. In the meantime, prompt countercyclical economic measures were taken with respect to trade, foreign-exchange, and domestic fiscal policies to mitigate the effects of the reduced net exports. These measures not only minimized the economic setback but stimulated an early recovery. Such policies can be increasingly effective as the Korean economy expands. But expansion and deeper penetration of foreign markets, in terms of both exports and imports, are a more important moderating force.

Financial Flows and Direct Investment

Changes in the international flow of capital appear to depend largely on fluctuations in trade, international differences in interest rates, and changes in exchange rates, and also on the availability of international capital which in turn depends largely on demand from and flow to other countries. The appreciation in the Japanese yen in 1972 and 1973, for example, encouraged a flow of capital out of Japan. Korea proved to be one of the most attractive countries to Japanese investors, and Japan accounted for all but a fifth of direct foreign investment in Korea in 1970–76. But foreign investment in Korea is still in an embryonic state—in 1976 it represented only 1.4 percent of total fixed capital formation. (Nor has investment in other countries been attractive to Koreans, since few countries offer better investment earnings.)

Because of high Korean interest rates, Korean borrowers find foreign capital very attractive. In 1970 and 1971, when demand for Korean exports was weak, imports were unusually strong, producing a large cumulative deficit in the current account (table 5-9). Korea met the shortfall in the basic balance by large increases in short-term capital and bank borrowings.

In 1972–73, thanks to a worldwide economic boom, the current account recorded an unusually low deficit. Net inflow of long-term capital maintained the same level as in the previous period, but both net short-term capital and net bank borrowings declined substantially. With the abrupt reversal in the current account to a cumulative deficit of nearly $4 billion in 1974 and 1975, short-term and long-term capital fell short of balancing the account. Bank borrowing was a very important element in the overall balance. Bor-

Table 5-10. Change in Korean Money Supply (M_1), by Sector, 1970–77

Billions of won

Source of change	1970	1971	1972	1973	1974	1975	1976	1977
Money supply	55.6	50.4	161.4	210.9	215.4	236.1	362.3	628.5
Government sector	−28.5	−15.9	80.9	15.4	103.4	202.5	−44.3	−104.7
Government agency	−2.0	2.0	2.0	9.0	−23.0	90.0	0	100.0
Private sector	75.0	139.0	12.9	29.0	680.9	77.5	36.4	119.4
Foreign sector	2.3	−72.4	64.7	197.1	−479.2	−53.4	512.4	656.1
Other sectors	8.8	6.8	0.9	−39.6	−66.7	−80.6	−142.2	−142.2

Source: Bank of Korea, Monthly Economic Statistics, vol. 32, no. 4 (April 1978), pp. 14–15.

rowings included $760 million in refinanced loans, $274 million in bank loans, and $286 million in credit from the International Monetary Fund.

As the world economies gradually recovered in 1976, Korea's current account deficit decreased substantially. Both net short-term capital inflows and net bank borrowings declined substantially.

The Payments Balance

In 1970–71 Korea recorded a deficit in its overall balance of payments and the money supply increased at a very low rate—less than 20 percent a year, compared with about 40 percent in the previous period. Domestic credit for the private sector was a major source of this increase in the money supply (table 5-10).

Foreign-exchange holdings were allowed to decline in 1971. Then, when the overall balance of payments swung around to a surplus in 1972–73, the Bank of Korea had to sell domestic money to buy foreign exchange, thereby creating high-powered money. About 70 percent of the increase in the money supply came from the foreign sector. Even though domestic credit was strictly limited, the squeeze was not enough to sterilize foreign-exchange earnings. Money supply increased at an annual rate of 45 percent and became one of the major causes of inflation in 1974–75. After the oil crisis, however, the situation was completely reversed. In 1974 the money supply stemming from both the private and government sectors increased drastically whereas money created by the foreign sector was substantially reduced and the overall money supply decelerated. This trend continued in 1975.

In 1976 the overall balance recorded a large surplus (earnings from construction ventures in the Middle East and receipts from tourism were major factors). Because of the increase in money supply from the foreign sector, a strong sterilization measure was adopted as part of an overall stabilization policy. Without controls on domestic credit, growth in the money supply would have easily exceeded 40 percent in 1976, considering the overall surplus and high rate of GNP growth. Excess money supply is likely to continue to be a problem for the Korean economy unless successful measures are devised to sterilize the money created from the foreign sector.

External Disturbances Caused by the United States and Japan

Although in recent years the percentage of Korea's total trade done with the United States and Japan has declined, the Korean economy still main-

Table 5-11. *U.S. and Japanese Contributions to Changes in Korean Trade Indexes, 1970–77*

Percent

Trade index and trading partner	1970	1971	1972	1973	1974	1975	1976	1977
Import unit value	3.7	−0.4	1.7	33.5	55.5	2.9	−2.0	2.2
United States[a]	1.7	1.0	0.7	4.7	6.7	3.1	0.8	1.1
Japan[a]	2.3	0.1	−0.7	3.5	14.5	0.6	−0.7	1.3
Others	−0.3	−1.5	1.7	25.3	34.3	−0.8	−2.1	−0.2
Export unit value	34.2	27.8	52.1	97.7	38.3	13.9	51.8	30.2
United States[b]	12.0	17.2	19.9	10.0	15.4	0.0	20.1	7.8
Japan[b]	21.3	2.9	14.0	78.7	3.5	−1.6	9.2	4.1
Others	0.9	7.7	18.2	9.0	19.4	14.6	22.5	18.3

a. Based on export unit value indexes of the United States and Japan.
b. Based on import unit value indexes of the United States and Japan.

tains close ties with both countries in trade, finance, technology, and other economic-related areas. Thus the economic fluctuations of these two countries exert a major impact on the Korean economy; the impact is readily discernible in two major economic variables in Korea—the import unit value and export value. From 1970 through 1972 the import unit value index rose at an annual average rate of less than 1 percent (table 5-11). The United States and Japan were the major sources of this small increase in import prices. The sharp rises in the annual rates of import unit value in 1973 and 1974 were the result of worldwide inflation caused by commodity shortages and the oil crisis. Since the United States and Japan were not major suppliers of these expensive raw materials including oil, direct responsibility for the rise in Korea's import prices was relatively small. In 1975 and 1976, prices for both raw materials and the exports of the two countries were stable.

The impact of both countries on Korea's export unit values varies from year to year, depending largely on their economic fluctuations and changes in exchange rates. In 1973, for example, both the United States and Japan had very high economic growth rates and contributed to the increase in Korea's export prices, though most of the increase was attributable to the appreciation of the Japanese yen. The contribution of these two nations was unusually small during the deep recession of 1974–75. Even in the recovery of 1976 and 1977, the contribution of other countries remained high because of the expansion of Korea's export market, particularly to the Middle East and Europe.

Before 1973, more than 70 percent of Korea's total exports went to the United States and Japan but their share declined to little more than 52 percent in 1977. Imports from these two countries, which were hovering around 70 percent of Korea's total imports during the same period, also decreased to less than 60 percent (see table 5-12). Though the direct impact of these two countries through trade has declined substantially in recent years, it remains significant. These two nations also have a strong indirect influence on Korea through close economic links with Korea's other trade partners. For example, increased industrial production in Japan and the United States has an indirect influence on Korea both because it causes world raw material prices to be bid up, which affects the cost of Korea's imports, and because it increases the income of raw-material-exporting countries, which then purchase more Korean exports.

During the 1970s the pattern of Korea's trade with the United States changed. The share of Korea's total exports that went to the United States decreased from 48 percent in 1970–71 to 31 percent in 1977, and the share of imports from the United States from 29 percent to 22 percent. This trend is typical of the changes in Korea's trade patterns as it has diversified its export markets. The appreciation of the Japanese yen and European currencies made exports to the United States slightly less attractive and thus to some extent Korea's export market shifted to Japan in 1973–74 and to European countries in 1975–76.

The composition of Korean exports to the United States shifted from semifinished materials to finished consumer products. The share of semimanufactured goods, such as textile yarn and fabrics, plywood, rubber manufactures, cement, and iron and steel, declined substantially from 30.8 percent in 1973 to 23.4 percent in 1975, and the share of such items as transportation equipment, machinery, and electrical machinery and appliances from 20.4 percent to 16.6 percent. However, miscellaneous manufactured articles, including clothing and footwear, increased from 44.7 percent of Korea's exports to the United States to 54.4 percent during the same period. The increasing share of consumer products is shortening the time lag between fluctuations in the U.S. gross national product and variations in Korea's exports. Imports from the United States of food and live animals decreased from 36.4 percent of imports in 1973 to 32.2 percent in 1975, while nonfood raw materials except fuels increased from 25.5 percent to 28.7 percent.

The share of Korean exports going to Japan decreased from 28.1 percent in 1970 to 21.4 percent in 1977, reflecting again the general trend toward diversification of Korea's export market. The jump in exports to Japan in 1973 and 1974 was due mainly to the yen appreciation in 1972 and 1973. Korea's imports from Japan, which hovered around 40 percent until 1974, declined to 35.3 percent in 1976. Since intermediate imports are inelastic

Table 5-12. *U.S. and Japanese Shares of Korea's Trade, 1970–77*
Millions of dollars and, in parentheses, percent of total

Year	Total trade		Trade with United States			Trade with Japan		
	Exports	Imports	Exports	Imports	Balance	Exports	Imports	Balance
1970	835.2	1,984.0	395.2 (47.3)	584.8 (29.5)	−189.6	234.3 (28.1)	809.3 (40.8)	−575.0
1971	1,067.6	2,394.3	531.8 (49.8)	678.3 (28.3)	−146.5	262.0 (24.5)	953.8 (39.8)	−691.8
1972	1,624.1	2,522.0	759.0 (46.7)	647.2 (25.7)	−111.8	407.9 (25.1)	1,031.1 (40.9)	−623.2
1973	3,225.0	4,240.3	1,021.2 (31.7)	1,201.9 (28.3)	−180.7	1,241.5 (38.5)	1,726.9 (40.7)	−485.4
1974	4,460.4	6,851.8	1,492.1 (33.5)	1,700.8 (24.8)	−208.7	1,380.2 (30.9)	2,620.8 (38.2)	−1,240.6
1975	5,081.0	7,274.4	1,536.3 (30.2)	1,881.1 (25.9)	−344.8	1,292.9 (25.4)	2,433.6 (33.5)	−1,140.7
1976	7,715.3	8,773.6	2,492.5 (32.3)	1,962.9 (22.4)	529.6	1,801.6 (23.4)	3,099.0 (35.3)	−1,297.4
1977	10,046.5	10,810.5	3,118.6 (31.0)	2,447.4 (22.6)	671.2	2,148.3 (21.4)	3,926.6 (36.3)	−1,778.3

Source: *Handbook of Korean Economy, 1978*, pp. 50, 54.

with respect to price,[10] the impact of the yen appreciation on the real value of imports was relatively small. Furthermore, the impact of the yen appreciation on the nominal value of imports was negligible because Japanese export prices increased in U.S. dollar terms.

The composition of imports from Japan has changed significantly in recent years. The share of crude raw materials decreased from 7.7 percent to 4.1 percent between 1973 and 1975, and the share of intermediate manufactured goods from 37.9 percent to 30.2 percent. Meanwhile, the share of chemicals rose from 12.3 percent to 18.9 percent of imports and the share of machinery and transport equipment from 34.5 percent to 38.5 percent. As the range of Korea's domestic industries expanded, some intermediate imports were replaced by domestically produced goods. Yet Korea will probably continue to import technology-intensive commodities such as chemicals and sophisticated machinery primarily from Japan for some time to come.

Korea's bilateral trade balance with the United States showed a deficit from 1970 through 1975. However, in 1976, thanks to a large increase in exports to the United States and stable import prices, Korea recorded a trade surplus with the United States of more than $500 million. Korea's bilateral trade balance with Japan differs from that with the United States because the Korean economy is heavily dependent on Japan for capital goods, semifinished intermediate manufactured goods, and chemicals. The bilateral trade deficit with Japan increased from the $600 million average in the early 1970s to nearly $1.3 billion in 1976. Thus unless Korea's exports to Japan increase markedly, the bilateral trade deficit with Japan will not be significantly improved. There will be some limitations on Korea's ability to diversify its imports because of geographical proximity and technological and structural ties with Japan. Korea should study the structural shifts in Japanese industries in order to determine where the Korean comparative advantage lies. Moreover, Korea should make a special effort to diversify its economic ties not only with Japan, but with the United States and the European countries where Korea has a trade surplus.

Monetary and Fiscal Policies

Korea's economic policy in 1970–72 was primarily concerned with the deterioration of the balance of payments and the danger of inflation, both of which were caused by the increased demand of the late 1960s. Thus when

10. Their elasticity is estimated to be 0.33 in 1964–73. Ibid.

foreign demand weakened in 1970–71, the Korean government could not work to stimulate domestic demand but rather had to impose very restrictive monetary and fiscal policies. Because of these lagged restrictive policies, the recession of 1970–71 was aggravated, and the average annual increase in the money supply was less than 20 percent compared to 36 percent over the previous four-year period.

Government budget expenditures in 1970 were allowed to increase only 3.4 percent whereas the average rise over the previous four years was 40 percent, and public investment and loans were held to a 5 percent increase compared to the earlier average of 59 percent. Gross fixed capital investment grew only 1.7 percent compared to an average of 35 percent in 1966–69. Government policies did not succeed, however, in stabilizing prices in 1970 because of the rise in utility rates and the devaluation of the won. Thus in 1971, fiscal policy was relaxed and budget expenditures rose by 26.3 percent. But weak foreign demand coupled with a less restrictive imports policy caused the deficit in the current account to rise very significantly, and restrictions were again placed on imports by the end of 1971.

Despite the restrictive policies, inflationary pressures continued in 1972. The economy suffered from the marked slowdown in real growth and the excess capacity in the manufacturing sector. The emergency economic decree of August 1972 provided several programs to help solve Korea's increased economic problems. Interest rates in the unorganized money markets were lowered from about 40 percent a year to 16.2 percent and in the organized market from 16.0 percent to 12.0 percent. Businesses were allowed to legally defer payment of existing unorganized private loans for up to five years and easy credit terms were established to make more loans available to them. Moreover, the government supplied special funds for industrial development and increased depreciation allowances by 40–80 percent. Within two months the money supply rose 18.2 percent. Government expenditures were also raised very significantly to provide additional stimulus.

The monetary stimulus and price controls of the August 1972 decree, coinciding with the fast worldwide recovery, caused the Korean economy to perform exceptionally well in 1973. Real output expanded by 16.7 percent, exceeding the highest growth rate recorded during the 1960s. The balance-of-payments deficit fell to $308.8 million. As a result, the economy overheated and inflationary pressures increased drastically, partly because of the strong foreign demand combined with the excess money supply—increasing at an average annual rate of more than 45 percent for 1972–73—and partly because of imported inflation brought on by the higher prices of imported raw materials.

The inflationary pressures induced by the oil crisis on the one hand and the ensuing worldwide recession on the other caused the government to introduce a series of measures to deal with the difficulties which included restrictive monetary policies early in 1974 to restrain aggregate demand and check the emergence of a serious balance-of-payments deficit. The special presidential measures promulgated in January included substantial reductions in taxes on wages and salaries and postponement of pension contributions to reduce the burden of inflation on low-income families. They also provided a large amount of funds for public works to create employment opportunities. Government expenditures, investment, and loans expanded substantially. During the first half of 1974, aggregate demand continued to be strong and real output grew at the high rate of 13.6 percent; in the second half, however, the growth rate declined very sharply because of a sharp decrease in exports and restrictive monetary policy. The rate of export expansion fell abruptly to 9.5 percent, the lowest real growth rate since 1967. Because of a rapid rise in import prices, nominal imports rose by 68.1 percent while nominal exports increased by 38 percent. The current account deficit—more than $2 billion—was the largest ever. It was not possible for the government to take further domestic expansionary measures, however, because the appropriate restrictive measures had not been taken during the boom period of 1972–73. If the overheated economy had been managed more effectively—if lagged policy responses had been set in motion during the boom—the efforts to overcome recession in 1974 and 1975 could have been more extensive.

To correct the payments deficit, the government adopted another special measure on December 7, 1974. It included the devaluation of the won to promote exports and provision of special funds for loans to business firms to lighten the repayment burden of short-term foreign loans. A special fund of 50 billion won was created to stimulate private investment and a fund of 69 billion won for low-cost housing projects, and manufacturers were offered a special depreciation allowance for using domestically produced materials. The measure stipulated that more than 60 percent of investment and loan projects funded must be implemented during the first half of 1975. Policymakers believed that foreign demand would start to recover by the end of 1975. The government's promptness in implementing appropriate measures —especially its requirement that specially funded projects be put in action in early 1975—helped Korea overcome the effects of the worldwide recession of 1974–75.

Even though recovery clearly got under way in the second half of 1975, the current account deficit for the year was high, at $1.9 billion. Real output increased by 8.3 percent and the money supply by a moderate 26 percent. Although the rate of inflation fell very significantly from the previous year, it remained high. The wholesale price index rose by 26.5 percent in 1975. Stabilization of prices and reduction of the balance-of-payments deficit were the main concern of policymakers in 1976. In spite of conservative monetary and fiscal measures, real output grew by 15.5 percent as exports at current prices increased 56.2 percent. Money supply rose at a rate of slightly more than 30 percent as a result of high net exports and receipts on invisible trade. The increase in money supply generated by the foreign sector became an important concern for aggregate monetary management. If the government wishes to sterilize the flow of foreign currency into the country, it can either reduce the budget, adjust interest rates on bank deposits, particularly for household savings, or require deposits of a portion of foreign-exchange earnings as a substitute for capital borrowing.

Foreign-Exchange Policy

Although Korea's foreign-exchange rate has not been adjusted simultaneously with changes in its determining factors, such as the relative value of local currency and the balance-of-payments situation, it has followed the general trend of changes in these determinants with some time lag. In the late 1960s when the economy became overheated, the won was overvalued which eventually contributed to price stabilization. However, during 1970–72, when the external economy was sluggish, this overvalued currency was devalued. This devaluation contributed to price rises which in turn became one of the obstacles to implementing proper expansionary economic policies. During 1973–74, external demand was very strong, and the local currency was again overvalued. The currency was devalued at the end of 1974 with the coming of the worldwide recession. In fact, the delayed 1974 devaluation aggravated the inflation in 1975.

It appears that Korea's delayed adjustment of the foreign-exchange rate helped reduce the excess foreign demand. However, the rather large price elasticity of the exchange rate means that any delay in adjustment of the rate has a relatively small impact on export demand. In fact, the slow policy response simply postponed the price rise of imported goods until the recession. It appears that prompt adjustment of the foreign-exchange rate to changes in its determining factors is the better choice when external demand is sluggish.

Direct Controls

In 1970–72 when the real growth of the Korean economy slowed down, those rates that were controlled such as public utility rates, rice prices, and exchange rates could no longer be suppressed because of the high pressure generated by the disequilibrium prices. As a result, in the second half of 1971 and first half of 1972 when the economy was at its lowest level of the recession, prices rose at a fast pace. Inflationary pressures necessitated restrictive monetary and fiscal policies throughout this period. The economy suffered from very low rates of real growth, together with severe excess capacity and high interest rates.

In an attempt to improve the competitive position of Korean exporters in this emergency, the government decided to limit wage increases and to hold price increases under 3 percent a year as measured by the wholesale price index (the current rate was 16 percent). The foreign-exchange rate and public utility prices were frozen since they were believed to be close to equilibrium values, but the price of rice was raised to help improve rural incomes. Interest rates also were substantially lowered by increasing the money in circulation. Although both imported inflation and excess money supply foreshadowed extremely high price rises in 1973, exceptionally stable prices were maintained. While the money supply expanded 46.6 percent, the wholesale price index rose only 7.0 percent. The combination of stable prices and unusually strong foreign demand stimulated Korean exports which in turn caused supply shortages in the economy.

In 1974–75 when foreign demand was extremely sluggish, the controls were lifted and the price rises were explosive. Indeed, the delayed policy response made the subsequent stagflation more serious. When the economy began to recover in 1976, prices were again suppressed. Yet price controls had not helped the economy combat inflation in the past but simply postponed the price rises until the recession. The postponements in fact aggravated the inflation.

In short, since the early 1970s the significance of the economic interdependence in the world has been recognized by the majority of economic decisionmakers of Korea. During the worldwide stagflation that occurred after the oil crisis, Korea was one of the most successful countries in overcoming its economic difficulties. The major factors behind this success were the prompt and effective economic ventures in the Middle East and the market expansions in the European countries.

The most serious shortcomings in the formulation of macroeconomic policy were in the lagged adjustments in prices, interest rates, and monetary and fiscal policies in response to changes in both the external and internal economic environments. From this experience it appears that Korea, because of its intensive interrelations with other countries, cannot avoid feeling some impact from an external disturbance. However, through use of domestic policy instruments, it has some leeway to channel the domestic impact of the external disturbance to either real income or prices. Korea has chosen to emphasize growth at the expense of inflation and has been very successful in achieving high growth rates. This strategy, however, requires giving prompt attention to inflation when external conditions permit. It appears that a lack of understanding of both domestic and foreign aggregate economic operations is one of the major factors responsible for the government's delayed policy responses. As international economic interdependence increases, more thorough research on overall operations and closer coordination among the economic ministries will be necessary to maintain a high and steady rate of economic growth for Korea and to improve social welfare.

CHAPTER SIX

Structural Change in the Philippines

ROMEO M. BAUTISTA

TOWARD THE END of the 1960s the Philippines was experiencing a severe foreign-exchange crisis precipitated by the need to service short-term credit that financed the trade deficits of the second half of the decade. In order to obtain a third credit tranche from the International Monetary Fund as well as longer repayment terms on debts to foreign banks, the government floated the domestic currency in February 1970; by the end of the year the exchange rate had moved from 3.9 pesos to 6.4 pesos per U.S. dollar. The dramatic developments in the world economy that shortly followed were further shocks to an economy only recently perturbed in its external sector and already adjusting to a new set of domestic price relationships.

The monetary and fiscal policies accompanying the de facto devaluation of the peso in 1970 failed to prevent a substantial increase in domestic prices.[1] Import measures were not liberalized as they had been when the peso was depreciated in 1962; continuation of controls effectively banned imports of some four hundred commodities. Thus, while the foreign currency price of imports rose by only 3.66 percent in 1970, the domestic wholesale price index of imports increased by 31.4 percent. The consumer price index rose 14.0 percent, the country's first postwar experience with double-digit

1. "The fear of further intensification of the social unrest that was triggered by price rises associated with the currency devaluation apparently led the government to fix the dollar value of the peso" in December 1970. R. E. Baldwin, *Foreign Exchange Regimes and Economic Development: The Philippines* (New York: National Bureau of Economic Research, 1975), pp. 80–81.

Table 6-1. *Percent Change in Various Philippine Price Indexes, 1956–76*

			Price index			
Year	Consumer	General wholesale	Export[a]	Export products, wholesale	Import[a]	Import commodities, wholesale
1956	2.84	3.19	1.47	4.39	1.29	8.67
1957	1.61	4.27	1.33	4.59	3.35	5.32
1958	3.40	3.39	4.06	10.60	2.16	4.01
1959	−1.10	1.37	8.33	13.06	2.11	9.00
1960	4.66	4.18	−1.46	−2.63	2.22	5.77
1961	1.27	4.92	−8.00	3.90	1.45	5.20
1962	5.65	5.06	−1.07	20.95	1.85	9.42
1963	5.74	9.74	5.31	19.71	6.72	6.14
1964	8.24	4.60	−0.81	−2.89	0.79	0.91
1965	2.42	2.25	1.73	2.77	1.69	0.50
1966	5.40	4.30	0.90	1.30	1.66	0.70
1967	6.41	2.59	1.78	6.12	2.27	0.10
1968	2.41	2.71	6.23	12.00	9.11	−0.30
1969	1.91	1.36	0.37	−1.74	1.81	3.18
1970	14.00	23.61	1.46	24.18	3.66	31.44
1971	15.06	15.69	−4.95	7.22	2.14	13.72
1972	10.01	10.11	−5.30	2.35	4.71	7.35
1973	14.00	24.52	45.90	53.91	28.80	27.94
1974	33.51	54.53	66.07	76.46	64.29	41.10
1975	8.15	2.87	−20.43	−30.56	3.78	18.04
1976	6.20	7.26	−12.45	2.53	−1.09	5.64

Source: Central Bank of the Philippines, *Statistical Bulletin, 1976.*
a. Based on U.S. dollar values.

inflation rates (table 6-1).[2] In 1971 the import wholesale price index climbed up 13.7 percent, contributing to a 15.1 percent increase in the consumer price index.

The 1950s and 1960s were a period of relative stability in the foreign trade of the Philippines, as is apparent in the fluctuations of export and import prices, volumes, and values (table 6-2). The standard deviation of both export and import price and value indexes is much higher in 1969–75

2. The consumer price index for Manila and suburbs is used in this study; it has been published since 1949 in the Central Bank's *Statistical Bulletin.* It is highly correlated with an index for the Philippines developed somewhat later and with the index for Manila and the entire country prepared by the National Census and Statistics Office since 1970. For a comparison of the two, see R. M. Bautista, "Inflation in the Philippines, 1955–74," in J. Encarnación and others, *Philippine Economic Problems in Perspective* (Quezon City: Institute of Economic Development and Research, 1976), pp. 178–213.

Table 6-2. *Change in Philippine Trade Variables, 1951–75*
Percent

Index	Mean change	Standard deviation	Mean change	Standard deviation
	1951–57		*1957–63*	
Export price	−2.65	13.55	1.55	5.17
Import price	−0.97	2.86	2.76	1.77
Export volume	5.10	8.55	7.96	7.44
Import volume	5.93	10.67	−2.52	7.52
Export value	1.32	19.02	9.79	12.36
Import value	4.91	11.14	0.20	16.25
	1963–69		*1969–75*	
Export price	1.44	1.77	9.91	38.59
Import price	1.59	0.72	19.77	24.89
Export volume	1.15	3.48	8.35	9.27
Import volume	9.49	8.76	3.37	4.30
Export value	2.44	3.61	24.63	40.71
Import value	10.95	9.37	23.57	232.95

Source: Calculated from data in Central Bank, *Statistical Bulletin, 1975.*

than in any earlier period. The dispersion of annual changes in export volume is greatest in 1969–75, but not markedly high. In sharp contrast, the standard deviation for the import volume index is at its lowest in 1969–75, the result of the import controls that had been in existence since World War II.[3]

Exports increased significantly after the 1970 peso devaluation, despite recessions in the United States and Japan. Export earnings had expanded only 17 percent during the entire six-year period 1963–69 but in 1970 they increased 24 percent, for the first time exceeding $1 billion in value. The change was due partly to the rise in dollar export prices of close to 10 percent, the export volume index therefore showing a 14 percent increase. In 1971 the volume of exports climbed 14.6 percent despite a discernible decline in the export price index. Exports of traditional commodities expanded impressively,[4] but there was also a significant expansion (28 percent) in exports of nontraditional manufactured goods, which had been the object of such measures as the Export Incentives Act of 1970.

Controls on import transactions and contractionary fiscal and monetary policies kept the rise in the value of Philippine imports to only 6 percent from

3. R. M. Bautista, "Import Demand in a Small Country with Trade Restrictions," *Oxford Economic Papers*, vol. 30 (July 1978), pp. 199–216.
4. Baldwin, *Foreign Exchange Regimes*, p. 81.

1969 to 1971 (despite a 12 percent increase in foreign currency import prices). The result was a substantial reduction in the country's merchandise trade deficit from $276.9 million in 1969 to only $38.1 million in 1971. Furthermore, for the first time since 1967, invisible receipts exceeded payments in 1971, reducing the deficit in the current account to $22.3 million.

Domestic investment suffered from the currency depreciation in 1970 but began a recovery in 1971 with an expansion in real terms of about 4 percent over 1970. Also, the gross national product increased by 5.4 percent in 1970 and 6.5 percent in 1971, discernibly higher than the average annual growth of 4.9 percent between 1963 and 1969. Thus, as the government's development plan for 1972–75 noted, the country had regained "economic composure from a gruelling adjustment period of FY 1970 and 1971 that saw some powerful policy-shifts redirect the development path."[5] The "brighter prospects" it forecast diminished, however, as the Philippine economy reacted to the shocks generated by the instability of the world economy in the first half of the 1970s.

International Disturbances in the 1970s

To facilitate its international trade and payments, a small open economy can benefit from pegging its currency to that of the country with which it has most of its trade and financial transactions.[6] If it has strong links with two large countries, no additional problem is created as long as the two maintain a fixed exchange rate between their currencies. During most of the postwar period the United States and Japan accounted for more than two-thirds of Philippine trade flows,[7] and until 1971 the exchange rate between the dollar and yen remained relatively stable. Since the initiation of greater flexibility in exchange rates among the world's dominant currencies, Philippine policymakers have had to contend with changes in the effective exchange rate of the domestic currency due to realignments of the U.S. dollar and Japanese yen.[8]

5. Philippines, National Economic Council, *Four-Year Development Plan, FY 1972–75.*

6. See R. I. McKinnon, "Optimum Currency Areas," *American Economic Review*, vol. 53 (September 1963), pp. 717–25; R. A. Mundell, *International Economics* (Macmillan, 1968), chap. 8.

7. The bulk of the remaining third was contributed by West Germany, the United Kingdom, the Netherlands, and Italy, as well as some Middle Eastern suppliers of crude oil.

8. R. M. Bautista, "Effects of Major Currency Realignment on Philippine Merchandise Trade," *Review of Economics and Statistics*, vol. 49 (May 1977), pp. 152–60.

Philippine export trade is, like that of most developing countries, concentrated in commodities. About four-fifths of the country's foreign-exchange earnings from merchandise trade since World War II has been contributed by ten principal export commodities, four of which could easily account for two-thirds of total export value in any given year. Several export commodities have been dependent to a significant degree on U.S. and Japanese markets, and all of the country's principal import commodities (except crude oil) have been supplied mainly by Japan and the United States.

Any change in the exchange rates of the dollar and yen thus can cause a redirection of Philippine trade flows as well as influence the magnitude of total exports and imports if the effective exchange rate of the peso is changed. Between 1971 and 1976 the peso depreciated 27.7 percent against the combined currencies of its six principal trading partners (expressed in pesos and weighted by the 1973–74 merchandise trade flows). The resulting changes in the prices of exported and imported goods affected domestic prices of both tradable and nontradable goods directly and indirectly. Moreover, the changes in prices and the magnitude of trade altered the gains and losses of importing and exporting industries and hence the pattern of income flows in those sectors.

The influence of externally determined export and import prices is likely to be significant in a small, open economy like the Philippines. Thus the rise in world commodity prices in 1972–74, which was both comprehensive and sharp, and the subsequent decline in most of them induced similar movements in the foreign currency price of Philippine exports and imports. The drastic price changes in some commodity groups were related to supply, in others to demand. Cereals, which the Philippines imports heavily (about $100 million average annual value for 1971–76), suffered crop failures in major producing regions beginning in 1972. In major Philippine export commodities (like copper, logs, and coconut products), demand reflecting simultaneous expansion in industrial countries caused prices to rise; the subsequent steep decline in demand brought a concomitant fall in prices. Growth in the world supply of sugar, one of the principal export products of the Philippines, lagged behind the growth in demand that accompanied the rapid rise in world income. Depletion of stocks resulted in sharp price increases in 1974, which led in turn to surprisingly large reductions in consumption that combined with the significant increase in production after 1974 to bring about the precipitous fall in the price of sugar in international markets.

Increases in world prices not only increase export earnings directly but indirectly through their effect on the volume of exports and thus on the country's capacity to import. Increases in the foreign currency price of imports negatively affect the capacity to import. Changes in the foreign currency price of exports and imports are reflected in the domestic prices of home-consumed exportable products and both imported and import-competing products; the changes also affect the costs of industries that use imported materials or buy from suppliers dependent on imports. As with exchange-rate changes, the repercussions of such changes in domestic prices are felt throughout the economy.

The increase in the import price of crude oil in 1973–74 was so drastic that it affected the country's economic performance in special ways and evoked particular policy responses. Oil is a commodity of crucial importance not only to the industrial sector but to agricultural production; high prices of fertilizers and pesticides induced by the oil problem could jeopardize the success of the "green revolution." Because the Philippines is dependent on oil imports for over 90 percent of its energy requirements, the severity of the oil price rise presented an enormous adjustment problem.

The oil price hike and the other changes in international commodity prices seem to have been related to the slowdown in world economic activity that began in early 1974. Whatever the underlying cause, the slowdown in the two developed economies with which the Philippines had strong trade links had a profound effect on export earnings. International capital movements, both public and private, were also affected. In the face of a recession and the economic hardships it entails, political considerations may reduce the willingness of developed country governments to extend development assistance. Moreover, since variations in economic activity influence the availability of capital and the relative profitability of investment, private capital flows may be adversely affected. Until 1972 the substantial part of net capital flows into the Philippines was in development loans; indeed net direct investment (excluding reinvestment of foreign companies)[9] showed an annual net outflow during most of the 1960s. Three-quarters of the total direct equity investment in 1970 was held by U.S. investors.[10] The United

9. An ILO report attributes the low level of direct foreign investment in the Philippines until 1972 to the "uncertain political situation, the rules stipulating Filipino ownership up to at least 50 percent . . . and the uncertain status of American-owned assets after termination of the Laurel-Langley Parity Agreement in 1974." International Labour Office, *Sharing in Development: A Programme of Employment, Equity and Growth for the Philippines* (Geneva: ILO, 1974), p. 281. After the declaration of martial law in September 1972, the Philippines adopted a policy of attraction of foreign investment.

10. Central Bank of the Philippines, Board of Investments, *Study on Foreign Investments.*

States and Japan also made the principal contributions to Philippine development assistance. During 1956–76, U.S. loans totaled $353 million (of which $171 million was via the Public Law 480 program), Japanese amounted to $332 million,[11] other countries' to $68 million, and multinational institutions' (principally the World Bank and Asian Development Bank) to $1,266 million.

Changes in the Exchange Rate

When the Japanese yen and most European currencies were appreciated relative to the U.S. dollar under the Smithsonian agreement in December 1971, the Philippine peso was already on a floating-rate system. The Central Bank's participation in the foreign-exchange market, however, effectively pegged the peso to the dollar. The stability of the peso-dollar exchange rate until March 1972 reflects what must have been a policy decision to depreciate the domestic currency with respect to the Japanese, Australian, New Zealand, and most European currencies, while appreciating it with respect to those of a few trade partners (Hong Kong, India, and Spain).[12]

Changes in relative exchange rates rather than in export prices (expressed in foreign currency) were responsible for many of the shifts in Philippine export trade with Japan and the United States between 1971 and 1974.[13] The 1971 realignment of major currencies appeared to be responsible for a 28–34 percent change in the relative values of the two export markets, and to have caused redirection of 11–17 percent of Philippine export trade.[14] The changes had significant effects on trade with Japan and West Germany because of the depreciation of the peso, and on trade in commodities with high price elasticities (in export supply or import demand).[15] Induced changes in exports and imports, estimated at $57.2 million and $32.3 million (at 1963 prices), imply an improvement in the country's merchandise trade balance—which is not surprising since the peso had been effectively devalued with respect to the currencies of most of its trade partners. While realignment of major currencies was partly responsible for the favorable balance, policy reactions to the external disturbance were also critically important.

11. C. P. Magno, "Notes on Development Loan Assistance to the Philippines, CY 1956–76," *Journal of Philippine Development*, vol. 3 (Second Semester 1976), p. 314.
12. See Bautista, "Effects of Major Currency Realignment," table 3.
13. R. M. Bautista and G. R. Tecson, "Philippine Export Trade with Japan and the United States: Responsiveness to Exchange Rate Changes," *Developing Economies*, vol. 12 (December 1975), p. 414.
14. Ibid., p. 413.
15. Bautista, "Effects of Major Currency Realignment."

Export and Import Prices

Philippine export and import prices in general fluctuated significantly during 1971–76 (table 6-1). Initially the country's exports suffered two consecutive years of declining prices in foreign markets. The commodity boom brought sharp increases in the export price index in March 1973 that lasted until October 1974. In the next twelve months the index dropped to about half its initial value as prices of leading export products fell in response to the world recession, and in 1976 it went down further by 12 percent. The import price index was rising moderately in the early part of the decade before the oil crisis pushed it up by 64 percent in 1974. Import prices increased a further 4 percent in the following year before registering a slight decline in 1976. The movement of the net terms of trade was therefore erratic—rising during the commodity boom of 1973–74 and falling in the succeeding two years, but by 1976 showing a considerable 30 percent deterioration from the 1971 level. The repercussions were apparent in the country's balance of payments and national income.

Individual export commodities followed roughly the time profile of the price index, most of them reaching peak prices in 1974 and 1975. On the other hand, the prices of principal imports did not rise in tandem with the drastic increases in the import price index which was dominated by the oil component.

The exogenous influences reflected in the prices of traded goods were only partly responsible for the double-digit inflation rates experienced in 1970–74. During 1970–72, internal factors were the chief causes of inflation. The 1970 devaluation moved the peso-U.S. dollar exchange rate by 72 percent and there was no accompanying import liberalization. Management of the exchange rate was mainly responsible for the substantial rise in the consumer price index in 1970 and for some part of the 1971 inflation.[16] In 1972 the peso fell another 10 percent in value against the currencies of the country's six most important trade partners, which would in part explain the 10.2 percent increase in the consumer price index during the year. The 7.4

16. T. A. Mijares, "The 1965 Interindustry Relations Study of the Philippine Economy," National Economic Council Workshop Series, 71-2 (University of the Philippines, School of Economics, November 24, 1971); based on the direct and indirect import dependence ratios computed from 1965 input-output table compiled by the Bureau of the Census and Statistics. A 60 percent devaluation would increase the price deflator in the gross national product by 13 percent in two years. R. M. Bautista, "Devaluation and Employment in a Labor-Surplus Economy: The Philippines," *Economia Internazionale*, vol. 26 (August–November 1973), pp. 543–59; this study is based on a dynamic, aggregative model of the Philippine economy. The GNP price deflator actually increased 31.2 percent from 1969 to 1971.

percent increase in the import price index must have had an inflationary effect, but the reduction in export prices of about 10 percent must have moderated the impact. Shortfalls in food supplies also contributed to inflation. Severe typhoons and floods in 1971 and 1972 and the widespread infestation of rice plants by the tungro virus disease kept production low in spite of the wider use of high-yielding varieties of rice and expansion in hectarage. Rice imports were instrumental in keeping the price rise of cereals relatively low (6.3 percent) in 1972.[17]

The impact of changes in the effective peso exchange rate after 1972 was relatively insignificant compared to the impact of the drastic increases in international commodity prices. The start of the export price boom, combined with substantial increases in import prices, explains a large part of the 1973 inflation. Again rice production declined (by 3.8 percent), still suffering from weather misfortunes; this time there was a marked rise in the cereal component of the consumer price index, reflecting both higher import prices and the government's substantial underestimation of import requirements.

Although in 1974 there were phenomenal increases in the world prices of traded goods generally, the bulk of the severe inflation in the Philippines can easily be attributed to the astounding increase in the import price of crude oil. Imports of 53.3 million barrels of crude oil during the first three quarters of 1973 at a c.i.f. cost of $152.7 million were matched by imports of 45.9 million barrels at a c.i.f. cost of $463.7 million between January and September of 1974—more than a threefold jump. The consequent rise in the domestic prices of refined petroleum products accounts for close to two-thirds of the 35 percent increase in the consumer price index from October 1973 to November 1974.[18] To be sure, the country faced increased prices of other imports in 1974 (perhaps induced in part by the supplying countries' oil problems). The rise in cereal prices was significant but the 1974 crop harvest (10 percent higher than the 1973 harvest) allowed a 50 percent reduction in rice imports. Undoubtedly a more significant contribution to the 1974 inflation was the continued export bonanza, which produced an 87 percent increase in prices paid for Philippine export products.

The dramatic decline of the inflation rate to only 8.1 percent in 1975 and 6.2 percent in 1976 reflected the sharp downturn in the country's import and

17. Central Bank of the Philippines, *Statistical Bulletin, 1976*. They mainly account for a 24 percent increase in the import value of cereals and cereal preparations in 1972.

18. Bautista, "Inflation in the Philippines." Static input-output calculations suggest a 22 percent effect on household consumption due to the oil price rise. While the analysis includes the doubtful assumption of constant mark-up pricing in each sector, its conclusion that the magnitude of the 1974 inflation was greatly influenced by the oil crisis seems reasonable.

export prices attributable to the world recession that began in early 1974. Prices of Philippine export products went down on the average by 20 percent and 12 percent in 1975 and 1976, while import prices rose 4 percent in 1975 and decreased slightly in 1976 (table 6-1). Moreover, agricultural production continued to expand, causing a very modest increase of 6.6 percent in the food component of the consumer price index in 1975 and 6.1 percent in 1976. Thus domestic food production and worldwide recession combined to reduce Philippine inflation substantially.

Effects on the Current Account

One striking feature of the Philippine external sector is the relatively more rapid expansion of real exports in the 1970s than in any other six-year period since 1950 (table 6-2). There was, however, also a high degree of variability, the annual growth rate of export volume showing the highest standard deviation during 1969–75. In sharp contrast the annual rate of increase in real imports in the first half of the 1970s was relatively low and far less variable. The divergence in patterns of export and import volumes might be attributed in part to concerted policy efforts to promote exports in the face of unstable world demand and to economize on imports in response to the sharp increase in import prices.

The volume of trade in most of the Philippines' principal commodity exports was highly erratic during 1971–76. Some commodities showed substantial net increases reflecting the favorable terms at which they were being sold in the later years. For certain commodities, volumes of exports decreased at times of higher prices—the unit value of copra, for instance, registered a historic peak in 1974 but exports declined sharply because of a very high floor export price established by the government. Market interference was likewise the reason for the decline of log exports after 1973 despite an improvement in export price, and the government assumed control over marketing the entire sugar crop with the termination of preferential treatment in the U.S. market in December 1974.

Exports of nontraditional manufactured goods generally expanded rapidly after the 1970 devaluation, with troughs in 1972 and 1974 compensated by high growth rates in other years.[19] Energy-intensive commodity exports, especially cement and paper products, seem to have lost momentum with the onset of the oil crisis, perhaps having their international competitiveness

---

19. The impressive performers were clothing, electrical machinery and appliances, transport equipment (mainly automotive spare parts), travel goods, and chemical products.

significantly impaired. Some consumption goods that were adversely affected in 1975 by the global recession recovered quickly the next year.

The pattern of Philippine import volume reflects different responses among commodities to price changes and to the country's capacity to import. Petroleum imports were relatively stable, disturbed mainly by the 8 percent reduction in 1974 when the full force of the oil crisis was felt.[20] However, they increased only 4.3 percent between 1971 and 1976, a drastic departure from an average annual rise of 10 percent in the 1960s. Cereal imports, needed to augment domestic food supplies in the early 1970s, dipped surprisingly in 1973. The reduction was due to the worldwide grain shortage— Thailand even canceled some Philippine orders on account of its own food problem. There were sharp reductions in imports of intermediate materials in 1975, reflecting a slowdown in the manufacturing and mining sectors but more importantly the relative severity of import restrictions in a year of substantial trade deficit.

In combination with the dramatic developments in export and import prices during the period, volume changes caused erratic movements in the Philippine merchandise trade balance. A growing deficit in the country's trade transactions in 1971 and 1972 was followed by a substantial surplus in 1973 as the explosion of international prices of primary commodities began to affect Philippine exports (table 6-3). The export boom continued late into the next year but its favorable effect on the trade balance was completely negated by the sharp increase in the import bill for crude oil—from $166.1 million in 1973 to $573.2 million in 1974. Total import value nearly doubled in 1974 and the trade deficit approached $500 million. In 1975 the world recession weighed heavily on the export sector, reducing the country's export earnings by 16 percent; that and the continued rise in imports jacked up the trade deficit to a record level of nearly $1.2 billion. While exports showed signs of recovery in the following year, total merchandise trade remained in deficit by slightly over $1 billion.

The country's merchandise trade balance was significantly influenced by the movement of the terms of trade. In 1971 and 1972 the trade deficit increased by $76.9 million and $116.7 million, respectively, as the terms of trade changed. During the commodity boom of 1973–74 the balance rose to $377.7 million, but it plummeted to a $913.2 million deficit in 1975–76. Over the six years the Philippine merchandise trade balance would have

20. Regression analysis of postwar annual data indicates a price elasticity of petroleum consumption of −0.45 and an income elasticity of 1.56. L. Gonzalo, "Petroleum Consumption in the Philippines: A Macroeconomic Analysis" (M.A. thesis, University of the Philippines, 1976).

Table 6-3. *Current Account in the Philippine Balance of Payments, 1969–76*

Millions of dollars

Account	1969	1970	1971	1972	1973	1974	1975	1976
Exports	874.6	1,082.8	1,147.9	1,138.0	1,871.4	2,693.8	2,262.6	2,516.9
Imports	−1,131.5	−1,090.1	−1,186.0	−1,260.0	−1,596.6	−3,143.3	−3,459.2	−3,633.5
Trade balance	−256.9	−7.4	−38.1	−122.0	274.8	−449.5	−1,196.6	−1,116.6
Transportation and merchandise insurance	−93.9	−91.2	−77.0	−87.4	−154.1	−271.2	−263.2	−258.0
Travel	−10.6	67.5	37.6	97.9	61.4	41.1	82.7	64.5
Investment income	−77.9	−129.7	−101.1	−101.1	−125.1	−54.3	−125.6	−253.5
Services rendered to U.S. military	58.9	30.6	36.1	40.9	41.6	47.9	49.6	53.0
Pensions from U.S. government	62.3	63.8	69.0	71.5	74.2	78.4	86.6	88.3
Private transfers	43.4	29.2	34.2	80.7	94.2	122.8	165.3	148.3
Other	−8.4	−18.6	17.0	19.2	165.0	202.9	211.9	135.1
Total	−283.2	−55.9	−22.3	−24.3	443.7	−281.9	−989.4	−1,138.9

Source: Central Bank of the Philippines, *Annual Report*, various issues.

been higher by $121.5 million annually on the average had the country's terms of trade remained constant.[21]

Nonmerchandise transactions partly compensated for the substantial trade gap generally registered during the period. Net receipts from private transfers (mainly remittances by Filipino emigrants) and from travel increased markedly.[22] The latter is attributable chiefly to intensified efforts by the government, particularly after martial law was declared, to attract foreign tourists as well as Filipinos residing abroad and to restrict foreign travel by Philippine residents. On the other hand, net disbursements for transportation increased substantially after 1973 reflecting higher freight charges occasioned by the oil crisis.

In total, current-account transactions in the Philippine balance of payments were close to being in balance in 1971 and 1972, produced a significant surplus in 1973, and deteriorated into increasingly large deficits through 1976.

Capital Flows

The external disturbances in the 1970s left an indelible mark on the country's capital account. The need to offset the large deficits in current transactions is reflected in the magnitude and direction of capital movements (table 6-4). Long-term loans, both official and private, increased progressively over the period, indicating relatively successful government efforts to sustain favorable credit standing abroad. One consequence was the nearly fourfold expansion of the country's external public debt from $1.0 billion in 1971 to $3.9 billion in 1976; during 1973–76 alone, an increase of $2.7 billion was registered.[23] For 1975 the ratio of short-term external debt to total export earnings was 0.377, which is more than double the corresponding ratio in 1973 (0.168). Private short-term capital, consisting mostly of im-

---

21. The effect on the trade balance B is expressed as $\Delta B = X(\Delta P_x/P_x) - M(\Delta P_m/P_m)$, where X and P_x are the export value and price index, and M and P_m the import value and price index each expressed in U.S. dollar terms.

22. The sharp reduction in travel receipts during 1973–74 was caused by a decline in rest and recreation expenditures of U.S. military personnel as the Vietnam War drew to a close.

23. It included substantial loans from the Oil Trade Financing Scheme as well as regular borrowing from the International Monetary Fund, the World Bank, and foreign commercial banks. The combined "gross publicized Euro-currency credits" to the Philippines during 1974 and 1975 amounted to $1.1 billion, which was exceeded only by credits to Brazil, Mexico, and Spain among developing country recipients. N. P. Sargen, "Commercial Bank Lending to Developing Countries," *Federal Reserve Bank of San Francisco Economic Review,* Spring 1976.

Table 6-4. Capital Account in the Philippine Balance of Payments, 1969–76
Millions of dollars

Account	1969	1970	1971	1972	1973	1974	1975	1976
Official grants and long-term capital	151.0	131.3	45.0	153.6	212.2	248.0	548.3	1,216.0
Reparations from Japan	35.3	13.1	26.4	-0.6	45.0	44.9	32.0	13.5
Other grants	13.6	13.4	4.9	15.2	32.3	30.3	34.2	18.9
Private loans	82.4	89.5	-34.4	-17.0	-5.1	32.2	126.0	336.5
Official loans	14.1	41.4	69.8	160.6	77.2	112.4	232.7	703.4
Other private capital	7.4	-24.3	3.9	-21.9	64.5	28.0	125.2	143.7
Other official capital	-1.8	-1.7	0.0	-3.8	-1.7	0.0	-1.7	0.0
Private short-term capital[a]	57.9	75.9	91.7	55.8	74.6	231.3	102.0	-95.9
Errors and omissions	-62.3	-147.2	-142.5	-107.0	-66.1	-87.4	-181.7	-145.0

Source: Central Bank, *Annual Report*, various issues.
a. One-year maturity.

port suppliers' credits and advances for exports, expanded in 1974 to more than three times the preceding year's value.[24]

Direct foreign investment ("other private capital" in table 6-4) was negligible in 1971 and negative in 1972, possibly because of the social unrest evident during those years and uncertainty about the status of American-owned assets after the scheduled expiration of the Laurel-Langley agreement in July 1974. With the imposition of martial law and the government's avowed policy of attracting foreign investment, a substantial flow of capital into the country began in 1973. After a noticeable decline in 1974, direct foreign investment grew rapidly in 1975 and 1976, perhaps because of the promotional efforts of the government that swamped any negative influence of the continuing world recession.

Overall, capital movements enabled the country to withstand the pressure on the balance of payments at least until 1974 and even raised the level of international reserves held by the Central Bank from about $0.4 billion in 1971 to $1.3 billion in 1976. The repercussion on the country's external debt (public and private) was quite severe, however; it moved from $2.2 billion in January 1971 to $5.6 billion by December 1976.

The Payments Balance

Reflecting the instability of the overall balance of payments, changes in international reserves and other monetary movements had varying effects on the country's money supply between 1971 and 1976 (table 6-5). In the surplus years 1971–74, large increases in the money supply from external sources prompted the monetary authorities to restrict domestic sources of credit in order to maintain a semblance of stability in the growth of money in circulation. The net changes in money supply were therefore due as much to the instability of the external sector as to the policy reaction to it.

The average rate of money expansion in the 1960s was 10.5 percent yearly, the standard deviation 6.5 percent. Between 1971 and 1976 the average annual growth of money supply was 20.4 percent—double the earlier average—but the degree of variability from year to year was the same 6.5 percent. In the external sector, however, variability during 1971–76 was far greater than in any other subperiod since 1950. The largest money supply increases of external origin occurred in 1973 and 1974; there was a contraction in public sector activities during both years, but an 85 percent increase

24. The net outflow of $96 million in 1976 was due to the "deposit with the U.S. Exim Bank of the proceeds from bond issues in New York for the country's nuclear power project." Central Bank of the Philippines, *Annual Report, 1976*, p. 44.

Table 6-5. *Change in Philippine Money Supply, by Origin, 1971–76*[a]

Millions of pesos

Origin	1971	1972	1973	1974	1975	1976
Internal	−85.9	662.8	−3,287.1	−321.7	5,236.2	3,135.9
Public sector	25.9	−419.1	−2,153.8	−2,768.5	4,865.7	3,652.0
Private sector	−111.8	1,081.9	−1,133.3	2,446.8	370.5	−516.1
External	605.9	566.4	4,643.0	2,389.3	−3,939.2	−1,375.8
International reserves	200.0	719.1	4,173.8	3,696.5	−380.4	394.6
Compensatory borrowing abroad	} 405.9	} −152.7	467.6	−937.5	−1,289.2	} 981.2
IMF credits used			−49.6	242.9	−872.5	
Foreign currency deposits			152.3	−118.1	−889.2	
Central Bank certificates of indebtedness			−101.1	−494.5	−497.9	
Net change in money supply[b]	520.0	1,229.2	1,355.9	2,067.6	1,307.0	1,760.1
	(10.1)	(23.7)	(20.9)	(25.4)	(14.5)	(17.1)

Source: Central Bank, *Annual Report*, various issues.
a. As of December 31; change from previous year.
b. Numbers in parentheses indicate percent change in money supply.

Table 6-6. *Percent Change in Philippine Gross National Product, by Sector, 1972–76*[a]

Sector	1972	1973	1974	1975	1976
Gross national product	4.9	9.6	6.0	5.8	6.3
Agriculture, fishery, and forestry	3.8	5.2	1.6	3.7	5.7
Industry	7.5	12.5	3.4	9.7	8.4
Mining and quarrying	2.5	4.1	1.8	1.4	2.4
Manufacturing	6.3	14.8	3.3	3.5	5.6
Construction	17.1	7.8	6.2	52.4	22.0
Utilities	3.1	5.7	2.9	6.4	7.4
Services	3.6	6.6	4.7	6.0	5.2
Transport	5.4	8.0	6.9	11.2	7.0
Commerce	2.9	5.5	3.5	5.5	5.3
Other	4.2	8.1	6.0	5.1	4.4

Sources: Philippines, National Economic Development Authority, Statistical Coordination Office, National Accounts Staff, "The National Income Accounts of the Philippines, CY 1971 to 1975" (September 1976), "CY- 1974–1976" (December 1976).
a. At 1972 prices.

in private domestic credits in 1974 contributed to a record-setting 25.4 percent expansion of monetary stock. In 1975 and 1976 the external sector was deflationary on account of the balance-of-payments deficit. Clearly the conduct of monetary policy was made difficult by the unpredictability of the external sector's effect on the country's overall balance of payments.

Domestic Activities

Gross national product during 1971–76 increased at an average annual rate of 6.5 percent, moving from the lowest to the highest rate in the first two years and then fluctuating around 6 percent for the rest of the period (see table 6-6). While potential GNP is a highly elusive concept for developing countries, an annual growth of 8–10 percent probably would have been plausible for the Philippine economy during the period if the external sector had been more stable. For one thing, the worsening terms of trade caused a substantial loss in real income. If the country's terms of trade had remained constant, the Philippine economy could have grown faster (in dollar terms) by about 1.3 percent annually on the average during 1971–76.

The natural disasters of the early 1970s had substantial effects on the agricultural sector from 1971 to 1976. The fall in output of food crops in 1972 and 1973, caused by poor weather and plant disease, was reversed by a combination of improved weather conditions and the government's massive food production campaign started in 1973 by the Masagana 99 program. But the external sector may also have had an influence on agriculture and the economy—in some places, farmers may have shifted from rice farming to more profitable production of sugar for the export market before the Masagana 99 subsidies on rice were introduced; the oil price rise in 1973–74 brought substantial increases in the price of fertilizers and agricultural chemicals and a significant rise in the cost of subsidizing food production.

The output of exportable primary commodities generally followed the pattern of export flows during the period. Hence instability in the world economy significantly affected production of export commodities, which account for about one-fourth of value added in the agriculture, fishery, and forestry sector. The same is true of the heavily export-oriented mining industry, which was hit hard during the recession years 1974 and 1975. Both mining and manufacturing output had grown rapidly after the 1970 devaluation. In 1974 and 1975 the growth of total production in manufacturing industries dropped steeply to 3.3 percent and 3.5 percent from a 14.8 percent increase in 1972. Within the sector there were large differences in performance, however. Output of industries making equipment for domestic use expanded at high rates through 1975, while export-oriented industries and those heavily dependent on oil lost ground. By early 1976, recovery was under way in both mining and manufacturing, underscoring the strong dependence of these sectors on the level of world economic activity.[25]

Among the industry groups in the national income accounts, construction exhibited the greatest variability in output during the period. Internal factors chiefly explain the pattern of activity. The extensive damage done by the severe typhoons and floods to infrastructure facilities, particularly in the food-producing regions, caused the government to step up its construction expenditures by 64.6 percent in 1972. The 17.1 percent growth in real value added to this sector represents a drastic departure from the average annual growth rate of only about 3 percent in the 1960s. Substantial increases in construction output occurred again in 1975 and 1976 (52 percent and 22 percent), led by hotel-building and other tourism-related projects which the private sector participated in but which were heavily underwritten by government financial institutions.[26]

25. The growth rate of value added in real terms from the first quarter of 1975 to the corresponding period in 1976 was 4.6 percent in mining and 4.3 percent in manufacturing.

26. Fourteen international standard hotels were constructed in 1975–76 at an estimated cost of $3,750 million for the immediate purpose of accommodating the delegates to the IMF-World Bank conference held in Manila in October 1976. A. Stretton, "The Building Industry and Employment Creation in Manila, the Philippines" (Ph.D. dissertation, Australian National University, 1977). As of September 1977 the fourteen hotel companies reportedly owed the Development Bank of the Philippines and the Government Service Insurance System 1.8 billion pesos, which debts were to be rescheduled. Philippine Daily Express, September 6, 1977.

Normally the level and allocation of domestic investment depend on the level of national income; in foreign-exchange-constrained economies that rely heavily on imports for physical capital accumulation, investment also depends on the capacity to import. Philippine data indicate that two-thirds of any increment in imports takes the form of investment goods. The average level of investment during 1952–75 indicates that the investment in 1974 and 1975 would have been far higher if it were not for the recession. In those years the rates of growth of both real GNP and imports were low, but capital formation expanded by 24 percent in 1974 and 20 percent in 1975. The reasons for the divergence in the level of investments probably would be apparent in a breakdown by industrial sector. The nearest approximation of such a breakdown is Central Bank data on investments of newly registered firms: in 1974, investments in agriculture increased by 39 percent over 1973, in forestry, fishing, and livestock by 121 percent, in manufacturing by 57 percent, and in construction by 43 percent; in 1975 there were sharp reductions in forestry and manufacturing, but a 100 percent increase in construction[27]—the latter in accord with the rapid expansion in construction activity during 1975–76. In the other sectors, only in the second year of the world recession were profit expectations sufficiently affected to deter large investments by prospective investors.

The impact of external disturbances on the use of labor is an especially important matter for labor-surplus economies like the Philippines. And because of the inequity in income distribution,[28] movements in the earnings of Filipino laborers are of significant interest. Though employment data from official household surveys are not available for the entire 1971–76 period, it is possible to postulate some effects of the recent instability on employment. Sectoral changes in production would suggest that employment in the primary export industries (including mining), as well as in manufacturing, was adversely affected by the 1974–75 recession. A Central Bank employment index for the mining sector showed a sharp increase in employment accompanying the export boom in 1973; the number of persons employed declined in 1974 and 1975 and even in the 1976 recovery the level of employment did not quite attain the 1973 mark.

In the manufacturing sector, employment increased in 1971 by 4.5 percent, then in the next two years by a remarkable 27.4 percent, reflecting the

27. Presumably the much expanded credit extended by government financial institutions to the construction sector accounts for the increase. For instance, while the total amount of loans granted by development banks (which are dominated by the government-owned Development Bank of the Philippines) trebled in 1974–75, loans to "real estate" increased more than sixfold.

28. E. Tan, "Income Distribution in the Philippines," in Encarnación and others, *Philippine Economic Problems*, pp. 214–61.

Table 6-7. *Indexes of Nonagricultural Wages and Salaries in the Philippines, 1971–76*

Index, 1972 = 100

Item	1971	1972	1973	1974	1975	1976
Manila and suburbs						
Money wage rates						
Skilled laborers	95.3	100.0	105.3	115.1	119.7	124.4
Unskilled laborers	94.3	100.0	102.7	110.8	120.1	126.2
Real wage rates[a]						
Skilled laborers	105.2	100.0	95.4	77.4	74.4	73.2
Unskilled laborers	104.0	100.0	92.8	74.5	74.6	74.3
Philippines						
Nominal earnings						
Salaried employees	93.4	100.0	111.1	121.6	136.9	154.7
Wage earners	90.6	100.0	112.2	110.9	124.4	145.1
Real earnings[a]						
Salaried employees	101.1	100.0	99.0	77.6	81.2	86.6
Wage earners	98.1	100.0	100.0	70.7	73.8	80.0

Source: Central Bank, *Statistical Bulletin, 1976.*
a. Nominal value deflated by the relevant consumer price index.

rapid growth of manufacturing value added in 1972 and 1973. A weakening of employment the following year follows the pattern of manufacturing output; there was even a decrease in employment level in 1974 by 1.1 percent.[29]

While employment data for 1974–76 are scarce, much information is available on worker earnings. Neither wage rates in industrial establishments in the Greater Manila area nor average earnings in nonagricultural industries in the Philippines (table 6-7) rose fast enough in 1971–76 to match the sharp increases in the cost of living (especially in 1973–74). Thus there was a general deterioration of real incomes during the period. Real earnings in nonagricultural industries in the Philippines did improve after 1974 as the inflation rate fell significantly. Skilled industrial workers in Manila suffered a loss in real purchasing power of 30 percent and unskilled workers a slightly smaller loss. Nonagricultural wage earners working outside Greater Manila were not as severely penalized, and salaried workers experienced the least (yet still significant) reduction in real income. The deterioration in earnings was not entirely due to a reduction in demand for labor caused by external

29. Employment data, 1971–74, are available in the Annual Survey of Establishments by the National Census and Statistics Office. A manufacturing census conducted in 1972 covered only establishments employing ten or more workers, precluding comparison with the Survey data.

disturbances. The various policies adopted by the government with respect to prices and wages failed to protect the real income of laborers.

The deteriorating effect of inflation on their real income might have impelled some workers to seek better job opportunities abroad. Indeed the overseas migration of Filipino workers expanded markedly in the 1970s; it is reflected in the substantial increases in net receipts from private transfers in the current account of the balance of payments (table 6-3). Instability in the world economy may have set in motion economic forces that encouraged domestic capital and technology to move out of the country (a disequilibrium invariably improves the economic opportunities in some places relative to others). Philippine accounting and development banking companies established and expanded subsidiary firms in other Southeast Asian countries in the early 1970s. And construction and engineering firms in recent years won contracts to set up infrastructure facilities in some Middle Eastern and African countries.

The Philippines' growing trade imbalance after 1973 accentuated the need to increase foreign-exchange earnings. In response, the government exerted much effort to promote tourism. The increasing flow of foreign visitors into the country may have affected the economic behavior of the local population and have had economic repercussions beyond that of raising foreign exchange. Tourism does present a dilemma, for while expenditures of foreigners provide direct benefits to the economy, the facilities and amenities that attract tourists also encourage luxury spending by the local population. Moreover, tourism-related activities may not even yield as high rates of return as other industries, as the investment in hotel-building in the Philippines seems to indicate.

The United States and Japan as Sources of Disturbance

Because of colonial ties dating back to the turn of the century, the Philippines has been highly dependent on the United States as a market for exports and a supplier of imports. Since the granting of political independence in 1946, however, the U.S. share in Philippine foreign trade has been gradually reduced. Trade with Japan, on the other hand, has increased so much that by 1970 it amounted to about the same proportion of total Philippine trade (30 percent of imports and 40 percent of exports) as trade with the United States. With the drastic increase in the crude oil share of the total bill, U.S. and Japanese imports dropped to about 50 percent; similarly their export shares fell to a total of about 60 percent after 1974.

Table 6-8. *Percent Change in Selected Japanese and U.S. Economic Indicators and Exchange Rate with the Peso, 1971–76*

Item	1971	1972	1973	1974	1975	1976
GNP[a]						
Japan	6.8	9.0	9.9	−1.2	2.1	6.3
United States	3.0	5.7	5.5	−1.7	−1.8	6.0
Industrial production						
Japan	2.8	7.2	15.6	−3.1	−10.6	11.0
United States	1.7	9.2	8.4	−0.4	−8.9	11.6
Export price index[b]						
Japan	0.7	−2.9	9.0	33.7	−2.9	1.0
United States	3.2	3.0	16.8	27.0	11.8	3.4
Exchange rate with peso						
Japan	22.2	8.0	9.1	−6.3	5.3	6.9
United States	8.6	3.7	1.3	0.5	6.8	2.7

Sources: U.S. Department of Commerce, *International Economic Indicators and Competitive Trends*, various issues; International Monetary Fund, *International Financial Statistics*, vol. 31 (May 1978).
a. At 1972 prices.
b. In national currency.

Such strong links make the Philippine economy inherently subject to shocks emanating from Japan and the United States. Indeed, they so dominate Philippine foreign trade and payments that a large part of the externally caused disturbances of the 1970s (with the exception of the oil crisis) can be traced to the economic instability in these two large countries. The severity of the shocks is due in part to the unusual synchronization of changes in their economies during 1971–76.

The sharp downturn in GNP and industrial production in 1974 in both countries was accompanied by a substantial increase in their export price indexes (table 6-8). Presumably, the simultaneous recession and inflation in the two countries affected adversely the foreign trade of the Philippines, and of other small economies strongly attached to the United States and Japan, in many ways. The impact on the Philippines' capacity to import, and hence on its trade balance, is apparent in the movements of the import price and export value indexes (table 6-9). Japan contributed more than the United States to the changes in the import price index from 1972 to 1974; in the latter year, when world oil prices quadrupled, the combined contribution of the two countries to Philippine imports was understandably small (38 percent). Annual fluctuations of Philippine export earnings during the period were quite severe, and the contributions of the United States and Japan to those changes very large. Indeed, for 1972 and 1975 the sum of their contributions is greater than unity; changes in Philippine export flows

Table 6-9. *Japanese and U.S. Contributions to Changes in Philippine Trade Indexes, 1972-76*
Percent

Year	Change in import price index		Change in export value index[a]	
	Japanese share[b]	U.S. share[b]	Japanese share	U.S. share
1972	0.469	0.070	0.818	0.411
1973	0.395	0.128	0.402	0.290
1974	0.110	0.068	0.322	0.636
1975	0.015	0.494	0.198	1.072
1976	n.a.	n.a.	−0.815	1.281

Source: Central Bank, *Statistical Bulletin, 1976.*
a. Ratio of percent change in trading partner's share to percent change in Philippine index, multiplied by trading partner's share of Philippine trade in 1974.
b. Based on trading partner's export unit value for manufactured goods.
n.a. Not available.

to the other countries balanced the changes.[30] Overall, significant export instability is attributable to the United States during 1974–76; on the other hand, Japan contributed heavily in 1972 and 1976, in the latter year serving to counterbalance somewhat the U.S. effect.

Philippine trade with the United States (table 6-10) was consistently on the surplus side during the period, except in 1975 when sugar exports fell drastically. There was a continuous deterioration of the trade balance with Japan because of Japan's progressive cuts in its imports after the export boom of 1973–74. The deficit of $355 million in trade with Japan in 1976 represented about one-third of the total merchandise trade deficit for that year. The principal export commodities heavily dependent on the Japanese market were adversely affected by the recession in Japan in varying degrees. In the case of copper concentrates, for instance, Japanese importers were widely accused of violating contract obligations as a way of reducing inventories at the height of the recession; by 1976 a fairly strong recovery of copper exports seemed under way.

There is no evidence that the pattern of loan assistance by the two countries, though it seems erratic (table 6-11), was significantly affected by economic instability in the 1970s, except possibly during 1976 when Japan's loans dropped sharply.[31] The substantial improvement in direct investments

30. The value of Philippine exports to each of these two countries declined slightly in 1972 and relatively sharply in 1975. In 1976, however, exports to the United States increased even as exports to Japan declined further.
31. Data for 1971–74 indicate that 5 percent of Japanese development assistance was in the form of grants, and 46 percent of U.S. aid was in grants. From multilateral sources, principally UN agencies, the average annual grant flow was slightly above $12 million. World Bank, *The Philippines: Priorities and Prospects for Development* (Washington: World Bank, 1976), p. 468.

Table 6-10. *Philippine Trade with the United States and Japan, 1971–76*

Country and year	Imports		Exports		Trade balance (millions of dollars)
	Millions of dollars	Percent of total	Millions of dollars	Percent of total	
United States					
1971	291.2	24.6	459.5	40.4	168.3
1972	312.6	25.4	446.6	40.4	134.0
1973	449.5	28.2	676.0	35.8	226.5
1974	733.0	23.3	1,156.7	42.5	423.7
1975	754.3	21.8	664.3	28.9	−90.0
1976	801.8	22.2	924.4	35.9	122.6
Japan					
1971	359.1	30.3	398.6	35.1	39.5
1972	390.8	31.8	373.4	33.8	−17.4
1973	518.5	32.5	674.5	35.8	156.0
1974	864.6	27.5	949.2	34.8	84.6
1975	966.3	27.9	865.0	37.7	−101.3
1976	976.4	26.9	621.5	24.1	−354.9

Sources: Central Bank, *Annual Report, 1976*, and *Statistical Bulletin, 1975*.

Table 6-11. *Japanese and U.S. Loans and Investment in the Philippines, 1971–76*

Millions of dollars

Item	1971	1972	1973	1974	1975	1976
Development loans						
Japan	48.56	57.07	61.74	56.20	60.35	33.01
United States[a]	28.88	69.12	26.20	36.50	50.06	70.68
Net direct investment						
Japan	0.56	−1.31	0.25	8.30	13.59	17.74
United States	−1.21	−13.16	51.23	36.41	112.64	47.77

Sources: Data provided by MEDIAD and Department of Economic Research, Central Bank of the Philippines.
a. Includes P.L. 480 loans.

from both countries after 1972 may be attributed to the new investment climate engendered by the imposition of martial law which also served to counteract any recessionary effects.

Monetary and Fiscal Policy

The conduct of Philippine economic policy from 1971 to 1976 was vitally affected by the policy adjustments made in the early part of 1970. Monetary and fiscal restraint was adopted to reduce domestic liquidity and counter the anticipated inflationary pressure. Reserve requirements against deposit liabilities of all banks were raised (by 2 percent in January 1970 and another 2 percent in April), rediscount ceilings of commercial banks were lowered, and certain liberal rediscount practices were restrained. Growth of money supply was held to a modest 6.2 percent. Domestic credit increased by 10.9 percent, with a major shift to the private sector as the source of support of export-oriented production. A sharp reduction in public works and other government expenditures turned the government's operating expenditures from a deficit of 934 million pesos in 1969 to a surplus of 107 million pesos in 1970.[32]

Restrictive monetary policy continued until the fall of 1972. The heavy flood damage to the major food-producing regions in July and August prompted adoption of a calamity financing program that could lend up to 200 million pesos to financial institutions in the stricken areas. "The large withdrawals of bank deposits experienced during the first weeks of martial law" caused the Central Bank in September to extend 375 million pesos to banks on an emergency basis in order to allay uncertainty among the general public.[33] As a result of the two actions there was a 24 percent rise in money supply and a 17 percent increase in domestic credit in 1972, roughly double the preceding year's increases. Fiscal policy apparently still aimed at reducing inflationary pressures even though government expenditures had to be made for reconstruction and rehabilitation; because of "the substantial growth in government balances" the public sector was a "disinflationary factor" in 1972.[34]

Shortfalls in rice production and failure to procure adequate rice imports contributed heavily to inflation in the early 1970s.[35] In May 1973 the government embarked on a massive credit expansion and fertilizer subsidy program, Masagana 99, to accelerate the recovery from damages to food crops and also in support of the long-held objective of food self-sufficiency. The program, designed for small farmers, extended 365 million pesos in credit in its first six months of operation. Otherwise, contractionary monetary and fiscal policy prevailed in 1973 as a reaction to the unparalleled expansion of the external sector (which resulted in a $664 million surplus in the balance of payments). The Central Bank reduced its own credit operations, raised its reserve requirements, and sold 2 billion pesos worth of certificates of

32. Central Bank, *Annual Report, 1970.*
33. Ibid., *1972*, p. 4.
34. Ibid., p. 6.
35. Bautista, "Inflation in the Philippines."

Table 6-12. *Philippine Export Tax Collections, 1970–76*

Millions of pesos

Year	Export tax collected		
	Stabilization	Premium	Total
1970	396.8	0	396.8
1971	548.7	0	548.7
1972	403.2	0	403.2
1973	286.9	0	286.9
1974	867.7	891.4	1,759.1
1975	581.8	872.9	1,454.7
1976	442.0	130.0	572.3

Source: Data provided by Revenue Collection Office, Central Bank of the Philippines.

indebtedness. The national government had an operating surplus of 2.1 billion pesos owing to an unprecedented 85 percent increase in tax and tariff collections (attributable to administrative reforms) against increases in operating expenses of only 30 percent. Mainly as a result of the large surplus in the external account, money supply expanded by 21 percent, total domestic credit increasing by 16 percent.[36]

In 1974, to moderate the expansion of domestic liquidity, the Central Bank sold close to 1.5 million pesos worth of certificates of indebtedness and raised interest rates on time deposits. However, rural credit programs continued to be encouraged (both Masagana 99 for rice production and a program for corn); higher maximum loans per hectare were set and banking institutions were required to set aside a minimum of 25 percent of their loanable funds for agricultural credit purposes. Thus domestic credit grew by 31 percent in 1974, its highest growth in twenty-five years. Money supply registered an increase of 28 percent despite a substantial surplus of 2.8 billion pesos in the government's cash operations; this was partly due to the balance-of-payments surplus of $100 million, in which substantial flows from nonmerchandise and capital accounts compensated for the trade deficit of $418 million.

The government was enabled by measures instituted in 1970 to capture a portion of the windfall profits from the export bonanza of 1973–74 (table 6-12). Temporary stabilization taxes (4–10 percent ad valorem), imposed on traditional exports in 1970 to siphon off the gains from the February devaluation, were made a permanent part of the customs and tariff code in 1973. In February 1974 President Marcos announced an additional tax on the premium derived from price increases that began in 1973. This premium

36. Central Bank, *Annual Report, 1973*.

export duty, applied to the difference between the ruling export price and the base price as of February 1974, became ineffective when the commodity price boom ended and even the regular export tax was temporarily withdrawn on the commodities hardest hit by the world recession.

With inflation showing signs of substantial deceleration in 1975 and 1976, expansionary monetary and fiscal policy served to compensate for the deflationary impact of the balance-of-payments deficit. Liquidity-increasing measures were adopted by the Central Bank, whose credits by December 1976 were nearly three times the 1974 level. Support for food production programs continued but sharp increases in Central Bank loans and advances were due "mainly to increased borrowings on the part of the Government Service Insurance System (GSIS) for hotel assistance and other government financial institutions for hotel financing under repurchase agreement."[37] Total domestic credit increased by 38 percent in 1975 and 24 percent in 1976. In the latter year the national government incurred a deficit of 1,850 million pesos in its cash operations—two-and-a-half times the deficit in 1975—relying chiefly on the issuance of treasury bills and other government securities to expand the money supply. Overall, money in circulation increased by 14 percent in 1975 and 17 percent in 1976.

The Philippines' monetary and fiscal policy between 1971 and 1976 developed mainly in reaction to the country's balance-of-payments problems and certain internal problems. The pattern of public expenditure and credit availment effectively benefited two sectors—food production after 1973 and tourist-related construction activities in 1975–76. Given the declared objective of food self-sufficiency, it was necessary that public works be oriented to the development of agricultural infrastructure and that credit facilities be slanted to the financing of food production. Indeed, the consequent improvement in food output contributed to the slowing down of inflation after 1974. The economic rationale for financing hotel-building and other tourist-related projects through loans by government financial institutions is difficult to discern. There is a large overcapacity in hotel buildings that is unlikely to be utilized before 1980; such tourist facilities, if Singapore's experience in the early 1970s is repeated, may then begin to pay their way.

Encouragement of construction activities in 1975 and 1976 might be viewed as a countercyclical policy to offset the decline in foreign demand that helped the Philippine economy to weather this period of world recession. However, such production activities as low-cost housing would have entailed less disbursement of foreign exchange and more employment creation.

Tax policy managed to deprive major export producers of part of their

37. Central Bank, *Annual Report, 1976*, p. 13.

windfall profits from both the 1970 peso devaluation and the export boom of 1973–74. The important feature of both the stabilization export tax and the export premium tax was their selectivity—larger windfall profits were taxed relatively more. There is merit in such a system (assuming that government spending contributes to social welfare more than does the spending of export producers), but it has not been followed in other policy areas—exchange-rate policy, for instance, aimed essentially at keeping the movements of the peso-dollar exchange rate stable; no policy actions were taken to offset undesirable gains and losses in some sectors that were a consequence of realignments of trade partners' currencies after 1971.[38]

Foreign-Exchange Policy

The Philippine peso was already in a floating-rate system when greater flexibility was introduced among the world's key currencies. After the de facto devaluation on February 21, 1970, the foreign-exchange rate—in practice, the peso-dollar exchange rate—depended on the trading between commercial banks. They took "the initiative in influencing or responding to demand supply conditions in foreign exchange."[39] Exchange rates with other currencies were determined by the previous day's rates in New York of those currencies vis-à-vis the U.S. dollar.

While it was officially claimed that a free exchange market had been created and that the Central Bank would refrain from intervening in the foreign-exchange market, the Central Bank (or an agent bank acting on its behalf) "stood ready to provide exchange at the current rate to maintain the stability of the exchange rate."[40] In 1972, for example, the amount transacted by commercial banks was $240.3 million; the Central Bank sold foreign exchange amounting to $129.0 million and bought $59.2 million. During 1972 the exchange rate was allowed to float only 4.5 percent away from the interbank guiding rate (the weighted average of exchange rates for all sales made on the preceding day).

The Central Bank's effective control of the peso-dollar exchange rate is also evident in the remarkable stability of the guiding rate between August and December 1971 (table 6-13) at the height of the dollar's weakening position in international exchange markets. A freely floating peso would have shown some improvement in its exchange rate with the dollar (in the Hong

38. Bautista, "Effects of Major Currency Realignment."
39. Central Bank, *Annual Report, 1971*, p. 67.
40. Ibid., p. 70.

Table 6-13. *Interbank Guiding Rate for Peso-Dollar Exchange, 1971–76*
Pesos per dollar

Month	1971	1972	1973	1974	1975	1976
January	6.4350	6.4350	6.7814	6.7310	7.0664	7.4856
February	6.4350	6.4350	6.7762	6.7189	7.0522	7.4693
March	6.4350	6.5460	6.7719	6.7234	7.0261	7.4583
April	6.4350	6.4350	6.7662	6.7216	7.0177	7.4354
May	6.4350	6.7220	6.7632	6.7174	7.0178	7.4304
June	6.4350	6.7718	6.7592	6.7184	7.0150	7.4309
July	6.4350	6.7778	6.7583	6.7346	7.2719	7.4298
August	6.4245	6.7795	6.7467	6.7428	7.5018	7.4297
September	6.4105	6.7795	6.7392	6.7473	7.5091	7.4290
October	6.4324	6.7812	6.7396	6.7724	7.5001	7.4283
November	6.4331	6.7806	6.7382	7.0670	7.4975	7.4282
December	6.4350	6.7804	6.7353	7.0623	7.4992	7.4282
Annual average[a]	6.4317	6.6687	6.7563	6.7881	7.2479	7.4403
		(3.68)	(1.28)	(0.47)	(6.78)	(2.65)

Source: Data provided by Department of Economic Research, Central Bank of the Philippines.
a. Numbers in parentheses indicate percent change over previous year.

Kong exchange market, the peso reached new lows in December 1971 in exchange rates with the dollar). In late 1973, however, when the dollar was again being depreciated relative to other important currencies, there was a discernible improvement in the peso exchange rate. This might have been due to the substantial improvement in the country's balance of payments in a year in which the Central Bank transacted a net purchase of foreign exchange amounting to more than $300 million.

The Central Bank circular that introduced the floating rate also restricted importation of certain commodities and remittance of invisibles, and placed capital movements under Central Bank control. In September 1972 a presidential decree restricted foreign travel by residents and shortly thereafter measures were adopted against blackmarketing of foreign currency by export-oriented and pioneer industries, remittance of royalties or rentals on trademarks, patents, and copyrights, and repatriation of foreign investments.

The movement toward liberalization was of course reversed in the subsequent years of worsening payments balances. "Prior referral to the Central Bank" was required for an increasing number of commodity imports. Nevertheless, it is surprising that the Philippine peso did not depreciate substantially. Only on two occasions (October–November 1974 and June–August 1975) did the exchange rate exhibit any sign of volatility. This indicates that the Central Bank's efforts to achieve a stable movement of the exchange rate were relatively successful. More fundamentally, however, the high level of international reserves being maintained (above $1 billion after March 1974) and the adequacy of the Central Bank's standby credit lines provided the safeguards against speculative activities in the foreign-exchange market.

Direct Controls

The government intervened to control prices and wages during 1971–76 in a variety of ways. Also in response to the external shocks, it assumed an increasing role in the supervision of and the participation in production and marketing activities, which the broad powers of martial law facilitated.

A price control law enacted in 1970 following the sharp price rises induced by the devaluation was extended by Congress in 1971 and by presidential decrees in 1973 and 1975. Price ceilings were set for a number of basic commodities. Price control was normally enforced through legal penalties but on occasion was also sustained by government subsidies or rationing. The practice of "socialized pricing" provided low ceiling prices for certain types of goods consumed by poor families at the same time that more expensive grades were left uncontrolled; it also froze rents on low-rent dwellings.

The government in 1974 declared that "all efforts shall be exerted to keep prices from increasing beyond 8 percent per year."[41] A few months later, when the consumer price index began to increase at unprecedented rates with the onset of the oil crisis, local producers and importers were quick to petition for price increases of commodities subject to regulation. Ceiling prices were frequently revised; it is doubtful whether they were very different from what free-market prices would have been. Socialized pricing only led to the discouragement of production of goods consumed by low-income families, and rent control to a significant shift in building expenditures toward luxury residential houses and high-rise buildings.[42]

Wage policy could have responded more actively to protect the real income of laborers. The wage and salary adjustments actually made were simply not adequate to match the erosion of purchasing power. Government must act to safeguard the welfare of workers since only a small portion (10 percent in 1971) of those employed are members of labor unions and an even smaller fraction (1.3 percent in 1972) are covered by collective bar-

41. Philippines, National Economic Council, *Four-Year Development Plan, FY 1974–77*, p. 27.
42. Stretton, "The Building Industry and Employment Creation."

gaining agreements.[43] Also, under martial law, strikes, picketing, and group assemblies of workers were prohibited. As consumer prices rose in 1974 and 1975, Philippine policies neglected the very significant need to offset the redistributional inequities brought on by inflation.[44]

The dramatic decline in the inflation rate in 1975–76 may appear to be due to the absence of a price-wage spiral, but the annual percentage changes between 1955 and 1965 in the consumer price index, the wage rate index for unskilled industrial workers, and the index of average monthly earnings indicate that is unlikely.[45] The main factors that brought forth the sharp fall in inflation rate during 1975–76 were the downswing in import and export prices and the marked increase in food supply.

Particularly after the imposition of martial law, government intervention in critical areas of the Philippine economy increased, with the creation of state enterprises charged with regulatory functions and sometimes with direct participation in production or marketing activities. Self-sufficiency in food supply became an overriding objective, resulting in the massive credit and fertilizer subsidy schemes as well as measures to assure food distribution. A fertilizer authority, given control over all aspects of the industry in 1973, set up a two-tiered system with much lower prices for fertilizer used in food production than for export crops. Another authority controlled all trade in wheat, rice, and corn.

The oil crisis, perhaps more than anything else, jolted Philippine policymakers into the realization that strategic sectors of the economy needed to be more tightly controlled. The petroleum industry in 1973 was heavily dominated by subsidiary firms of major international oil companies. The government took a substantial, direct role in the importation of crude oil, refining, and distribution of petroleum products when it formed the Philippine National Oil Corporation. Government-to-government contracts accounted for about 45 percent of crude oil requirements in 1976, and only 75 percent of imports were from the Middle East (as opposed to 95 percent in 1973). Pricing of petroleum products roughly followed the increases in the import price of crude oil;[46] in early 1974 an acute shortage of oil was

43. J. Encarnación, G. A. Tagunicar, and R. L. Tidalgo, "Unemployment and Underemployment," in Encarnación and others, *Philippine Economic Problems,* pp. 136–77.

44. Bautista, "Inflation in the Philippines," pp. 201–02.

45. M. L. Treadgold, "Economic Growth and the Price Level in the Philippines, 1964–65" (Ph.D. dissertation, Australian National University, 1969), p. 197. However, because price and wage changes during 1955–65 were relatively moderate, the possibility of a more sensitive price response to large wage increases cannot be ruled out.

46. See Bautista, "Inflation in the Philippines."

met in a fairly orderly fashion by gasoline rationing. An Energy Development Board, created by presidential decree in March 1976, recommended that to reduce dependence on imports for 95 percent of its petroleum, the Philippines develop nuclear, geothermal, and hydroelectric energy sources, but also continue exploration for oil. Presidential decrees that liberalized the requirements for foreign participation in the search for indigenous petroleum deposits called for production sharing to replace the concession arrangements for exploration that were characteristic before 1973.

Government intervention in strategic economic sectors is not without danger. Lack of experience and expertise may lead to poor decisions being made. Indeed, some important policy measures appear to have been adopted without careful analysis; for instance, the ten-year power program for Luzon, part of the national energy plan, was judged by the World Bank to be "very costly . . . and its construction schedules, particularly those for geothermal and nuclear plants . . . optimistic."[47] The Bank recommended a smaller and less expensive program that it claimed reflected "more closely the demand projected" in the Philippines' power plan.[48]

External Trade Arrangements

As an ad hoc response to trade fluctuations, the Philippine government intensified its efforts to diversify export markets and import sources. In 1973 the Philippines applied for membership in the General Agreement on Tariffs and Trade, in order to gain most-favored-nation treatment in its trade with other members. The government also embarked on tax negotiations and investment treaties with key trading and investment partners. In 1974 the preferential treatment for Philippine exports to the United States expired and the government faced the likelihood that it would be replaced by the kind of concessions given to developing countries generally. Preferential treatment in the Japanese market became a theme of efforts to renegotiate Philippine trade agreements with Japan, and the "colonial" nature of Philippine trade became a sore point as the Philippine trade deficits with Japan grew.[49] Moves to promote other bilateral and multilateral trade arrangements thus became significant.

Favorable political developments made trade relations with Communist

47. World Bank, *The Philippines,* p. 506.
48. Ibid.
49. Bautista and Tecson, "Philippine Export Trade with Japan and the United States."

countries possible and opened areas of trade cooperation with other members of the Association of Southeast Asian Nations (ASEAN). Trade with Russia, which began in 1972, amounted to $89 million in 1976 (sugar was the main export commodity in 1976). Trade with the People's Republic of China began in 1971; by 1976, exports had reached $43.6 million and imports $53.8 million (including significant amounts of crude oil). Although China and Russia accounted for only 3.5 percent of Philippine trade in 1976, the trade involved commodities of special interest in years of trade instability.

Trade with other ASEAN countries (Indonesia, Malaysia, Singapore, and Thailand) constituted only 5.2 percent of the total value in 1976. But in a 1976 ASEAN meeting, preferential trading arrangements were discussed, and rice and crude oil were the first basic commodities identified for "priority of supply and priority of purchase . . . in times of shortage and of oversupply, respectively."[50] An industrial cooperation program got under way, and various other measures were agreed on for study—long-term (quantity) supply contracts, preferential interest rates on financing of purchases, preference in government procurement, and extension of tariff preferences. Machinery was established within ASEAN for dialogues with other countries, such as Australia, New Zealand, Canada, the United States, and Japan, and with regional groupings, such as the European Community and COMECON.

New institutional ties in ASEAN and elsewhere may be the Philippines' best hope for protecting its economy in future bouts of instability. Better domestic policy can provide some relief, but changes in external policy may also be necessary since the source of many of the Philippines' recent difficulties has been the instability of its major trading partners.

50. Report of the Second Meeting of the ASEAN Economic Ministers, Kuala Lumpur, March 8–9, 1976.

CHAPTER SEVEN

Agriculture, Thailand's Mainstay

NIMIT NONTAPUNTHAWAT

AN ECONOMY as small as Thailand's could not avoid being buffeted by the crises of the 1970s. Its only recourse in such circumstances is to take measures that minimize the destabilizing effects of the disturbances and hope that it is strong enough to weather the turbulent period. The task of ending the crises has to be left to the larger countries. The early 1970s were especially difficult for the Thai economy, for this period, the most tumultuous in the modern history of Thailand, witnessed the October 14, 1973, students' uprising and the Communist takeover of its eastern neighbors in early 1975.

Thailand is an open economy. Between 1965 and 1975 the size of the foreign sector was generally slightly larger than two-fifths of the economy and was expanding slightly faster than the economy as a whole.[1] Expansion in the size of the foreign sector relative to gross national product in 1966–70 was due mainly to the rapid increase in foreign-exchange receipts from the United States in return for the provision of military-related services by the Thai government. Thereafter it was the result of a rapid expansion in the volume of exports, a rise in the prices of Thailand's principal exports, and an increase in prices of imports occasioned by the fourfold increase in the price of crude oil. As the foreign sector grew, the channels through which foreign disturbances can be transmitted to the country also broadened.

The ratio of exports to production is high for nearly all of Thailand's

1. Exports and imports of goods and services accounted for 40.9 percent of the gross national product in 1966–70 and 45.1 percent in 1971–75. Bank of Thailand, *Monthly Bulletin,* various issues.

181

major export commodities. Between 1965 and 1975 more than nine-tenths of the total production of rubber and maize was exported, more than two-thirds of jute and kenaf, two-thirds of tapioca products, and virtually all tin metal production. The ratios are lower but never below 10 percent for all other major export products. Producers of export commodities are highly susceptible to price and demand fluctuations in the world market, and domestic prices tend to fluctuate in response to world prices.

Like most countries that export primary commodities, Thailand has a relatively high degree of commodity concentration. In 1960, about 70 percent of exports consisted of rice, tin, rubber, and teak, all traditional exports. By 1975, Thailand had been very successful in diversifying its exports, but only fourteen commodities exceeded 500 million baht in export value. Export sales were also concentrated heavily on a few countries.

Thailand is an agricultural country whose agricultural technology is still fairly primitive. In 1975, agriculture provided the livelihood of 32.2 million Thais, approximately 75 percent of the population, but it accounted for only 30 percent of national income. About two-thirds of the country's exports, however, were foodstuffs and raw materials. Such a dependence has advantages as well as disadvantages. By being a food surplus country and the largest exporter of food grains in Asia, Thailand avoided the hunger riots that plagued many of its less fortunate neighbors in 1976.

Thailand is located in one of the most unstable regions of the world, where the United States, the Soviet Union, the People's Republic of China, and more recently Japan, all seek to extend their influence. The Thai economy cannot avoid being affected by changes in the economic and political policies of these four powers. For example, the decision to withdraw U.S. troops from the Indochinese peninsula had an immense impact on foreign and domestic investment in Thailand, as did the fall of Laos, Cambodia, and Vietnam to communism. In an attempt to counter the influence of their Communist neighbors and the major world powers, Thailand and other free-market economies in Southeast Asia have begun to coordinate their political and economic actions. The formation of the Association of Southeast Asian Nations is one step in this direction.

The structure and stage of development of the Thai financial system do not allow the use of conventional instruments to control the economy. The ratio of privately held government securities to money supply was approximately 0.5 in 1975. The capital market is still in an embryonic stage. There are virtually no secondary markets for any of the financial assets and a substantial portion of the economy remains uncommercialized. Because operations in the open market cannot be used as a means for monetary control, the government has relied on changes in the required reserve ratio. And it has used the discount rate to channel cheap credit to industries it wishes to promote rather than to regulate the expansion of credit by commercial banks. The ceiling rates the commercial banks can pay to their depositors as well as the ceiling rates on various forms of commercial bank credit are used to maintain an artificially low interest rate in the belief that cheap credit is essential for growth. The ratio of capital assets to risk assets is used to assess the solvency of the banking system. Little effort is made to control money supply, and the Bank of Thailand's ability to manipulate money supply in the short run is limited.

The Thai Economy in the Late 1960s

The 1960s were a decade of stable and rapid growth for the Thai economy. Thailand was one of the fastest growing developing countries, with a growth rate of 8.5 percent from 1964 to 1969. Meanwhile, the annual increase in the consumer price index was only 2.5 percent, and unemployment in the nonagricultural sector was not a problem. Thailand experienced a balance-of-payments deficit only near the end of the decade, although its balance of trade was in deficit throughout the 1960s and became very large in the second half of the decade. The trade deficit was offset by receipts from tourism, direct investment, and military and other services to the U.S. government.

The decade witnessed major changes in the economy. The first five-year development plan provided domestic stimulus early in the 1960s. The direct involvement of the United States in the Vietnam War and the subsequent increase in the number of air bases in Thailand also had great economic and social impacts on the Thai economy. A fourfold increase in the trade balance deficit during the second half of the 1960s was due mainly to the stagnation of exports; imports continued to increase at the compounded annual rate of 10 percent. Thailand's terms of trade improved substantially from 1967 to 1969 but fell sharply in 1970 as a result of the precipitous fall in prices of exports and of rice in particular.

Among the factors responsible for the rapid increase in the volume of imports were substantial expenditures in the latter 1960s under the second national economic development plan for capital goods, which grew from about 30 percent of total imports in 1965 to approximately 35 percent in 1970. The Thai Board of Investment gave tax breaks in the 1960s to companies that needed to import raw materials and capital goods to start factories. The aim was to reduce imports of finished goods, but new production was more than offset by imports of capital goods, intermediate products, and raw materials. The new industries became dependent on foreign suppliers, thus impeding the development of tertiary and capital goods industries. Imports of intermediate products increased from about 20 percent of total imports in 1965 to 25 percent in 1970. Military and nonmilitary expenditures by American forces also affected Thai imports, which increased to meet the demands both of the Americans and of Thais whose incomes increased as a result of U.S. spending.

Generally speaking, the Thai economy performed satisfactorily with a high rate of growth in the second half of the 1960s. Near the end of the decade, however, there were some disturbing developments. In 1969 Thailand's balance of payments showed a deficit of 914 million baht, the first in that decade. During the first six months of 1970 the deficit reached 683 million baht, more than three times that of the corresponding period in 1969. In response, the government in June 1970 promulgated a Custom Tariff Emergency Decree raising many tariffs and reducing a few. Its primary objective was to restrict imports of nonessential goods.

The unequal growth rates of the various sectors of the economy were another sign of future trouble. In the 1960s the agricultural sector had an average annual compound rate of growth of only 5.6 percent. This was approximately one-half the growth rate in the industrial sector and slightly more than half the rate in the commercial sector.

The distribution of income between regions and between urban and rural areas became increasingly unequal as a result of the rapid growth of the 1960s and to a lesser extent the U.S. expenditures in Thailand during the Vietnam War. The high growth activities such as industry, commerce, and services were concentrated in urban areas and especially in Bangkok and the four surrounding provinces, which caused them to have a much higher rate of growth than the rest of the country and widened the income gap between urban dwellers and the villagers. Growth was also higher in provinces that had U.S. bases and in certain industries such as services and construction that were concentrated in Bangkok and capitals of the provinces with bases.

The relatively slow growth and low incomes of the agricultural sector led to migration problems as people moved from villages to cities. During the 1960s a significant portion of the migration was seasonal; the farmers undertook construction work in the cities during the dry season and returned home to farm when the rains came. As industrial development increased toward the end of the decade, so too did the percentage of the migration that was permanent. The migration to the metropolis brought with it problems usually

Table 7-1. *Percent Change in Real Gross National Product of Thailand, 1961–76*

Year	Change in GNP	Year	Change in GNP
1961	8.5	1969	7.8
1962	8.5	1970	7.4
1963	9.9	1971	7.9
1964	6.0	1972	4.0
1965	7.9	1973	10.3
1966	12.2	1974	5.4
1967	7.9	1975	5.0
1968	8.6	1976	5.7

Source: Bank of Thailand, *Monthly Bulletin*, various issues.

associated with poverty, poor sanitation, and inadequate housing. But the problems never became acute because of the low food prices in Thailand. The fact that the migrant laborers knew little about labor laws and regulations contributed significantly to the labor unrest in the later period.

Thus, near the end of the 1960s there were signs that the Thai economy would encounter major difficulties in the future. These difficulties helped bring about one of the most unstable periods in the modern history of Thailand. Between October 1973 and October 1976, Thailand had six governments and three prime ministers. There were frequent clashes between groups with different interests, and almost daily demonstrations. Most labor disputes ended in work stoppages. It is difficult to distinguish the economic damage caused by internal disorder from that brought on by external disturbances.

Economic Performance of Thailand, 1971–76

The performance of the Thai economy between 1971 and 1976 was not as good as it had been in the second half of the 1960s. The real GNP growth rate fell from an average 8.8 percent in 1966–70 to only about 6.4 percent in 1971–76 (table 7-1). The rate of inflation, as measured by the consumer price index for urban areas, increased from a negligible 1.5 percent to about 9 percent (table 7-2).

The growth rate of real GNP had a drastic fall from 7.9 percent in 1971 to only 4 percent in 1972. Among the many factors responsible were a crop failure in 1972 and a slowdown in the growth rate of gross fixed capital formation. The decline in capital formation is difficult to explain, but two major

Table 7-2. *Percent Change in Various Thai Price Indexes, 1968–76*

Year	Price index			
	Consumer[a]	Wholesale[b]	Export	Import
1968	1.8	n.a.	−0.3	−5.2
1969	2.4	3.3	3.5	−2.2
1970	−0.1	−0.5	−5.5	8.1
1971	0.4	0.3	−3.8	5.2
1972	4.8	7.9	4.1	5.6
1973	15.5	22.8	57.0	16.7
1974	24.3	28.8	47.9	61.8
1975	5.3	3.8	−13.3	11.5
1976	4.2	3.9	−0.2	2.1

Source: Bank of Thailand, *Monthly Bulletin,* various issues.
n.a. Not available.
a. Consumers Price Index for Urban Area by Group, Whole Kingdom. Food accounts for 49.5 percent of indexed items.
b. Domestic products account for 69.23 percent of items indexed.

factors were the slowdown of U.S. activities in the country and a brief abandonment of the Thai Board of Investment's policy of issuing promotional incentives for new industrial ventures.

The effect of the restriction of imports in 1970 combined with the economic slump of 1972 and the de facto devaluation of the baht following the first dollar devaluation was to turn the balance-of-payments deficit of 2.7 billion baht in 1970 and 0.33 billion baht in 1971 into a surplus of nearly 4 billion baht in 1972.[2] The baht devaluation caused a rise of 5.6 percent in the import price index. In addition, the poor harvest raised the food component of the consumer price index 6.7 percent above the 1971 level.[3] As a result, the rate of inflation rose from a negligible 0.4 percent in 1971 to 4.8 percent in 1972.

The gloomy picture of 1972 suddenly became brighter in 1973, when the full effects of the commodity boom were felt. The worldwide crop failure in 1972 caused a great increase in the 1973 export prices of cereals, Thailand's major export commodity. The export price index increased 57 percent between 1972 and 1973. The commodity boom and the return to a more normal level of crop production revived economic activities and investment and put the economy back on the path to rapid growth. Real GNP increased 10.3 percent and private gross fixed capital formation 44.7 percent.[4]

2. Total exports expanded by more than 30 percent while imports increased by only 15 percent.
3. Bank of Thailand, *Monthly Bulletin,* various issues.
4. Thailand, Office of the Prime Minister, National Economic and Social Development Board, *National Income of Thailand.*

As a result of the sudden increase in aggregate demand and a second de facto devaluation of the baht following the dollar devaluation of February 1973, the price level rose considerably and Thailand had a double-digit inflation rate for the first time since World War II. The consumer and wholesale price indexes jumped 15.5 percent and 22.8 percent, respectively, between 1972 and 1973. The balance of payments continued to show a surplus but the size of the surplus was reduced to 864 million baht as the economic boom increased imports by 37.4 percent and the crop failure in 1972 reduced the export quantum index by 8.7 percent.

With the oil embargo and the subsequent fourfold increase in the price of crude oil, the Thai economy was plunged into a recession. The higher oil prices added to existing inflationary pressures. The growth rate of real GNP fell by half (5 percentage points) from its peak in 1973. The consumer and wholesale price indexes increased at the unprecedented rates of 24.3 percent and 28.8 percent, respectively. Thailand was, however, more fortunate than most countries because the prices of its export commodities continued to increase until mid-1974 and declined gradually in the last two quarters. Thus the average level of export prices was high throughout 1974. As a result Thailand enjoyed a record balance-of-payments surplus of 8 billion baht even though its petroleum import bill nearly tripled (from 4.7 billion baht in 1973 to 12.6 billion baht in 1974).

The years 1975 and 1976 were recession years. In spite of large-scale fiscal stimulation, the real GNP growth rate fell to 5 percent in 1975 because of the withdrawal of U.S. forces in 1975, the downward trend in export prices, and importing countries' reduced demand during the worldwide recession. A 10 percent decrease in the value of exports with only a slight increase in imports produced a huge balance-of-payments deficit of nearly 2.9 billion baht in 1975.[5] Several factors finally brought the inflation under control: the recession, the contractionary effect of the balance-of-payments deficit on the money supply, direct price controls, and fiscal measures designed to slow the rate of price increases. The consumer and wholesale price indexes increased by only 5.3 percent and 3.8 percent, respectively, in 1975. The continuation of fiscal stimulation together with recovery in the industrial countries raised the growth rate slightly to 5.7 percent in 1976. In that year the consumer price index fell to 4.2 percent and the wholesale price index to 3.9 percent. The balance of payments, however, continued to have a deficit. Even though the export drive managed to reduce the deficit in the merchandise trade by approximately 8 billion baht from the 1975 level, the drastic fall in the net receipts of other accounts—namely, U.S. expenditures in

5. Bank of Thailand, *Monthly Bulletin,* various issues.

Thailand, net private services, and net private transfers—made the overall deficit slightly over 2.2 billion baht.

The Exchange Rate and Trade Prices

For many years before 1969 Thailand enjoyed balance-of-payments surpluses and consequently had accumulated a sizable amount of foreign-exchange reserves. Because the foreign-exchange crisis occurred when Thailand's balance of payments changed to a large deficit, the Thai government decided to maintain the old rate of exchange between the baht and the U.S. dollar after the Smithsonian agreement of December 1971. This de facto devaluation of the baht certainly contributed to the increase in Thailand's import prices, but unit import values had started to rise even before the formal devaluation of the dollar. The revaluation of the German mark in October 1969 and the floating of the mark and other strong European currencies in May 1971 helped to raise Thailand's import price index in 1970 and 1971 by 8.1 percent and 5.2 percent, respectively (table 7-2). The Smithsonian agreement formally revalued the currencies of Thailand's most important trading partner, Japan, by approximately 17 percent and of its third most important trade partner, West Germany, by about 14 percent, helping to raise the index another 5.6 percent in 1972.

The second devaluation of the dollar by 10 percent in February 1973, and the Thai government's decision to depreciate the baht by the same percentage, combined with the floatings of other major world currencies, further reduced the value of the baht against the currencies of its twenty major trading partners. By July 1973, the baht had dropped 11.34 percent below the Smithsonian par value. As a result, import prices made a record jump of 14.2 percent in the second quarter of 1973.[6]

Taking into consideration inflationary pressure from abroad and the country's comfortable reserve position, the Thai government decided to revalue the baht by 4 percent on July 15, 1973. The revaluation of the baht together with the increasing strength of the dollar to which the baht was tied when the oil crisis occurred limited the increase in import prices in the third quarter of 1973 to only 10.6 percent above the second quarter's level. The oil crisis pushed the import price index up another 12.8 percent in the fourth quarter, and by the end of the year to an increase of 16.7 percent. After the multifold increase in crude oil prices in 1974, the index skyrocketed to a record 61.8 percent above the 1973 level. Import prices increased slightly in the recession years of 1975 and 1976 even though the substantial appreciation of the

6. Ibid.

effective exchange rate of the baht in 1975 and 1976 moderated the inflationary impact of the oil crisis.

When the worldwide drop in food crop production sent food prices soaring in 1973 and 1974, Thailand's major export commodities captured unusually high prices in the world market. Thus the export price index increased by a massive 57 percent in 1973 and 48 percent in 1974 (table 7-2). The sharp increase in the export prices of cereals turned into a rather sharp decline in 1975 when world production of food crops returned to a more normal level. The export price index fell 13.3 percent in 1975 but only marginally in 1976.

Movements in the prices of traded goods influence the prices of nontraded goods through their effect on income and demand for substitute products and directly through the products and capital equipment used in the production of nontraded goods. An econometric study relating the prices of international and domestic goods found that marginal propensities to consume the two kinds of goods are about the same (0.35 for international goods and 0.37 for domestic goods).[7] It found also that the effect of a rise in the price index for international goods is substantially larger than that of a fall in the index. Applying the study's regression results to 1971–76 increases of 113.7 percent in international prices (the average of import and export unit values) indicates that domestic prices would rise at least 77 percent.[8]

The appearance of inflation in 1972 (table 7-2) was primarily due to the tying of the baht to the depreciating U.S. dollar and to the increase in food prices resulting from the shortfall in food supplies. The double-digit rate of inflation in 1973 was again the product of the baht devaluation and the increasingly high price of food. The buoyant export-led growth of 10.3 percent in 1973 (table 7-1) indicates that the increase in domestic demand was also very likely one of the factors contributing to the higher prices.

The high price of crude oil and the continued shortage of food grains in the world market were the two major factors responsible for large increases in consumer and wholesale price indexes in 1974. On the other hand, foreign-exchange fluctuations and the government budget became restraining fac-

---

7. See Supachai Panitchpakdi, "Inflation: The Case of External Disturbances," in Prateep Sondysuvan, ed., *Finance, Trade and Economic Development in Thailand*, Essays in Honour of Khunying Suparb Yossundara (Bangkok: Sompong Press, 1975); and Werner Baer and Isaac Kerstenetsky, eds., *Inflation and Growth in Latin America* (Yale University Press, 1964).

8. Panitchpakdi, "Inflation," tested the effect of varying P_i, the price index of international goods (agricultural, mining, and manufacturing sectors), on P_d, the price index of domestic goods (all sectors not included in P_i). With increasing rates for P_i, P_d equaled $49.09 + 0.68\ P_i$, and with decreasing rates equaled $98.18 + 0.40\ P_i$ (in both regressions, R^2 was 0.99).

tors, the former because of the increasing strength of the U.S. dollar in the aftermath of the oil crisis and the latter because of the budget surplus generated mainly by the expanding tax base and the difficulty of implementing planned expenditures.

The sharp reduction in the inflation rate in 1975 and 1976 reflected a return to more normal demand for and supply of food in both domestic and world markets and a slowdown in international and domestic economic activities. The rate would have been even lower if fiscal and monetary policies and an agricultural price-support program had not been adopted to stimulate the economy.

The devaluation of the baht following the dollar devaluations favored farmers and the producers and exporters of other commodities at the expense of importers and city dwellers who spend a larger portion of their income on imported products. Skyrocketing prices of food exports also benefited farmers and exporters. Windfall gains were siphoned off, however, by the imposition and variation of government premiums on exports. The effects of the oil crisis fell heavily on nonfarmers because their daily lives depend on oil more than do farmers' lives. However, the government's policy of subsidizing oil, electricity, and water supply during the period of increasing oil prices softened the impact on city dwellers.

Thai farmers, especially rice farmers, suffered little from the economic recession in the industrial countries because demand for their products is income inelastic and also because the industrial countries are not their most important markets. Salaried and skilled workers were the groups hardest hit by the 1973–74 inflation because wages failed to increase as fast as prices. The laborers, however, apparently did not fare as badly as the salaried and skilled workers because between 1973 and 1975 the minimum wage was doubled from 12 baht to 25 baht per day.

Terms of Trade

Thailand's terms of trade registered a precipitous fall in the early 1970s, the index moving from 128.3 in 1969 to 101.5 in 1972.[9] The deterioration in 1971 and 1972 was due mainly to a decline in export prices but also to the weakening of the U.S. dollar. Then in 1973 the situation was suddenly reversed. Despite an 8 percent devaluation of the baht, Thailand's terms of trade improved nearly 35 percent in 1973 as a result of the world food shortage and commodity boom. Export prices had another huge increase during 1974, but higher oil prices overwhelmed the gain and terms of trade fell 8.6

9. Bank of Thailand, *Monthly Bulletin,* various issues.

Table 7-3. *Indexes of Thai Merchandise Trade, 1961–76*

Index, 1958 = 100

Year	Export index			Import index			Terms of trade index
	Volume	Unit value	Value	Volume	Unit value	Value	
1961	146.2	106.1	155.1	122.8	101.7	124.9	104.3
1962	141.7	104.3	147.8	146.3	95.5	139.7	109.2
1963	146.3	102.6	150.1	164.4	94.5	155.4	108.6
1964	185.1	103.4	191.4	182.9	94.6	173.0	109.3
1965	191.5	104.8	200.7	196.8	95.2	187.4	110.1
1966	202.7	107.9	218.7	241.2	93.1	224.6	115.9
1967	205.1	107.1	219.7	290.9	92.6	269.4	115.7
1968	198.7	106.8	212.2	332.5	88.0	292.6	121.4
1969	206.6	110.5	228.3	366.1	86.1	315.2	128.3
1970	218.8	104.7	229.1	352.2	93.1	327.9	112.5
1971	265.3	100.9	267.7	332.9	97.9	325.9	103.0
1972	332.3	105.0	348.9	362.5	103.4	374.8	101.5
1973	303.3	164.8	499.9	424.3	120.7	512.1	136.5
1974	316.9	243.7	772.4	398.1	195.3	777.5	124.8
1975	324.4	215.1	697.8	372.5	217.8	811.3	98.8
1976	470.1	200.6	943.0	411.3	215.1	884.7	93.3

Source: Bank of Thailand, *Monthly Bulletin*, various issues.

percent from the 1973 peak. The decline continued in 1975 and 1976 when the index fell to 98.8 and 93.3.

Thailand's agricultural production responds quickly to price incentives as new crops can be planted to take advantage of changing prices. Thus Thailand was able to exploit the rise in commodity prices and enjoy a period of rapid growth. The increase in the export volume index from 1970 to 1972 (table 7-3) was a record in the modern history of Thailand. The index reveals two indigenous strengths of the Thai economy. One is its ability to quickly double export production, as it did in the relatively short time of six years (which included 1972, a year of unfavorable weather conditions). The other is its relative freedom from the unfavorable effects of the economic recession in the industrial countries, as evidenced by the continued increase in the index in 1975, the year of deep recession.[10] The first strength originates from the flexibility of the Thai agricultural export sector, and the second from the fact that world demand for cereals, the country's primary exports,

10. Since Thailand uses very small amounts of fertilizer and pesticides per acre, price rises during the oil crisis had little effect on agricultural production. The fertile land, the nonintensive nature of production, and the low prices of the products do not warrant more intensive use of the land.

Table 7-4. *Important Items in Thai Balance of Payments, 1961–76*
Millions of baht

Year	Merchandise trade			Services		Transfers		Foreign capital flow				Errors and omissions	Balance of payments
	Exports	Imports	Balance	Government[a]	Private	Government	Private	Direct investment	To private sector	To government sector	Other		
1961	8,923	-10,192	-269	301	19	443	98	121	563	107	76	196	1,655
1962	9,434	-11,397	-1,963	504	5	805	106	156	1,341	23	22	342	1,295
1963	9,578	-12,695	-3,117	576	110	993	145	347	1,285	4	10	596	949
1964	12,165	-14,126	-1,961	745	-12	644	131	473	1,002	271	-3	240	1,430
1965	12,663	-15,219	-2,536	1,309	135	650	146	870	281	282	231	636	1,985
1966	13,817	-18,296	-4,479	3,363	743	748	216	571	494	362	93	1,195	3,304
1967	13,888	-21,958	-8,150	4,619	1,294	1,024	174	894	1,012	482	-158	102	1,313
1968	13,808	-23,878	-10,650	5,094	1,054	1,407	140	1,240	717	602	-115	959	449
1969	14,254	-25,565	-11,311	4,591	1,363	1,098	89	1,058	1,571	329	-48	357	-914
1970	14,270	-26,515	-12,245	4,441	1,595	954	57	891	1,092	498	-8	66	-2,652
1971	16,692	-26,633	-9,941	4,113	1,289	773	131	808	568	357	299	1,266	-335
1972	21,750	-30,615	-8,865	4,925	1,658	608	631	1,427	2,027	189	301	1,090	3,991
1973	31,252	-42,054	-10,801	4,589	2,247	570	2,399	1,605	971	362	-1	-1,076	864
1974	49,002	-63,304	-14,302	3,920	3,681	541	4,376	3,836	5,116	102	0	742	8,012
1975	44,365	-64,526	-20,161	3,216	2,946	498	1,134	1,745	5,928	82	-2	1,756	-2,858
1976	59,860	-71,735	-11,873	1,608	35	362	101	1,614	5,658	2,144	167	-369	-83
1971–76	222,921	-298,867	-75,946	22,373	11,856	3,352	8,772	11,035	20,268	3,236	764	3,409	9,591

Source: Bank of Thailand, *Monthly Bulletin*, various issues.
a. Includes services provided to the U.S. government by the Thai government.

fluctuates less than demand for industrial raw materials. The tendency for cereal prices to rise rapidly during a period of supply shortage such as occurred in 1973 and 1974 and to fall following a period of bumper crops also helped stabilize the export earnings of the country. The data in table 7-3 indicate that the volume and unit indexes for exports fluctuated more than the value index in the 1971–76 period of world instability.

Thailand has been a model for successful export diversification. It began to diversify in the early 1960s and became one of the few developing countries that could boast six commodities that each consistently earned substantial amounts of foreign exchange annually for the country. Changes in export prices were strongly correlated with changes in production. Sugar is the most impressive case of export response to prices. Before 1970 Thailand's sugar exports were negligible; by 1976 its exports of 1.2 million tons made it the sixth largest exporter in the world.

In 1970 the Thai Board of Investment changed from its policy of encouraging import substitution to one that emphasized export promotion. Exports of both light and heavy manufactured goods increased very rapidly after 1971, with a one-year pause during the economic recession in 1975. As a percentage of total exports, manufactured goods exhibit an almost uninterrupted upward trend until 1973, then a temporary fall during the oil crisis, the worldwide recession, and the period of high cereal prices. Their share of total exports rose again with the economic upswing in 1976. Judging from the fact that exports of manufactured products (excluding tin metal) as a percentage of total exports nearly quadrupled between 1970 and 1976,[11] the export promotion program seems to have been successful.

The picture of Thai trade from the import side is just the opposite of that from the export side. The volume of imports increased rapidly in the second half of the 1960s while exports stagnated, causing a huge deficit in the balance of trade (tables 7-3 and 7-4). This prompted the government to increase tariffs on commodities in mid-1970, which in conjunction with the de facto baht devaluation led to a reduction in import volume in 1970 and 1971. The second baht devaluation and higher export prices for cereals in 1972 and 1973 helped to keep the deficit in the merchandise trade account below the 1970 level until 1974. With an oil import bill increase from 4.7 billion baht in 1973 to 12.6 billion baht in 1974 despite a drop in the petroleum import volume from 55.9 million barrels to 48.2 million barrels, the record increase in the value of exports was outstripped and the deficit went to more than 14 billion baht. In 1975 the fall in export prices of grains and the worldwide recession contributed to a record deficit. With the export drive

11. From 4.5 percent of total exports to 17.0 percent.

and world recovery in 1976 the deficit decreased to approximately the same level as in 1970.

The extent to which the baht devaluations in 1971–73 contributed to the improvement in the balance of trade and thus the balance of payments is difficult to measure. However, if a price elasticity of −0.86 for rice exports[12] is used as a proxy for the price elasticity of total Thai exports, and an estimate of 0.90 is assumed to be the import price elasticity,[13] then the sum of the price elasticities of exports and imports would be 1.48, substantially greater than unity. The baht devaluation therefore can be assumed to have led to the improvement of Thailand's balance of trade and balance of payments, a conclusion that seems to be well supported by empirical data.

The surplus in the service account was an important source of foreign exchange for Thailand. The foreign exchange received for the Thai government's services to the U.S. military establishment was large enough to offset the deficits in the merchandise trade account in the 1960s and 1970s. The private service account also showed a net gain which can be largely attributed to the steadily increasing earnings from tourism from the outbreak of the Vietnam War until 1975. This growth initially was due mainly to the increase in the number of U.S. servicemen visiting Thailand on the rest and recreation program (the number went from zero in 1965 to more than 70,000 in 1969, but fell rapidly to 8,000 in 1972), then to the increase in other visitors, especially from Japan and neighboring countries. By 1972, tourism was bringing in about 2 billion baht worth of foreign exchange annually, making it the second or third most important earner of foreign exchange for the country. The higher cost of travel after the oil crisis and the worldwide recession did not have a noticeable effect on the tourist industry. The importance of tourism as a foreign exchange earner continued with tourism earning almost 4.5 billion baht in foreign exchange in 1975.

Capital Flows

Net foreign transfers to the Thai government declined rapidly after 1969 as the United States withdrew its troops from Vietnam and as Thailand's economic growth made it ineligible for grants and advantageous loans from the international agencies and lending countries. Aid from the United States fell steadily from about 1.2 billion baht in 1968 to only 138 million baht in 1976. With the decline in grants from other countries, receipts by the Thai government fell steadily in the 1970s (table 7-4). The foreign exchange re-

12. From Veerapongsa Ramangkura, "The Chulalongkorn Econometric Model," Faculty of Economics, Chulalongkorn University (1976).
13. From Kriengsak Yothaprasert, "An Empirical Study of Thailand's Imports, 1960–70" (M.A. thesis, Thammasat University, 1970).

ceived through private transfers became excessively large between 1972 and 1975. It is generally accepted in banking circles that the sudden increases in private transfers were from earnings from smuggling, notably of rice and sugar, during the time of high commodity prices, and from transfers of funds by persons in the three former French Indochinese states in anticipation of the Communist takeover.

Table 7-5 shows the flow of medium- and long-term private capital into Thailand in 1971–76. The flow of suppliers' credits (medium-term trade credits of three to five years duration which are closely related to imports of producer and, to a lesser extent, consumer durables) decreased consistently from 1971 through 1973. Stagnation in private gross fixed capital formation in Thailand and the uncertainty in the foreign-exchange market played an important role in reducing the inflow. However, the fact that the decrease continued through 1973, a year of unusually rapid economic growth in Thailand, indicates that the foreign-exchange market is probably the more important factor. Credit from other sources in 1971 and 1973, years of great instability in the foreign-exchange market, was abnormally low. Flows of both medium-term credits and loans rose markedly in 1974 in response to the rapid increase in the import bills and the more stable foreign-exchange market. The recession of 1975 and 1976 reduced both types of trade credits.

The instabilities of the 1971–76 period influenced the level of foreign investment in Thailand in different ways. For example, the foreign-exchange crisis encouraged countries with large surpluses in their balance of payments or large accumulations of U.S. dollars in their foreign-exchange reserves to adopt policies that favored the outflow of dollars, either through direct foreign investment or through loans to foreign countries. On the other hand, the oil crisis caused a slowdown in economic activity in the investing countries as well as in the host countries and reduced the previously abundant reserves which discouraged foreign investment in all countries including Thailand. The U.S. withdrawal and the fall of three neighboring states to communism undermined investors' confidence in Thailand. The political instability and labor and social unrest in Thailand made investors particularly wary of projects with a long pay-back period.

Foreign direct investment followed approximately the same pattern as gross fixed capital formation in the private sector. The only difference is that the absolute level of foreign investment, measured in either constant or current prices, fell in 1975 and 1976, the years of world recession.

The flow of capital out of the country is determined by the terms of credit and the size of trade debts incurred in the past and by the remittance of profits and debt repayments on direct investment to parent companies. For-

Table 7-5. *Sources of Medium- and Long-Term Capital Received by Thailand, 1971–76*
Millions of baht

Year	Japan			United States			Other	All sources
	Public	Private	Total	Public	Private	Total		
1971	322	787	1,109	−30	320	290	273	1,672
1972	204	466	670	−102	1,360	1,258	1,336	3,264
1973	198	−119	79	1	334	335	1,073	1,487
1974	198	764	962	224	1,778	2,002	4,960	7,924
1975	565	302	867	274	253	527	3,762	5,156
1976	834	350	1,184	718	590	1,308	3,992	6,484
1971–76ᵃ	2,231	2,550	4,871	1,085	4,635	5,720	15,396	25,987

Source: Bank of Thailand, *Monthly Bulletin*, various issues.
a. Cumulative net receipts.

eign firms that received promotional incentives from the Thai government during 1971–76 were for the most part new firms that needed to reinvest a large share of their profits. Profits repatriated during the period were made largely by firms that had been in the country long before the inauguration of the investment promotion activities.

The flow of capital to the public sector (table 7-4) increased in 1976 when the government deficit produced by expansionary fiscal policy was partially financed from abroad. One of the factors that led the government to increase its borrowing in 1976 was the continued deterioration in Thailand's balance of payments during the year. Though total government debt stood at 16.6 billion baht (approximately $0.8 billion) by the end of 1976, it amounted to only 42 percent of official foreign-exchange reserves and approximately 28 percent of total exports. Even during the oil crisis, Thailand never had a serious debt servicing problem. The government had long had a policy of requiring profit-making state enterprises to repay both the principal and the interest on their foreign loans. The only help it extended to these enterprises was to guarantee the loans. This policy meant that direct government debt totaled only 7.1 billion baht in 1976; but the government also guaranteed loans of 9.5 billion baht.

Japan and the United States as Transmitters of Disturbance

Japan and the United States are Thailand's two most important trade partners as well as foreign investors. Thus changes in the growth rates, price levels, and policies of these two countries are bound to have an effect on the performance of the Thai economy. However, the roles of the two in the Thai economy are not quite the same. The Thai and the Japanese economies have become more and more complementary since the Japanese economy is geared toward heavy and knowledge-intensive industries. The colossal and diversified economy of the United States has become more and more competitive with the Thai economy because both are major exporters of cereals. Furthermore, disposal of tin from the gigantic U.S. stockpile raises stiff competition for Thailand, a major tin producer.[14]

14. Jindarah Phangmuangdee, in "Analysis of the United States' Tin Disposal" (M.A. thesis, Thammasat University, 1975), found that tin prices are highly sensitive to the United States' tin disposal program and that the program occasionally generates speculative trading. Ramangkura, "Chulalongkorn Econometric Model," found that U.S. sale of rice under the surplus agricultural commodities program affects Thailand's rice exports. Frequent complaints by Thai rice exporters led to an agreement that the U.S. government would consult with the Thai government before selling rice in Thailand's traditional rice markets.

Table 7-6. Flow, Balance, and Distribution of Thai Trade, 1966–75

	1966–70					1971–75				
	Imports		Exports		Trade balance	Imports		Exports		Trade balance
Trading partner	Millions of baht	Percent of total	Millions of baht	Percent of total	(millions of baht)	Millions of baht	Percent of total	Millions of baht	Percent of total	(millions of baht)
Pacific basin countries[a]	74,025	62.9	46,481	65.1	−27,544	134,468	58.3	110,467	66.2	−24,001
Japan	42,154	36.1	15,766	22.1	−26,848	77,759	33.7	42,617	25.5	−35,142
United States	19,126	16.2	9,705	13.6	−9,421	32,765	14.2	17,289	10.3	−15,499
ASEAN	4,053	3.4	13,074	17.5	9,021	6,142	2.7	29,883	17.9	23,741
Singapore	1,385	1.2	5,336	7.5	3,953	3,564	1.5	14,051	8.4	10,487
Malaysia	981	0.8	5,324	7.5	4,343	1,795	0.8	8,335	5.0	6,540
Philippines	290	0.2	593	0.8	303	374	0.2	2,324	1.4	1,950
Indonesia	1,399	1.2	1,821	2.6	422	409	0.2	5,173	3.1	4,764
Other major partners	8,692	7.4	7,936	11.1	−756	17,829	7.7	20,698	12.4	2,869
Hong Kong	2,013	1.7	5,206	7.3	3,193	2,827	1.2	11,095	6.6	8,265
Australia	3,272	2.8	304	0.4	−2,968	6,667	2.9	1,453	0.9	−5,224
Taiwan	2,768	2.4	2,351	3.3	−417	6,337	2.7	7,022	4.2	685
Korea	639	0.5	75	0.1	−564	1,986	0.9	1,128	0.8	−760
European Community	28,761	24.4	10,894	15.2	−17,867	40,816	17.7	26,151	15.6	−14,615
United Kingdom	8,847	7.5	2,070	2.9	6,777	12,391	5.4	2,618	1.6	−9,773
West Germany	12,669	10.8	2,823	4.0	−9,846	15,723	6.8	4,197	2.5	−11,526
France	1,387	1.2	736	1.0	−651	4,741	2.1	1,582	0.9	−3,159
Italy	2,480	2.1	1,350	1.9	−1,130	3,835	1.7	1,674	1.0	−2,161
Belgium	1,020	0.9	491	0.7	−329	1,844	0.8	1,098	0.6	−746
Netherlands	2,358	2.0	3,424	4.8	1,066	2,282	1.0	14,982	9.0	12,700
OPEC[b]	4,424	2.8	1,413	2.0	−3,009	17,100	7.4	5,327	3.2	−11,773
Miscellaneous other	10,560	8.9	12,635	17.7	2,075	38,318	16.6	24,928	14.9	−13,390
Total	117,770	100.0	71,425	100.0	−46,345	230,732	100.0	166,815	100.0	−63,914

Source: Bank of Thailand, *Monthly Bulletin*, various issues.
a. Omits countries included under Miscellaneous other.
b. Omits Indonesia, which is included under ASEAN.

Japanese influence on Thailand's economy in 1971–76 was exerted in part through trade and trade credits. The United States, being an important world capital market, was able to exert its influence through the capital account somewhat more than Japan. The impact of both countries on domestic price levels was considerable. Their effects on Thailand's balance of payments went in opposite directions—Japan's huge trade surplus with Thailand had a negative influence, whereas the U.S. impact was favorable until 1975.

Japan is clearly Thailand's most important trade partner. During 1966–70, 36 percent of Thailand's cumulative imports were from Japan, and during 1971–75, 34 percent, while 22 percent and 25 percent of its cumulative exports were to Japan during these two periods (table 7-6). The United States is a distant second—in both periods, cumulative imports from the United States were less than half those from Japan, and in 1971–75 Thai exports to the United States were also less than half those to Japan. In fact, the European Community as a group does more trade with Thailand than the United States. Furthermore, both the ASEAN countries and the group of countries classified as other major partners in the Pacific basin are more important export markets for Thai products than the United States. Judging from the trade accounts, economic disturbances in Japan would affect the Thai economy much more than disturbances of the same magnitude in the United States.

The proportion of total Thai exports to Japan declined in 1971 and 1972. Taking into account the fact that the target volume of Japan's imports from Thailand is negotiated one year in advance, it is very likely that the recession in Japan that began in mid-1970 and continued through 1971 was a major factor responsible for the decline. The depreciation of the baht against the yen by about 20 percent between 1970 and 1972 did not seem to have a significant positive effect on Thai exports to Japan. The recession in Japan in 1974 and 1975, on the other hand, did not seem to adversely affect Thailand's exports to Japan, because the recession was worldwide.

The effect of the recession on Thailand's exports to the United States was erratic. While the United States had negative growth rates in both 1974 and 1975, the U.S. share of total Thai exports fell only in 1974 and was back to a more normal level in 1975. The 1974 decline was probably due more to the very high share of cereals in Thai export values, little of which were exported to the United States, than to the recession.

On the import side, the appreciation of the yen against the baht between 1970 and early 1973 did have a noticeable negative effect on Japanese exports to Thailand. Japan's share of Thailand's imports declined rapidly after 1973, as the proportion of imports from Saudi Arabia, the major supplier of

Table 7-7. *Influence of Japan and the United States on Price Stability in Thailand, 1971–76*

Percent

Year	Share of Thai import market		Change in export price index		Share of change in Thai import prices[a]	
	Japan	United States	Japan	United States	Japan	United States
1971	37.67	14.21	3.3	3.2	1.2	0.5
1972	36.93	15.67	10.7	3.7	4.0	0.6
1973	35.74	14.02	23.3	17.7	8.3	2.5
1974	31.39	13.49	24.9	28.3	7.8	3.8
1975	31.55	14.31	−4.6	10.0	−1.5	1.4
1976	30.88	14.32	1.5	3.4	0.5	0.5

Source: Bank of Thailand, *Monthly Bulletin*, various issues.
a. Calculated as the product of the share of Thai import market and the change in export price index.

crude oil to Thailand, increased. The U.S. share of total imports did not fall after the oil crisis. The United States at that time was doing better than both Japan and West Germany in the Thai market, probably as a result of the dollar devaluation.

The United States influences Thai export prices not through purchases from Thailand, but rather through its role as a major supplier and price leader of certain export commodities such as maize and soybeans. Since changes in world supply have been frequent, they are more important than world demand in determining the prices of export crops. Thus U.S. supplies have a greater impact on Thai export prices than does the considerable Japanese demand for those commodities.

As measured by the effect that changes in U.S. and Japanese export price indexes have on Thailand's import prices, Japan was much the more important transmitter of inflation to Thailand from 1971 to 1974 (table 7-7), both because of its much larger share in the Thai market and because of the appreciation of the yen. However, continued increases in U.S. export prices during the recession of 1975 and 1976 made the United States the more important transmitter of inflation to Thailand in those years.

U.S. Military Expenditures

The presence of American military personnel and U.S. expenditures on the construction of air bases and other military-related facilities were a remarkable stimulus to the Thai economy in the second half of the 1960s. Total U.S. expenditures accounted for 4.5 percent of Thailand's national in-

Table 7-8. *U.S. Military Expenditures as Percent of Thai National Income and Exports, 1966–76*

Year	Thai income (billions of baht) National	Thai income (billions of baht) Export	U.S. military expenditures (billions of baht)	U.S. expenditures as percent of Thai national income	U.S. expenditures as percent of Thai export income
1966	78.74	13.82	2.72	3.45	19.68
1967	89.59	13.81	4.33	4.83	31.35
1968	95.35	13.23	5.33	5.58	40.29
1969	104.58	14.25	4.91	4.69	34.46
1970	110.60	14.09	4.58	4.14	32.50
Average, 1966–70	95.78	13.84	4.37	4.54	31.60
1971	116.87	16.70	4.03	3.45	24.13
1972	133.68	21.75	4.47	3.34	20.55
1973	178.62	31.25	4.22	2.36	13.50
1974	219.91	49.00	3.40	1.55	6.94
1975	239.10	44.36	2.64	1.10	5.95
1976	264.93	59.86	0.76	0.29	1.27
Average, 1971–76	192.19	37.16	3.25	1.69	8.75

Source: Bank of Thailand, *Monthly Bulletin*, various issues.

come and over 30 percent of the foreign exchange earned from exports (table 7-8). After 1972 they declined consistently and by 1976 had fallen to an insignificant level. Approximately one-fifth of U.S. military expenditures in Thailand during 1966–70 is estimated to have been spent on directly induced imports—for example, on equipment and materials for construction projects—and the other 80 percent to have been spent locally. Each dollar of U.S. military expenditures in Thailand is calculated to have eventually led to an increase in income of $2.90 and an increase in imports of approximately $0.77—$0.20 worth directly induced, and the other $0.57 worth indirectly induced.[15] Those estimates applied to U.S. military expenditures in 1971–76 (table 7-9) indicate the impact of the American withdrawal on the Thai balance of payments. The reduction in U.S. military expenditures had very little effect on the growth of national income during 1971–73 (table 7-10). After 1973, however, the negative effect became significant, and by 1976, when the withdrawal was completed, the effect was substantial.

15. Boonkong Hunchangsith, "Economic Impacts of the U.S. Presence in Thailand, 1960–1972" (Ph.D. dissertation, Claremont Graduate School, 1974), using the Keynesian multiplier model, found that the marginal propensity to import and the income multiplier are about 0.25 and 2.9, respectively.

Table 7-9. *Impact of U.S. Military Withdrawal on Thai Balance of Payments, 1971–76*
Millions of baht

Year	U.S. military expenditures	Induced imports[a] Direct	Indirect	Total	Contribution to balance of payments
1971	4,030	806	2,297	3,103	927
1972	4,470	894	2,548	3,422	1,028
1973	4,220	844	2,405	3,249	971
1974	3,400	680	1,938	2,618	782
1975	2,640	528	1,505	2,033	607
1976	760	152	433	585	175

Source: Bank of Thailand, *Monthly Bulletin.*
a. Calculation based on estimates by Boonkong Hunchangsith, "Economic Impacts of the U.S. Presence in Thailand, 1960–1972" (Ph.D. dissertation, Claremont Graduate School, 1974).

Table 7-10. *Effect of Changes in U.S. Military Expenditures on Thai National Income, 1971–76*

Year	Difference in U.S. military expenditures from mean for 1966–70 (billions of baht)	Difference in national income generated by U.S. military expenditures Billions of baht[a]	Change from previous year Billions of baht	Percent
1971	−0.34	−0.884	...	−0.7
1972	0.10	0.238	1.122	0.2
1973	−0.15	−0.299	−0.537	−0.2
1974	−0.97	−1.633	−1.334	−1.0
1975	−1.73	−2.830	−1.197	−1.7
1976	−3.71	−5.780	−2.950	−3.3

Source: Table 7-8.
a. Calculations based on estimates by Hunchangsith, "Economic Impacts."

At the height of the American involvement in the Vietnam War, American bases in Thailand were probably the single largest source of employment in the country. The direct employment of Thai nationals at American air bases reached a peak of 44,000 workers in 1966–67 (approximately 1.5 percent of the nonagricultural labor force) when military construction was most active. In 1972 the number had dwindled to 31,000 persons. By the end of 1976, when all of the air bases had been turned over to the Thai government, almost all employees had probably been laid off because the Thai government did not have enough money to maintain the bases. About 45 percent of the Thai workers employed in the bases in 1969 were professional, semiprofessional, and skilled workers, the segment of the labor force most plagued by employment problems in the 1970s.[16] Assuming that every workingman has to support five dependents, the U.S. withdrawal would have affected the livelihood of about 150,000 persons, not a very large portion of a population of 40 million. But if indirect unemployment, especially of bar girls and employees of other "soft service" businesses whose customers were mainly U.S. servicemen, is taken into account, the impact of the U.S. withdrawal would have been stronger.

The number of soft service establishments fell from 652 in 1966 to 499 in 1972, and owners of establishments still in operation complained of a fall in revenues. Some of the entertainment businesses, however, reported an increase in the number of Thai customers as their American customers disappeared. This imitation of the American soldiers' way of life is one of the many negative aspects of the American presence. Most of the ill effects are of a social or political nature, but one probable negative economic effect is that of misallocated resources. American bases were able to bid professional and skilled workers and other scarce resources away from other more productive undertakings. In addition they encouraged the undesirable migration of Thais to the base areas.

Capital Flows and the Balance of Payments

Japan and the United States each supplied almost one-quarter of net medium- and long-term capital for Thailand in the 1971–76 period (table 7-5). Japan was the most important lender to the Thai government and government enterprises and the United States, as one of the most important capital markets in the world, was the most important source of capital for the private sector. The flow of capital fluctuated from year to year but fell to a very low level in 1973, the year when uncertainty in the foreign-exchange market reached a peak. Flows to the private sector were responsible for that drop and for the decline in 1975 and 1976, the years of worldwide recession.

Thailand has had a balance-of-trade deficit with both Japan and the United States for decades. The huge annual trade deficit with Japan in the 1971–76 period greatly exceeded the surplus in the capital account in every year. As a result, there was a net foreign-exchange outflow from Thailand to Japan of approximately 34.4 billion baht during the period (table 7-11).

16. The unemployment rate among graduates of technical and teacher training schools was about three times the national average, while the rate for university degree holders was slightly above the national rate. Data on employment in U.S. bases are from ibid., which relies on Conrad Bekker, "SID Panel on Impact of U.S. Military Spendings" (Bangkok, U.S. Embassy).

Table 7-11. *Thailand's Balance of Payments with Japan, 1971–76*
Millions of baht

Year	Trade account	Capital account	Total
		Balance	
1971	−5,819	1,109	−4,710
1972	−6,741	670	−6,071
1973	−6,668	79	−6,589
1974	−7,249	962	−6,287
1975	−8,665	867	−7,798
1976	−5,500	1,184	−4,316
1971–76	−40,642	6,263	−34,379

Source: Bank of Thailand, *Monthly Bulletin*, various issues.

The chronic balance-of-payments deficit with Japan threatens to impede growth unless it is offset from other sources. A reduction of imports would also adversely affect growth since the imports are mostly capital goods and intermediate products needed for industry.

Thailand had a balance-of-payments surplus with the United States until 1975, but the surpluses were due mainly to U.S. military expenditures and to an occasional jump in net capital flows from the United States (an oil concessional fee in June 1974 caused such a jump). A sharp rise in the trade deficit in 1974 combined with the rapid fall in U.S. military expenditures in Thailand and U.S. grants to Thailand produced Thailand's first deficit in the overall balance with the United States (table 7-12).

Direct Foreign Investment

Despite the publicity accorded it, direct foreign investment is not a significant portion of total Thai investment. The cumulative direct investment from Japan and the United States during 1971–76 amounted to 3.3 billion baht and 5.9 billion baht, respectively. These amounts were less than 1.4 percent and 2.5 percent of the cumulative private gross fixed capital formation (240.9 billion baht) during the period.

Employment generated by their investments was not substantial. The 34,582 Thai workers employed by the firms Japan invested in made up 0.25 percent of Thailand's total labor force or 1.6 percent of employment in the manufacturing sector in 1975. The corresponding figures for the nineteen firms receiving American investment were 0.06 percent and 0.36 percent. The relatively small number of jobs created is due in part to the capital-intensive production methods employed by these firms. The average value of

Table 7-12. *Thailand's Balance of Payments with the United States, 1971–76*
Millions of baht

			Balance		
Year	Trade account	Capital account	Government services[a]	Transfer account	Total
1971	−1,546	290	4,115	519	3,378
1972	−2,004	1,258	4,925	418	4,597
1973	−2,654	340	4,589	356	2,631
1974	−4,697	2,002	3,920	229	1,454
1975	−4,598	527	3,216	116	−739
1976	−4,400	1,308	1,608	138	−1,346
1971–76	−19,899	5,725	22,373	1,776	9,975

Source: Bank of Thailand, *Monthly Bulletin*, various issues.
a. Represents U.S. military and nonmilitary expenditures in Thailand.

fixed assets per employee in Japanese-Thai joint ventures was 158,000 baht, in U.S.-Thai ventures 83,200 baht.

The contribution of the Japanese- and American-financed firms to the increase in exports is also very small. The value of exports by fifteen recipients of American investments was only 3.1 billion baht, and for the twenty-three firms in which the Japanese invested only about 234 million baht—about 7 percent and 0.5 percent, respectively, of total Thai exports in 1975. Japanese investments are more concentrated in import-substitution industries than are American investments. However, the big difference in their contributions to the growth of exports seems to be due mainly to American investment in the tin-smelting industry, which would be an important export industry even if there were no American investment.

The contribution to Thai economic growth of both Japanese- and American-financed firms is also very limited. Japanese-Thai ventures imported about 69 percent of their material inputs, American-Thai ventures 29 percent. Again the difference is due mainly to the tin-smelting industry, which uses domestic tin concentrates. American-financed firms seem to be concentrated in the mineral-product industries while Japanese-financed firms are often in the textile industry, which uses a high proportion of imported materials.[17]

Thailand's high degree of dependence on imported capital equipment and

17. Bank of Thailand, Department of Economic Research, "The First Survey of Production, Investment, and Employment Conditions in Industrial, Commerce and Service Sectors" (1976); and Board of Investment, *Survey of Promoted Firms 1975;* see also, Seiji Naya and Narongchai Akrasanee, "Thai-Japan Economic Relations: Trade and Investment," in Ecocen, Study Paper no. 9 (1974).

intermediate inputs plus the fact that domestically procured inputs of both Japanese- and American-financed firms were mostly raw materials indicate that foreign investment does little to stimulate industrial activity in the manufacturing sector of Thailand. Foreign investment does not seem to contribute significantly to the saving and earning of foreign exchange because of the great dependence on imported inputs and the fact that some export industries merely increased the degree of processing of their products.

The impact of foreign investment on the transfer of technology is probably not great. Most of the training in foreign-financed firms is on-the-job training of three months or less. Some skilled and professional employees are sent to the firms' home country for training, but seldom for more than three to six months. American firms are more inclined to employ skilled and professional workers from the local labor force than are Japanese firms. It is difficult to determine whether the practice of hiring trained workers from the domestic labor force is beneficial to the Thai economy. American-financed firms generate employment income and improve the marketing and managerial skills of the local labor force, but they also bid away this resource from local firms by offering higher wages.

Response to Foreign-Exchange Crisis

The foreign-exchange crisis in the second half of 1971 occurred when Thailand was suffering a period of balance-of-payments deficits for the first time in recent history. In 1970, import tariffs on over two hundred commodities were increased to reduce the deficit to a manageable level. Given this deficit, it is not surprising that the Thai government decided not to change the value of the baht vis-à-vis the U.S. dollar when the dollar was officially devalued toward the end of 1971. The index of the external value of the baht weighted by the values of merchandise exports and imports of twenty major trading partners was down by an average of 7.06 percent right after the Smithsonian realignment. When the dollar was devalued by another 10 percent on February 12, 1973, the Thai authorities again decided not to change the value of the baht vis-à-vis the dollar. When major world currencies were floated against the dollar after the devaluation, the value of the baht fell a further 4.61 percent. According to the Bank of Thailand, the 1973 devaluation was needed to control the huge trade deficit that had plagued Thailand since the mid-1960s. The baht value was also allowed to fall in order to keep the income (in domestic currency) of exporters and farmers from falling and to increase the competitiveness of Thai export commodities, both reasonable moves for an economy in which a high proportion of farmers' income is used to buy domestically produced goods and in which prices respond to the world market.[18]

In mid-1973 the Bank of Thailand decided to appreciate the baht. The rise in the cost of living brought on by the rapid increase in the prices of imported products had provoked a public outcry for immediate steps to stop the inflation. Commercial banks had begun a panic sale of U.S. dollars to the Exchange Equalization Fund (an organization within the Bank of Thailand whose major function is to intervene in the foreign-exchange market to stabilize the external value of the baht) in anticipation of further depreciation of the dollar. Moreover, in academic circles it was argued that Thailand's reserves could support a baht revaluation.

In July 1973 the baht was revalued from 20.80 to 20.00 per dollar, the official rate that continued through 1976. The trade-weighted value of the baht was down slightly more than 1 percent in September 1973. By the end of 1975 it had gone up by nearly 5 percent, as the oil embargo and increase in crude oil prices strengthened the U.S. dollar and hence the baht. The weakening of the dollar brought the value of the baht down by more than 1 percent by the end of 1976. Despite the baht's devaluation by approximately 10 percent following the second dollar devaluation in February 1973, its value with respect to the currencies of Thailand's twenty trade partners declined only 4.9 percent, 2.4 percent, and 3.9 percent from the Smithsonian value at the end of 1974, 1975, and 1976, respectively.[19]

Response to the Commodity Boom

The worldwide crop failures in 1972 placed a heavy burden on food-shortage countries, but they were a boon for Thailand, a food-surplus country and an important supplier of rice for East Asia. Although the large increase in the prices of cereals was short-lived, it provided Thailand with breathing space to adjust to the new world environment. It also prevented a radical deterioration in Thailand's balance of payments, terms of trade, and foreign-exchange reserves after the multifold increase in the price of crude oil.

Because the supply of rice in a particular year depends on production a year earlier, the severe drought and other natural disasters in 1972 reduced

18. Data on changing value of the baht are from Bank of Thailand, *Annual Economic Report,* various issues.
19. Bank of Thailand's calculations.

the world food supply in 1973. In Thailand the production index of cash crops fell from 150.2 in 1971 to 141.2 in 1972. The effects of unfavorable weather on the production of rice and maize were most acute, the indexes falling from 135.3 to 122.8 for rice and from 271.3 to 151.6 for maize.[20]

The reduced production of cereals in 1972 pushed their prices in the world market up spectacularly in 1973 and 1974. Both export and farm prices of four major food crops affected by the price rises—rice, maize, tapioca products, and sugar—either had exhibited a downward trend or had been stagnant before 1971. The export price of sugar started to rise sharply in 1972 and prices for the other three crops turned sharply upward a year later. In 1974 the average export prices of rice, maize, tapioca products, and sugar were approximately 3.2, 2.2, 2.5, and 3.6 times the average for 1967–70.

The shortage of rice in the world market coupled with Thailand's sharply decreased production and increased exports in 1972 threatened to force domestic rice prices up to a level that was unacceptable to both the government and consumers. Realizing that consumers would not easily accept a change in the government's policy of maintaining low prices for rice, Thailand's staple food, the government decided to continue its policy. This forced the government to intervene extensively in the rice market in 1973 and 1974. It used a premium—an export tax levied on rice exporters—to insulate the domestic market from the inflationary impact of excess demand. The premiums and domestic wholesale prices of rice rose and fell together from September 1972 until June 1975, when a new farm price-support program caused the wholesale price to rise despite a fall in export prices.

Export quotas and a rice reserve program were used to insure a sufficient supply of rice for domestic consumption. Upward pressure on domestic prices caused the government on June 12, 1973, to ban all rice exports, with the exception of those under government-to-government contracts. The ban was lifted in early 1974 when the substantially larger 1973 crop came on the market, but exports continued to be restricted throughout 1974 while domestice rice stockpiles were being replenished.

Government measures succeeded, despite strong world pressure, in keeping domestic prices at an acceptable level. Between April 1971 and March 1974, the average local price of rice increased about 3.0 times while the export price increased 5.3 times. However, when world production improved after 1974, the world price was only marginally higher than the domestic price.

20. Bank of Thailand, *Monthly Bulletin*, various issues; 1963 = 100 for all indexes of agricultural production.

The Thai government also imposed export quotas on sugar to insure an adequate domestic supply and employed the same tactics as with rice to keep the domestic price low. Between 1971 and 1975 the average export price of sugar increased nearly 4.5 times, with most of the increase occurring in 1974. In early 1974, sugar was placed under price control; by November the world price of white sugar was approximately six times the controlled price. As a result of the difference, smuggling became widespread and a lucrative black market was created in Thailand. A premium levied on exports in mid-1974 lasted until January 1976 when the export price dropped below the level of the premium.

Response to the Oil Crisis

There is no doubt that Thailand was adversely affected by the higher oil prices. Virtually all of the oil consumed in the country is imported, and it is estimated that 85 percent of the country's energy requirement is met by oil. In the long run the skyrocketing price of oil tends to turn the terms of trade against primary exporting countries like Thailand because they are unable to pass higher production costs on to importing countries in the form of higher export prices.

The price of crude oil started rising in April 1973 when OPEC increased its price 5.7 percent in response to the February devaluation of the dollar. Since the value of the baht was tied to the dollar, the price Thailand had to pay for the imported crude oil increased by the same percentage. By the third quarter of 1974 the price of imported crude oil had approximately quadrupled.

Because Thailand was classified as a neutral country, its imports of Arab oil were not cut off during the embargo in late 1973, but they were reduced by the same rate as OPEC's oil production. The government responded immediately to the threat of insufficient oil supplies by adopting measures to restrict domestic oil consumption and by finding other sources of supply. Short-run conservation measures ranged from rationing the limited reserves to restricting the hours of the entertainment businesses to reducing the number of neon lights and advertising signs on the streets.[21]

As is usually the case, the rationing hurt small users and new customers most. In the last quarter of 1973 and the first quarter of 1974 the activities

21. Plans were developed for the construction of two nuclear plants to generate electricity, but opposition from environmental groups and other difficulties made progress slow.

of the small coastal fishing boats, which account for nearly 30 percent of the total marine fish catch, were practically paralyzed. The tin-mining industry was also hit hard. Many small mine owners were forced to shorten work hours or to stop operating altogether, and investment in new mines fell. As a result, the production of tin concentrates declined sharply from 28.6 billion tons in 1973 to 27.8 billion in 1974 and 22.4 billion in 1975.[22] The conservation measures and economic slowdown reduced the growth rates of the electricity-generating and service industries. Electricity consumption in Bangkok and its environs dropped 0.6 percent in 1974 in contrast to a growth of 12.3 percent in 1973. In the services industry the rate of growth fell from 9.9 percent in 1973 to 7 percent in 1974, but recovered to 8.1 percent and 8.6 percent in 1975 and 1976, respectively, when the oil conservation controls were lifted.

Fiscal and monetary measures as well as direct price controls and subsidies were employed first to counter the inflationary impact of the crude oil price increases in the first half of 1974 and later to stimulate the economy when the oil crisis plunged the world into a deep recession. The concentration on conservation led the government to raise the excise tax on certain petroleum products and the property tax on owners of passenger cars. When the oil embargo was lifted in early 1974, the immediate problem became inflation and possibly hyperinflation. Thus the Thai government abandoned the fiscal measures aimed at restricting consumption and adopted direct price controls over both wholesale and retail prices. The controls were aimed at minimizing consumption of products that were not available from domestic sources. In addition, a National Energy Administration was established to handle the energy problem.

The wholesale prices of all types of petroleum products were allowed to increase but retail prices were not. The government shared the burden as the gap between wholesale and retail prices shrank by reducing the business taxes and custom duties on many petrolum products. When OPEC announced a 10 percent increase in the price of crude oil in October 1975, the government decided to subsidize the oil distributors directly and keep the retail prices of all petroleum products at their current levels.[23] The government managed through controls and subsidies to keep the price of petroleum products in Thailand lower than in most of the non-oil-exporting countries and thus lessened the inflationary pressure on the general price level.

22. Part of the sharp reduction in 1975 was due to the suspension of the right granted to Temco to do offshore mining in the Andaman Sea.

23. By March 1977 the government had paid more than 1 billion baht in subsidies. The burden of subsidizing the oil distributors and the urgent need for larger national defense expenditures led the new government to abandon the subsidies and allow the retail prices of all petroleum products to rise on March 15, 1977.

Monetary policy was also employed to combat the sudden jump in the price level after the oil embargo. The rapid rise in the price level together with the unusually high rate of bank credit expansion in 1973 (42.9 percent above the 1972 level whereas the average rise in 1966–72 was 15.8 percent) and the widespread belief that some of the bank credits were used to finance speculative inventory holdings persuaded the Bank of Thailand to take measures to restrain credit expansion by commercial banks. In January 1974 the Bank of Thailand raised its lending rate to commercial banks from 10 percent to 11 percent and elevated the ceiling rates on all types of commercial banks' credit by 1 percent. In March the required reserves ratio on all types of deposits was raised from 7 percent to 8 percent and commercial banks were allowed to increase the rates paid on all types of deposits except demand deposits by 1 percent.

These measures brought about a quick retraction in the rate of bank credit expansion, to only 13.4 percent above the level at the end of 1973, and a liquidity shortage in the banking sector developed. The shortage was attributed partly to the high cost of borrowing from abroad (another important source of funds for Thai commercial banks) owing to high interest rates around the world, and partly to the restrictive measures taken by the Bank of Thailand. The liquidity shortage together with the economic slowdown in the industrial countries after the oil crisis convinced the Bank of Thailand to switch to an expansionary policy, and in September 1974 it reduced the required reserve ratio from 8 percent to 7 percent and raised the amount the commercial banks could borrow from the bank.

Response to Economic Recession

The most important factor responsible for the economic slump Thailand experienced between 1974 and 1976 was the economic recession in the industrial countries, though the fall of the former French Indochinese states to communism and the American military withdrawal from Thailand in 1976 were contributing factors. Thailand was shielded somewhat from the adverse effects of recession in the industrial countries because only two of its seven major export commodities were significantly affected. These two commodities, tin and rubber, accounted for only 15.7 percent of the total value of exports in 1972; furthermore, only 5.8 percent of total export earnings came from manufactured goods excluding tin metal, and a large portion of the manufactured exports, with the possible exception of textiles, went to neighboring or other developing countries.[24] The fall of Laos, Cambodia, and

24. Bank of Thailand, *Monthly Bulletin,* various issues.

South Vietnam to communism was not a severe economic blow since none was an important trade partner of Thailand. While official figures show that trade with Laos fell by half from 1974 to 1975,[25] there was a sizable border trade that went unrecorded, as there was with Cambodia. The withdrawal of U.S. military personnel caused the proportion of Thai imports from the United States to fall from 16 percent in 1972 to 13 percent in 1976.

The rapid slowdown in economic activities in 1974 forced the Thai government to use fiscal policy for the first time to stabilize short-run aggregate demand. Little effort had been made before then to use either discretionary monetary or fiscal measures to stabilize demand. Changes in money supply were determined by endogenous factors such as the balance of payments, bank credit expansion, and government budget deficits or surpluses which, in turn, had been determined by developmental needs, administrative costs, and expected tax revenues. Occasionally a tariff rate change was made to correct external imbalances. Fiscal policy that affects money supply (for example, the financing of the budget deficit) had been governed by a long-run growth plan rather than by Keynesian short-run aggregate demand stabilization.

After consistently showing a deficit in the preceding three years, the Thai budget turned to a surplus of about 2 billion baht in 1974. The government had in fact planned for a deficit of about 10 billion baht, but inflation had caused tax revenues to increase dramatically while planned expenditures had been suspended because of inflated construction costs. The government announced its determination to use the 1975 budget as a means to stimulate the economy even if it meant incurring a deficit. Many short-run projects were undertaken, such as job creation programs in rural areas, farm price-support programs, low-cost housing projects, and programs to provide cheap credit to farmers. Planned government expenditures increased from 36 billion baht in 1974 to 50.5 billion baht in 1975 and finally to 62.7 billion baht in 1976. The planned deficits for those years were 9.8 billion baht, 11.5 billion baht, and 14.0 billion baht.[26] Even though expenditures in 1975 and 1976 were substantially lower than planned, the deficit in 1976 was about 2 billion baht more than planned because tax revenues were less than expected.

The government tried to finance as much as possible of the budget deficits of 1975 and 1976 with loans from commercial banks, government savings banks, and other financial institutions because it was less inflationary than

---

25. Ibid.

26. Thailand, Office of the Prime Minister, National Economic and Social Development Board, *The Third National Economic and Social Development Plan, 1972–1976.*

borrowing from the central bank or drawing down the Treasury's cash balance. At the same time, a large tax reduction was enacted to stimulate private consumption and investment, but it was implemented carefully to cause the least inflation possible. In January 1974 the government announced a reduction of custom duties. Business excise taxes on fishing equipment were also reduced to help the depressed fishing industry. Then in February 1975 a temporary large-scale reduction in import duties was announced. On the monetary side, cheap and long-term credits were provided for industries—principally textiles and mining—suffering from the higher costs of production and depressed demand.

These measures appear to have been relatively successful, for the Thai economy did not fare as badly as many developing countries did during the worldwide recession. Thailand's rate of growth in 1975 was 5.0 percent, slightly lower than the 5.4 percent rate achieved in 1974 (table 7-1). By 1975 the inflation was largely under control so the inflation rate was not much higher than it was during the relatively normal period in the second half of the 1960s. Because of the reduced inflation rate, the rate of growth improved slightly in 1976.

The high level of government investment in 1975 and 1976 was responsible for an increase in the rate of growth of capital formation. Gross fixed capital formation had been stagnant between 1969 and 1972 (it declined from 13.9 percent in 1969 to 6.4 percent in 1970 and to 0.3 percent in 1971, then increased to 3.8 percent in 1972, but still was far below pre-1970s rates).[27] In 1973 it rose rapidly with the expansion caused by the commodity boom. The high level of investment in 1973 and 1974 was the result of growth in the private sector (investment expenditures in the government sector were actually declining). Government fiscal measures in 1975 and 1976 countered some of the deflationary pressures in the private sector and probably played a part in the better than average performance of the Thai economy during that difficult period.

Policy Evaluation and Recommendations

Most of the policy measures implemented in Thailand during 1971–76 were not part of an overall macroeconomic program but were adopted to counter particular economic problems at particular times. There is little doubt that the measures lessened the pain but it is questionable whether they cured the wounds. Indeed, the aftereffects of some of the special measures

27. Thailand, Office of the Prime Minister, National Economic and Social Development Board, *National Income of Thailand,* various issues.

may even prove to be detrimental to the economy in the long run. The costs and benefits of policy measures as well as the feasibility of administering them must be weighed carefully before they are put into effect. While there may be numerous arguments in support of particular measures in the short run, those benefits must be weighed against long-run costs to the economy.

The complete ban on rice exports by private rice exporters, for example, insured sufficient supply in the domestic market and perhaps lower prices, but it made long-standing customers suffer more. This was one of the major reasons for the gradual loss of Thailand's traditional rice markets such as Hong Kong to other producers such as the People's Republic of China. Thailand must always remember that under normal circumstances it sells its export products, which are mainly agricultural products, in a buyer's market. The uninterrupted supply of rice is more important than anything else to the importing country. Thus, during a period of worldwide food shortages, Thailand must provide its good and long-standing customers with food even if this entails higher costs to domestic consumers. Higher prices for cereals, especially rice, might even be beneficial to the Thai economy in the long run if they improve the distribution of income in favor of farmers, the poorest group in the country.

Rice premiums proved to be an effective means of controlling the domestic price of rice in 1973–75. If the domestic price had risen to the world level during the period, then the well-being of the urban poor would have been severely affected. Nevertheless, it should be asked whether it is fair to let the farmers bear the burden of feeding the urban poor and be deprived of the windfall gain from the high commodity prices. In the interest of long-run political and social stability, a gradual elimination of the rice premium should be given serious consideration and other measures found to help the urban poor.

During the 1973–76 period Thailand's price control program was far from being well managed. Lack of manpower to administer the program and to prevent speculative inventory holdings turned the program, especially for the products with many retailers and wholesalers such as rice, sugar, eggs, and meat, into nothing more than an announcement of the controlled price levels. Prices in the markets were usually above the controlled levels, and sometimes much higher. Among the many undesirable effects of the program was the increase in speculative inventory holdings following the announcement of the price control program. The announcement also caused goods to disappear from the market and created black markets, thereby further aggravating the inflationary pressures. It is probably better to let prices work themselves out than to try to implement a poorly planned and poorly managed price control program.

The attempt to keep the retail price of petroleum products low by reducing business taxes and subsidizing distributors certainly helped reduce the rate of inflation but probably also increased the inequality of the distribution of income because the rich consume more oil than the poor.

While some of the policy measures may have done more harm than good in the long run, others were definitely a step in the right direction. Those that promoted the development of the rural areas are good examples. Firms that chose to locate their factories outside of metropolitan Bangkok were given the largest promotional incentives. Several programs to aid the rural population were started: a village council program, a program to increase the credit commercial banks extend to the agricultural sector, a farm price-support program, and a land reform program. There was much talk about the latter two but very limited implementation. The programs, especially the village council program, were not well planned and were widely perceived as politically motivated. Yet the programs were a bold innovation in the economic policy of Thailand and a move in the right direction.

Improving Thailand's Stabilization Policy

Malaysia's success in revaluing its currency vis-à-vis the U.S. dollar to reduce the inflationary pressure from abroad during 1971–74 is often cited as an example for Thailand. But the structure of the Thai economy makes the country susceptible to balance-of-payments deficits, and its balance-of-payments surpluses have been due to factors exogenous to the economic system.[28]

The foreign exchange received from U.S. military expenditures and to a lesser extent from loans and direct investment enabled Thailand to avoid balance-of-payments deficits in the 1960s. The first signs of balance-of-payments problems appeared near the end of the decade and they were dealt with by massive restrictions on imports. The skyrocketing of commodity prices caused by worldwide crop failures and the speculative holding of raw materials temporarily eliminated Thailand's balance-of-payments problems. But with the oil crisis and the return to more normal levels of food production the problems reappeared. Even if there had been no oil crisis and the ensuing high oil prices, Thailand would have had balance-of-payments problems that would have impeded growth had it not been for the commodity boom. Thus luck was on the Thai side in the second half of the 1960s and in the first half of the 1970s with respect to the balance of payments. Thai-

28. See Nimit Nontapunthawat, "Thailand's Foreign Exchange Reserves Position in the Past Fifteen Years" (Bangkok: U.S. Agency for International Development, 1975).

land enjoyed reasonable rates of growth during the decade even though the annual deficit in the merchandise trade account never fell below 8 billion baht. However, to insure the continuation of this rate of growth, the trade gap must be reduced or capital inflows must be encouraged to eliminate the balance-of-payments deficit. To close the trade gap by import restrictions al⟨ ⟩e is not possible because imports of capital goods, intermediate inputs, and petroleum products, which accounted for 81 percent of total imports in 1976, are essential for domestic production and cannot be reduced without a reduction in the level of production. Therefore, an increase in exports is required to close the trade gap.

The chronic deficit in the trade account is partly due to the import substitution policies of the 1960s. The high tax cuts offered as inducements for domestic production of goods created industries that were heavily dependent on imported capital goods and intermediate inputs. In 1960, intermediate products accounted for only 18 percent of total imports. By 1970 the share had grown to 25 percent. The balance-of-payments problems in 1968 and 1969 convinced policymakers that the decade of import substitution policies had not resulted in a reduction in imports but rather only in a change in the form of imports—from finished products to intermediate products. The Board of Investment after a review of its industrialization policy ended incentives to import intermediate products and switched the emphasis to incentives for industries that produce for export. The export value of manufactured products did increase from 2.3 billion baht in 1970 to 8.8 billion baht in 1975. A large portion of the fourfold increase, however, was probably due to inflation.[29] Greater efforts must be directed toward increasing exports in order to prevent the balance-of-payments problem from becoming an obstacle to growth.

Past experience should have taught policymakers that the inflow of foreign capital should not be promoted without regard to the costs involved. The structure of industrial production is the product of past policy. The resilience of the structure established with incentives to foreign and domestic investors is evidenced by the fact that the share of intermediate inputs in total imports increased from 25 percent in 1970, when import incentives were eliminated, to 28 percent in 1976. Although the increase is probably due to the appreciation of the yen vis-à-vis the baht, the change in the structure of industrial production after 1970 is probably small.

When the Thai government revised its investment promotion law, it set up

---

29. More significant perhaps is the fact that manufactured exports grew only slightly faster than total exports. Manufactured exports were 16.2 percent of total exports in 1970 and 20 percent in 1975.

a center to advise foreign investors on customs and financial matters and to help them to get visas, licenses, work permits, and trademarks without having to cut through the red tape of several different ministries. But if fiscal incentives given to foreign investors and protection given to the industries become excessive, they could foster industries that are highly inefficient and that would never be able to compete in the world market or even in the protected domestic market. The belief that tax incentives are crucial to induce foreign investment should be discarded. As Meier put it, "The foreign investor is less likely to be attracted by the prospect of receiving an exemption after a profit is made than he is by being sure of a profit in the first place."[30] Political, social, and economic stability and a clearly stated long-run policy toward foreign investment are probably more important than fiscal incentives.

The ability of the Thai economy to withstand wave after wave of economic disturbances from abroad during 1971–76 was due to both its inherent strength and good luck. It was luck that the exchange-rate and oil crises happened to coincide with the worldwide food shortage. Thailand's strength lies in the fact that it is a rice bowl of East and Southeast Asia as well as a major supplier of other cereals to the densely populated eastern Asia. As long as the world faces the problem of feeding its inhabitants, being a food surplus country will be one of Thailand's greatest strengths. The problem of insufficient food supply seems likely to worsen rather than improve despite the increased yields of the new strains of grains. For example, as an increasing number of nations extend their territorial waters to the two-hundred-mile limit, consumption will shift from fish to meat, which will increase demand for animal feeds such as maize and tapioca products, both of which are important exports of Thailand.

Unless Thailand's export promotion effort is successful or another export rice boom occurs, balance-of-payments deficits will probably be an obstacle to the country's economic growth. Import restrictions will reduce the growth rate but this probably cannot be avoided. The high growth rate of the 1960s will be difficult to achieve unless the ASEAN countries join forces and bargain collectively with the bigger nations in trade negotiations or a substantial volume of oil and gas is discovered in the Gulf of Thailand and the Andaman Sea.[31] Either of these events would push the country back on the rapid growth path of the 1960s.

30. Gerald M. Meier, *The International Economics of Development: Theory and Policy* (Harper, 1968), p. 149.
31. Natural gas has been discovered in the Gulf of Thailand and there are encouraging signs of substantial crude oil deposits in the northeastern region of the country.

CHAPTER EIGHT

Economic Interaction in the Pacific Basin

THE RESPONSES of the six Pacific basin countries to the four world crises varied with their particular economic and political circumstances and with the economic structure of each country. Responses also depended on whether a country had a role in originating the crisis, as did the United States and Japan in the breakdown of the Bretton Woods system, or were just reacting to the event, as all six were to the oil crisis.

Natural resources—both endowment and the particular content—accounted for the most important structural difference among the countries. Japan and the Republic of Korea, both poor in natural resources, are forced to import raw materials and food and must export processed and manufactured products to pay for them. The United States has an abundance of some natural resources, but a shortage of others; it thus exports agricultural products, imports petroleum, and both exports and imports manufactured products. Australia while having substantial manufacturing capacity is particularly rich in natural resources and thus exports primary products and imports manufactured goods. By way of contrast, both the Philippines and Thailand have abundant natural resources, the former more heavily involved in minerals and tree crops and the latter in agricultural products, but neither is as advanced as Australia is in manufacturing.

The Breakdown in the International Monetary System

The United States and to a smaller extent Japan had central roles in the breakdown of the Bretton Woods system and its replacement by managed floating exchange rates. For them, interactions in the Pacific basin added little to the crisis. Economic relations with Japan and the United States were primarily responsible for the impact of the crisis on the other countries.

Small countries in general found the Bretton Woods system of pegged exchange rates quite congenial to their needs. It permitted them to capture the economic benefits of being part of an optimal currency area without seriously constraining their ability to make balance-of-payments corrections through changes in exchange rates. While the breakdown of the system had few direct consequences for Australia, the Republic of Korea, the Philippines, and Thailand, fluctuations in the exchange rate of the yen and dollar did. Once the yen-dollar rate became disturbed, exchange-rate changes became an important vehicle for transmitting economic impulses among the countries.

Under the rules (or lack of rules) of a managed floating exchange-rate system, small countries have the option either of pegging their currency to another currency, to a special basket of currencies, or to special drawing rights, or of floating independently. Seldom are their capital markets sophisticated or deep enough for them to allow private demand and supply to determine their exchange rate, so they generally choose to peg in one form or another. Optimally a small country would peg its currency to that of its principal trading partner (although it still must encounter transaction costs as long as it maintains an independent currency). However, if it has two or more trading partners of about equal size and their bilateral exchange rate is unstable, as the dollar-yen rate was in the 1970s, the small country faces a dilemma. In the 1970s Korea and Thailand pegged their currencies rather rigidly to the U.S. dollar, the Philippines showed somewhat greater variance, and Australia allowed its dollar to move more independently of the U.S. dollar over the years (table 8-1).

During the Bretton Woods era, Australia nominally pegged its currency to the British pound, but by 1967 the Australian dollar was actually pegged to the U.S. dollar, as was evident in Australia's completely offsetting the British devaluation. While the old system was breaking down, Australia's real economic growth continued at a good pace, even though its currency was becoming undervalued and creating the risk of domestic inflation. The undervaluation attracted foreign capital, which swelled the country's foreign reserves and stimulated domestic monetary expansion. Furthermore, pegging to the U.S. dollar meant that in 1970 the Australian dollar was effectively devalued 1 percent on a trade-weighted basis—just the opposite of what was needed. At the end of 1971 when the U.S. dollar was formally

Table 8-1. *Fluctuations in Exchange Rates of Australia, Japan, Korea, the Philippines, and Thailand against the U.S. Dollar, by Quarter, 1970–77*

Year and quarter	Japan	Australia	Korea	Philippines	Thailand
1970					
First	0.00280	1.120	0.00327	0.20040	0.04808
Second	0.00280	1.120	0.00323	0.16321	0.04808
Third	0.00280	1.120	0.00321	0.15980	0.04808
Fourth	0.00280	1.120	0.00317	0.15620	0.04808
1971					
First	0.00280	1.120	0.00312	0.15550	0.04808
Second	0.00280	1.120	0.00306	0.15601	0.04808
Third	0.00299	1.130	0.00270	0.15620	0.04808
Fourth	0.00318	1.165	0.00270	0.15620	0.04808
1972					
First	0.00325	1.1910	0.00262	0.15558	0.04808
Second	0.00325	1.1910	0.00252	0.14921	0.04808
Third	0.00325	1.1910	0.00251	0.14761	0.04808
Fourth	0.00325	1.2750	0.00251	0.14761	0.04808
1973					
First	0.00352	1.3464	0.00251	0.14743	0.04808
Second	0.00377	1.5143	0.00251	0.14771	0.04778
Third	0.00377	1.4336	0.00251	0.14806	0.04908
Fourth	0.00364	1.4826	0.00252	0.14826	0.04908
1974					
First	0.00342	1.4843	0.00251	0.14853	0.04908
Second	0.00358	1.4840	0.00251	0.14859	0.04908
Third	0.00339	1.4757	0.00251	0.14900	0.04908
Fourth	0.00333	1.3125	0.00234	0.14275	0.04908
1975					
First	0.00341	1.3477	0.00207	0.14192	0.04908
Second	0.00342	1.3417	0.00207	0.14227	0.04908
Third	0.00335	1.2891	0.00207	0.13303	0.04908
Fourth	0.00329	1.2623	0.00207	0.13322	0.04904
1976					
First	0.00331	1.2569	0.00207	0.13382	0.04902
Second	0.00334	1.2353	0.00207	0.13446	0.04902
Third	0.00344	1.2422	0.00207	0.13444	0.04902
Fourth	0.00341	1.1664	0.00207	0.13445	0.04902
1977					
First	0.00350	1.0926	0.00207	0.13481	0.04902
Second	0.00363	1.1059	0.00207	0.13488	0.04902
Third	0.00376	1.1108	0.00207	0.13507	0.04902
Fourth	0.00405	1.1269	0.00207	0.13524	0.04902

Source: International Monetary Fund, *International Financial Statistics*, various issues.

Table 8-2. *Percent Change in the Effective Exchange Rates of Six Pacific Basin Countries, by Quarter, 1971–77*[a]

Year and quarter	Australia	Japan	Korea	Philippines	Thailand	United States
1971						
First	n.a.	n.a.	n.a.	n.a.	n.a.	n.a.
Second	−0.6	3.3	−43.0	−0.8	−1.4	2.3
Third	−2.9	32.0	−12.6	−10.6	−13.5	−9.0
Fourth	−0.4	20.6	−16.1	−13.0	−15.2	−8.6
1972						
First	−8.6	12.2	−19.3	−5.8	−7.4	−4.3
Second	3.0	6.2	−14.0	−19.8	−0.4	−0.0
Third	0.3	0.3	1.3	−0.0	−0.8	1.2
Fourth	35.2	−1.7	0.5	0.4	0.8	2.7
1973						
First	14.7	42.3	−23.3	−21.8	31.0	−17.3
Second	−8.6	−3.9	−2.8	−3.8	−8.1	−8.7
Third	24.0	−3.0	0.1	−0.7	9.4	2.2
Fourth	15.4	−16.3	11.1	11.9	15.9	11.3
1974						
First	−5.8	5.4	−4.4	−3.8	−5.6	−6.0
Second	4.6	−10.8	4.3	4.9	4.8	3.0
Third	−32.7	−13.6	9.7	6.1	9.0	9.2
Fourth	1.5	1.5	−53.8	−17.5	−4.3	−0.8
1975						
First	0.6	7.0	−5.1	−2.6	−7.2	−2.6
Second	0.0	−0.3	1.6	2.0	3.0	7.7
Third	−1.3	0.8	6.3	−18.5	14.1	14.3
Fourth	1.1	−2.2	1.3	1.4	−1.0	0.5
1976						
First	1.0	9.5	−3.7	−0.7	−4.2	3.3
Second	2.1	6.6	−1.1	0.3	−0.4	4.0
Third	1.3	16.0	−6.5	−6.3	−8.4	15.8
Fourth	−39.7	−2.0	2.9	1.2	0.2	7.8
1977						
First	0.3	26.5	−8.8	−7.7	−7.5	10.0
Second	−0.1	17.7	−5.8	−3.3	−5.7	2.2
Third	−5.3	4.7	−1.6	−2.3	−1.9	1.5
Fourth	−9.5	46.8	−16.3	−13.0	−18.6	−5.7

Source: U.S. Federal Reserve Bank of San Francisco, *Pacific Basin Economic Indicators*, various issues; changes are compound annual rates of change.

n.a. Not available.

a. Minus sign denotes a devaluation.

devalued as part of the Smithsonian agreement, Australia's adjustment in its exchange rate with the U.S. dollar was not large enough to prevent its effective exchange rate from depreciating another 8 percent (table 8-2). Australia's Liberal-Country party government was not prepared to appreciate the currency because of its negative effect on farmers' incomes and thus by implication preferred to accept domestic inflation as an adjustment mechanism. Inflation occurred in part because of rising prices of Japanese goods brought on by the yen appreciation. In December 1972, following the election of a Labor government, Australia appreciated its currency by 7 percent in terms of the U.S. dollar (yielding an effective appreciation of about the same amount). By then, though, the inflation problem could not be headed off.

Australia continued to peg its currency to the U.S. dollar despite the beginning of managed floating in March 1973, but also appreciated its dollar twice against the U.S. currency during the course of 1973; by January 1974 the effective exchange rate was fully 20 percent above its mid-1970 value. With the worsening of domestic economic conditions in September 1974, Australia devalued its dollar by 12 percent and shifted from a policy of pegging to only the U.S. dollar to one of pegging to a special trade-weighted basket of currencies. The effective exchange rate remained fairly stable for two years while the Australian dollar depreciated against the stronger world currencies. But in November 1976 a huge devaluation of 17.5 percent was undertaken to improve the balance of payments and increase incomes of primary producers. Subsequently a modified independent float was adopted. The Australian dollar appreciated about 2 percent at the beginning of 1977, but then depreciated about 4 percent in the last quarter of the year.

The usual policy of the Republic of Korea has been to change the exchange rate of the won (which is pegged to the U.S. dollar) to adjust for inflation. Since the inflation rate of Korea consistently has been quite high, the won has only declined against the dollar. Thus the devaluation of the won in 1970 was quite unrelated to international monetary events. Korean trade has been very responsive to devaluations of the won and the trade balance has improved.

Economic fluctuations in the United States and Japan and changes in the yen-dollar exchange rate have great impacts on Korea. The won was devalued against the dollar even as the dollar was itself declining at the end of 1971 and devalued again along with the dollar in February 1973 (table 8-1). The massive change in the won's value vis-à-vis the yen caused exports to Japan to increase greatly, but it also meant an increase in the price of Japanese imports which caused inflationary pressure in Korea. The won was devalued once more against the dollar at the end of 1974 and then rigidly pegged for three years. Thus the effective rate of the won rose and fell with the dollar (table 8-2).

The Philippines in February 1970 became one of the first countries to float its currency when it moved to correct a growing balance-of-payments deficit. The peso devalued about 40 percent before it stabilized at the end of 1970. Exports did increase sharply after the devaluation despite the recession in the United States and Japan. At the same time, inflationary pressure was generated, particularly because import policy was not liberalized along with the devaluation (in an earlier devaluation it had been). Concern over inflation led to restrictive demand management policy. The peso was de facto pegged to the U.S. dollar, but it was permitted to float down 6 percent vis-à-vis the dollar during the first half of 1972 and then again at the end of 1974 and in the second half of 1975.

Fluctuations in the yen-dollar exchange rate cause difficult problems for the Philippines. About 35 percent of Philippine trade is with the United States and an equal volume with Japan. Even if the Philippines were to peg the peso to a basket of currencies heavily weighted by the dollar and yen, domestic instability would still come from both major trading partners because of the differences in the goods they buy from and sell to the Philippines. Since full stability is no longer an option for the Philippines, it seeks partial stability by pegging softly to the dollar. It has strong links with the U.S. economy through capital transactions as well as trade flows.

The deterioration in the performance of the economy of Thailand in the early 1970s had little to do with world monetary instability. Though Thailand had fewer traditional economic ties with the United States than either Korea or the Philippines, its economy was so strongly influenced by U.S. military expenditures related to the Vietnam War that the baht was more strictly pegged to the U.S. dollar than were other currencies. Indeed in 1970–77, the baht exchange rate showed more stability against the U.S. dollar than did the Australian dollar, the yen, the won, or the peso. The baht-dollar rate was stable before and after the Smithsonian agreement and thus they were devalued together, as they were again in February 1973. The baht's only adjustment against the dollar was a 4 percent appreciation in July 1973. Thailand should perhaps have ceased to peg the baht so rigidly to offset the inflation caused by the 1972–74 commodity boom. Even in 1973 when the current account was in its best position, Thailand continued to have large deficits in its balance of payments; thus it appeared as if an effective devaluation of the baht was necessary.

The breakdown of the Bretton Woods system caused a serious problem for both the United States and Japan basically because it fueled inflationary fires that persisted for many years, and from 1971 onward the instability of the dollar-yen rate caused difficulties for Australia, Korea, the Philippines, and Thailand. Though stability in exchange rates is desirable, it should not be allowed to perpetuate a disequilibrium. If an exchange-rate correction, which is bound to occur eventually, is very fast, adjusting to it is difficult and there is likely to be some overshooting (especially if the adjustment has been long delayed). Greater stability in the yen-dollar rate should be sought by reducing the divergencies between the economies of Japan and the United States and by prompt adjustment to the divergencies that do occur.

Small countries must have some flexibility in pegging their exchange rates as a means of insulating themselves from external disturbances, even though such insulation has not proven very successful in the past. However, the exchange rate cannot be used as a domestic policy instrument even by a relatively small country without hurting other countries. For instance, the sharp depreciation of the Korean won in 1974 had serious consequences for the economy of Taiwan, one of its competitors for export markets whose interests were not considered in the policy decision.

The Bretton Woods system left a legacy of excessive use of the U.S. dollar in the Pacific basin. Japan's trade in the region is greater than that of the United States, yet currencies continue to be tied to the dollar and most trade to be denominated in dollars even when it involves Japan and not the United States. As more countries peg their currencies to a weighted basket of currencies, more trade is invoiced in yen, and more financing is arranged in Tokyo, the balance between the yen and the dollar is improving. Moreover, the Japanese government has begun to encourage the opening up of Japan's capital market to enhance the process. However, private asset owners as well as central banks in the Pacific basin must increase the share of yen in their reserves and reduce the share of dollars. Their portfolio adjustment can lead to a weakening of the dollar relative to the yen unless the Bank of Japan increases the growth of its money supply to accommodate demand for yen and the U.S. Federal Reserve reduces the growth of the dollar money supply to match the reduced demand for dollars.

The 1972–74 Commodity Boom

The United States and Japan were equally to blame for the 1972–74 commodity boom and subsequent collapse. The U.S. role was greater in creating the preconditions for the boom while Japan was more directly involved in pushing up world prices as the major purchaser of commodities in the Pacific basin. Both had rapid expansions in 1972–73 which when added to the expansions in other OECD countries resulted in excess demand for raw materials.

Inflation in the United States was significantly worsened by the rise in prices of commodities. Furthermore the rise of import prices helped undermine the mandatory price-control system, which was the principal instrument for fighting inflation. When price controls were lifted, the suppressed inflation burst forth. Price rises of internationally traded commodities also added to inflation in Japan, but less so than in the United States. The delayed improvement in Japan's terms of trade as a result of the 1971 appreciation in the yen meant that the yen price of imported raw materials rose less than the dollar price, making the situation more manageable in Japan.

In Australia, the Philippines, and Thailand, all producers and exporters of raw materials, the impact of the commodity boom was marked and somewhat similar. The increase in external demand for Australia's raw materials started in March 1972 and the terms of trade improved rapidly for about a year. The rise in raw material prices was transmitted directly into the economy through three separate channels. Domestic prices of exported goods rose somewhat even though there existed a tax mechanism for automatically stabilizing the domestic prices of such commodities. Real incomes rose greatly, particularly in the mineral industries, increasing demand for labor and pushing wages up in all industries since little slack existed in the labor market. Furthermore the commodity boom came during a period in which monetary policy was permissive. Thus when Australia's balance-of-payments surplus increased sharply, the domestic money supply expanded and became highly inflationary. As a further consequence of the commodity boom, long-term contracts governing minerals exports caused tension between Australian exporters and Japanese importers. In some cases the contracts were modified and prices raised.

Australian monetary policy was very slow to react to the threat of inflation. Given the surplus in the balance of payments, monetary stringency could only have been enforced with a change in the exchange rate; the government's unwillingness to appreciate the currency meant that when the Australian dollar was finally revalued at the end of 1972, it was too late to head off the inflation. Further policy action, in the form of an across-the-board 25 percent reduction of import tariffs in mid-1973, came after most of the damage had been done. Australia's exports are heavily concentrated in a few mineral industries and the equilibrium exchange rate is dependent on the success of those industries. There is thus no assurance that adjustments in the exchange rate alone will permit the continued prosperity of secondary manufacturing where many Australians are employed. Sophisticated use of many policy instruments may be necessary to sustain domestic balance.

Prices of the particular metal ores that the Philippines exports did not increase until March 1973, but the commodity boom led to strong export performance and rapid economic growth in 1973. The balance of payments also recorded a large surplus. The commodity boom merely perpetuated the inflation the Philippines had been suffering since early 1970 when the peso was devalued and raised it slightly by encouraging a gigantic increase in the domestic money supply—the internal reflection of the balance-of-payments surplus. The internal tax system on commodities, geared to export prices, did however drain off some of the income windfall that would otherwise have gone to the minerals industry.

Import prices also rose for the Philippines as a result of the commodity boom. They went up a little earlier than export prices because of the need to import rice in 1972–73, but in the end both rose about the same amount. Thus the Philippine terms of trade were rather erratic, first falling, then rising in 1973–74, and then falling again.

Thailand benefited from the boom in its minerals exports and even more so in its food exports, and the boom had a strong expansionary impact on the economy in 1972 and 1973. While some of the expansionary pressure led to inflation, much of it generated real output as Thailand, in contrast to Australia, had an elastic supply of labor. The domestic money supply was permitted to rise to finance the expansion and the higher level of inflation.

Both Thai and world food production were disappointing in 1972, so that both domestic and foreign demand for Thailand's output increased. To insulate the domestic market from the commodity price inflation, the government instituted an export-price premium and reserved most of the rice crop for domestic consumption. Though the domestic price of rice did rise, it was limited to an acceptable level by controls. Early in 1973, however, all rice exports except those under government-to-government agreements were banned and private export contracts for rice were not fulfilled. In the long run, forcing the adjustment onto customers of Thai rice proved a very serious matter indeed. A similar system to control the distribution of sugar was disastrous; it led to domestic smuggling and a black market.

In contrast to the commodity-exporting countries, Korea immediately suffered the consequences of the commodity boom. Korea is heavily dependent on imports for raw materials and thus the commodity boom raised the price of imports and added to domestic inflation. Korean real income was also adversely affected since Korea's terms of trade deteriorated persistently throughout the period. Nevertheless real economic progress continued in Korea. In fact, 1973 was a particularly good year. Korean exports to both Japan and the United States grew very rapidly both because of economic expansion in those countries and because of Korean policies promoting exports. Thus the balance-of-payments deficit actually declined. Korea was able to absorb some of the burden of higher import prices by increasing the volume of production and by just passing along higher import prices in higher export prices. As long as Korea can buy raw materials in a competitive market—that is, pay the same price for them that its industrial competitors pay—Korea need not be seriously injured by rising import prices.

Controlling inflation had been a major problem for the Korean government and the commodity boom made the job more difficult. The government attempted to use direct price controls but rising import prices put greater pressure on the control system. To avoid serious distortions the government was forced to moderate the controls. Still the major causes of Korean inflation were domestic, principally rapid growth of the money supply; the import price problem merely made the situation marginally more difficult.

With the possible exception of Japan, all of the countries in this study tried to moderate the impact on their domestic economies of the inflation caused by price rises in the commodity boom. None of them achieved much success, in part because of the failure to perceive the rises as temporary. If the 1972–74 increase had been merely the first stage of a rising trend of raw material prices, as many in Australia and elsewhere believed, then the policy of doing very little would have been correct. None of the countries had an effective instrument to deal with the problem. Appreciations of exchange rates were of limited help in insulating the raw-material exporting countries from the real external disturbance. In the face of world price rises in response to increased demand for key export commodities, an appreciation of a country's currency sufficient to maintain balance-of-payments equilibrium and to insure domestic price stability would be so drastic as to disturb its industrial sectors. But even if successful, it would force all of the inflation onto importing countries since obviously all countries cannot appreciate their currencies simultaneously. Export taxes are often imposed as a partial alternative to currency appreciation. But they introduce additional uncertainties into the pricing of internationally traded commodities and also complicate the problems of importing countries, possibly causing trade disputes. When commodity prices rise because of a decline of supply rather than increased demand, as was the case for Thai rice, it is inappropriate for the exporter to force consuming countries to bear the full force of the loss of supplies and the inflation burden as well.

Domestic politics also interfered in the adjustment process in the Pacific basin; in Australia and the United States restraining policies were not adopted because of constituent problems and the approach of elections. The success of an adjustment policy should not depend on ad hoc decisions being taken at the appropriate moment. A policy approach must be adopted that circumvents national tendencies to sacrifice long-term needs for short-run imperatives.

The Oil Crisis

The oil crisis that began with the embargo in the autumn of 1973 and the fourfold increase in prices early in 1974 was bound to have serious consequences for all countries. Japan, the one most seriously affected of the countries in this study, not only suffered a temporary physical shortage, an increase in inflation, a contraction in real activity, a deterioration in the balance of payments, and an increase in the relative price of energy, but the Japanese people were seized by panic. For some time the government was unable to quiet fears that led to a buyers' panic and a shortage of goods in the stores—even of toilet paper. The panic made it all the more difficult to deal with the significant problems of inflation and structural changes necessary to accommodate energy price rises.

The U.S. response to the oil crisis was as bad as or possibly worse than Japan's. The United States was less dependent on petroleum for energy than Japan and possessed substantial domestic oil resources, even if not enough for self-sufficiency. Yet a comprehensive energy program was not legislated until 1978 and it did not deal with petroleum. The lack of an adequate response reflected the inability of both President Ford and President Carter to convince the American people that the problem was serious and to develop a consensus on how to share the burden of the domestic adjustment.

The Philippines and Thailand, which have few oil resources or reliable alternative sources of energy, avoided some of the difficulties that could have occurred in the oil crisis and dealt immediately with their problems. Thailand, like the United States and Japan, was subjected to the supply reductions instituted by the Arab oil producers. The government responded by restricting oil consumption. This severely reduced the operations of small fishing boats and small tin mines and reduced electricity consumption.

Thailand's terms of trade deteriorated only slightly in 1974 because of the lingering effects of the commodity boom. Crude oil imports rose from $173 million (8.3 percent of total imports) in 1973 to $436 million (13.8 percent of imports) in 1974, thus worsening the balance of payments. The Thai government instituted detailed price controls on oil products to restrain overall inflation, to cut retail profit margins, and to discourage consumption of petroleum products not locally refined. It also adopted restrictive fiscal and monetary policies in January 1974 to fight the inflation, but they were eased when the world recession deepened. In October 1975 it offered subsidies to keep domestic oil prices stable despite an increase in the international price; those subsidies were reduced in March 1977 for fiscal reasons.

When the oil crisis struck, the Philippines instituted policies to make the country less dependent on highly integrated, multinational oil companies. It promoted exploration for petroleum, invested in nuclear power, introduced excise taxes and a rationing system for gasoline to promote conservation, and purchased control of the Philippine facilities of a multinational oil company. The government also sought to diversify its sources of oil imports. Though Philippine imports of oil rose from $209 million and 11.7 percent of total imports in 1973 to $619 million and 17.8 percent in 1974, the impact was cushioned by the residual effects of the commodity boom. The 74.5 percent rise in import prices was partially offset by a 45.7 percent rise in export prices. After 1974, however, Philippine export prices declined, but oil prices did not. Domestic inflation worsened considerably. Higher oil prices accounted for two-thirds of the 35 percent rise in the Philippine consumer price index between October 1973 and November 1974.

The Korean government was much more concerned about the longer run implications of the oil price rise than about the prospects of a temporary supply interruption. Since the country was heavily dependent on imported oil as a source of energy for industry, as a direct input into petrochemicals, and as a fuel for heating, the government was well aware of the dangers inherent in the oil crisis. In 1973, crude petroleum imports amounted to only $277 million or 6.5 percent of total imports. They rose dramatically to $966 million in 1974 and $1.3 billion in 1975, representing 14.1 percent and 17.5 percent of total imports in the two years. Korea was particularly concerned about the negative impact of the rise in oil import prices on the real economy, domestic inflation, and the balance of payments.

In January 1974, the Korean government undertook a special program to counter the decline in domestic economic activity with measures that included public works spending and income support for low-income families. This policy was reasonably successful as the economy grew rapidly in the first half of 1974, but slowed down in the second half because of declining exports. Domestic inflation, however, could not be contained and price controls previously adopted were removed to prevent further distortions. Monetary policy was tightened instead, to provide some measure of price restraint. To combat the serious deterioration of the balance of payments and domestic growth, the won was devalued in December 1974 and special loans were offered to business to ease the foreign debt burden and stimulate investment. Low-cost housing investment was also encouraged. In addition, the government began to explore the possibility of selling Korean goods and services to the newly enriched oil countries. All of the policies except those aimed at controlling domestic inflation were successful.

The oil crisis had no serious direct impact on the Australian economy. Australia was close to self-sufficient in petroleum and an exporter of coal and uranium. In order to cushion any inflationary consequences, domestic crude oil prices were maintained at the pre-1974 level even in 1976. With the relatively low domestic prices of energy and petrochemical materials, Australia's international competitiveness in manufacturing should have improved to some extent. The rise in world crude oil prices also had a favorable effect on Australia since it caused the price of coal and uranium to rise. Nevertheless, Australia did suffer indirectly from the oil crisis. In the subsequent world recession, which the oil crisis exacerbated, the demand for Australian exports fell notably. The fact that Japan's long-term prospects appeared decidedly less promising after the oil crisis may have discouraged foreign direct investment in Australia as well as domestic investment.

It is an interesting question whether raw-material-exporting countries or industrial countries have the greater difficulty in adjusting to the oil crisis. Part of the answer rests on which would find it easier to offset the deterioration in its terms of trade (because of higher import prices for petroleum) by increasing the price of its own export products. Factors in the production of raw materials are perhaps not so well organized that they can counter the tendency of fluctuations in world supply and demand to alter commodity prices, whereas factors involved in industrial production, such as labor unions or industrial oligopolies, can prevent price declines because they are well organized and in a good position to defend their real incomes. On the other hand, because of industrial countries' greater dependence on petroleum, an increase in the relative price of energy is more likely to raise costs, disrupt production processes, and pose a threat to their way of life than it is for developing countries. Thus the secondary repercussions would tend to be much greater in industrial countries than in primary-producing countries. The ability to adjust to an oil crisis does not seem to rest on industrial prowess; indeed, adjustment to the 1974 crisis was much easier for the developing countries than the advanced countries.

Worldwide Recession and Weak Recovery

The severity of the worldwide recession that commenced in most countries in 1974 arose from the inflationary distortions created during the unusually synchronized expansion among industrial countries in 1972–74. The oil crisis not only worsened the inflation, it caused real incomes to decline. It also made fighting the recession difficult because of its adverse impact on the industrial countries' payments balances. As it turned out, the lingering inflation was the most serious factor inhibiting recovery.

The recession hit bottom in the United States during the first half of 1975 in response to stimulative monetary and fiscal policies, though American imports continued to decline until the fall. Once recovery took hold, the expansion continued quite steadily (with some quarter-to-quarter variance). The upturn of industrial production in Japan preceded that in the United States by a month or so. After a strong start, recovery proceeded haltingly and was very weak compared to earlier recoveries. Both the Japanese and the U.S. recoveries occurred well in advance of those in European countries and were much more robust. This was particularly beneficial to the countries of the Pacific basin since they depend on Japan and the United States for economic stimulus.

In the first half of 1974, the foundation of Australia's growing prosperity collapsed. Because of the world recession, Australia's export prices declined and export volume fell drastically. Not even the minimum level of exports specified in the long-term contracts with Japan could be sustained because excess inventories were accumulating in Japan. Furthermore, rising wages continued to push up Australian costs which intensified the unemployment problem. In response to the rapid rise of unemployment, the Labor government devalued the Australian dollar, eased fiscal policy, and adopted a permissive monetary policy. The easier money accommodated the inflation, but neither it nor the devaluation could stimulate output in the face of weak world demand. The seriousness of the inflation caused the government to tighten its monetary policy in the second quarter of 1974 which made the recession worse, and the fiscal 1974–75 budget was made fairly restrictive. By mid-1975 the government had adopted a gradualist approach toward the reduction of both inflation and unemployment. However, a new government came to office in November more committed to fighting inflation than to easing unemployment. But within its first month, unemployment rates began to rise again, and the Liberal-Country party government responded by depreciating the Australian dollar and simultaneously taking measures to stimulate the tradable goods industries, while still maintaining a general anti-inflation policy. As these policies gradually took hold in 1976, unemployment declined slightly. Despite the devaluation, the balance of payments remained in deficit. Thus Australia failed to find the combination of policies that would simultaneously control inflation, reduce unemployment, and maintain balance-of-payments equilibrium.

Like Australia, Korea suffered a reduction in export volume in 1974 and a decline in its GNP growth to an annual rate of 5.1 percent in the second half of the year. In contrast to Australia, however, Korea began to recover in early 1975, mainly because of fiscal stimulants enacted at the end of 1974. The expansion of the Korean economy after midyear, led by a marked increase in exports, seems attributable to the won devaluation, to the government's support to business firms, and to the business recovery in the United States. Though export volume increased, the balance-of-payments position did not improve substantially because of the deterioration of the terms of trade.

In 1976, economic performance was even better, as exports to the United States and Japan both expanded greatly. Moreover, prices remained reasonably stable (by Korean standards) as the rises of the wholesale and consumer price indexes were kept at 12.1 percent and 15.4 percent. The current account deficit decreased to its lowest level since 1970 and was easily offset by long-term capital inflows. Korea further improved its trade position by increasing its exports to Europe and the Middle East. The most distinctive feature of the Korean economy is the crucial role that changes in exports play in determining demand. The stagnation from mid-1974 to mid-1975 was explained by the slowdown of exports, and the rapid economic expansion afterwards was led by the increase of exports.

The deflationary impact on the Philippine economy as the commodity boom ended and the world recession took hold was particularly strong in 1975. Despite various governmental measures to protect low-income households, employment in manufacturing began to decline in 1974 and real wages were actually reduced in 1975. The inflation moderated in 1975, with the CPI rising 8.2 percent and the WPI only 5.4 percent. Seizing the opportunity to stimulate the economy, the government offered incentives for agricultural production and invested heavily in the tourist industry, financing a massive expansion of hotel-building. Economic growth did recover, but the balance-of-payments deficit worsened. The deficit was financed by capital inflows, and in 1976 was somewhat relieved by the partial recovery of exports, especially of manufactured goods.

Thailand also felt deflationary pressures from the world recession, but even more so from other restraints. Its export prices did drop. But export volume held up fairly well since Thailand's exports are foods, which are less cyclically sensitive than other products. Furthermore, Thailand exports to other developing countries and thus its trade is less affected by recessions in industrial countries. One of Thailand's particular difficulties in the recessionary period was adjusting to the Communist victory in its neighbors Cambodia, Laos, and Vietnam.

The direct impact was a sharp drop in Thailand's border trade with these countries after 1974 (though unrecorded trade may have replaced recorded trade). The indirect effect of the Communist victory was considerable, since the confidence of Thai and foreign entrepreneurs was undermined and investment suffered. Domestic political instability may have reduced confidence even further. And the American military withdrawal, even though gradual, may have played a major role in weakening the economy. The withdrawal meant the end of substantial American expenditures in Thailand. It also exposed the misallocation of certain investment that was geared to American needs.

The creation of a budget deficit in 1974 to stimulate the economy was the first conscious attempt of the Thai government to use fiscal policy. Expenditures were raised in January 1974 and tax reductions were added at the end of 1975. These measures were designed in such a way as to minimize their inflationary impact. Furthermore, monetary policy was selectively eased to stimulate particular industries. The Thai economy responded to the challenge and performed remarkably well. Government measures had their intended effect and government investment increased.

All six countries during the 1974–76 recession attempted active demand management policies and some took supply-stimulating measures as well. Furthermore all were prepared to finance their balance-of-payments deficits on current account rather than restrain their economies or let changes in the exchange rate make the entire adjustment. The weights that different countries assign to the various dimensions of macroeconomic performance —growth, inflation, and the balance of payments—differ, of course, as do the challenges facing them. Thus the outcomes of their efforts to deal with the crises of the 1970s differed.

Macroeconomic Performance in the 1970s

Until 1973, all six of the Pacific basin countries achieved the rate of growth they had established in the 1960s (see table 1-3). However, a decided break occurred in 1974 with the onset of the world recession.[1] Subsequently Korea, the Philippines, and Thailand once again achieved their earlier rates, but Australia, Japan, and the United States did not. Though it is possible that Korea is in a phase of accelerating growth, so that its potential growth now exceeds the 1964–69 standard,[2] it nevertheless had a remarkably high rate of growth in 1970–77, in the face of challenges no less severe than those affecting the industrial countries. For the Philippines and particularly Thailand the challenges on balance were no easier, although they benefited from the commodity boom (as did Australia); but Thailand had the additional difficult adjustment to the U.S. military withdrawal.

Despite its long recession, the United States came a bit closer to reaching its pre-1970 potential than either Australia or Japan. It is indeed possible that the potential growth of these three countries is now below their 1964–69 standards. For the United States the change of trend may have taken place in 1967.[3] Though the low U.S. growth rate may be a result of declining potential, that does not improve the situation; it does, however, redirect attention toward structural factors in the economy and away from demand management. Japan's potential may also have been reduced drastically, to 6–7 percent a year in the 1970s, because it reached the end of its catching-up process, but actual growth was still below that level. While Australia's growth potential also appears to have fallen, the factors behind its decline are unclear.

When account is taken of the interaction among the countries, the dichotomy between the high and low achievers becomes more remarkable. Korea, the Philippines, Thailand, and Australia are heavily dependent on growth in Japan and the United States and they were given less support, yet with the exception of Australia they were able to achieve their potential growth rates while the advanced economies fell short of their potential.

Countries differ in the level of inflation they normally suffer (see table

1. The break in Australian growth was delayed one year.
2. Kazushi Ohkawa and Henry Rosovsky, *Japanese Economic Growth: Trend Acceleration in the Twentieth Century* (Stanford University Press, 1973), analyze the phenomenon of such growth for Japan.
3. *Economic Report of the President, January 1979*, chap. 2. Also see Edward Denison, *Growth, Productivity, and the Sources of Their Retardation* (Brookings Institution, 1980).

1-7) as they do in growth potential. Japan in the 1960s exhibited a relatively high rate of inflation because of the dual nature of its economy; however, the phenomenon was confined to retail prices. For somewhat the same reason, Korea also had a history of high inflation, but the level was much higher than Japan's and showed up in wholesale as well as retail prices; yet Korea's pattern of inflation was not duplicated in Taiwan's similar economy. The other four countries had reasonably low inflation rates in the 1960s with consumer price increases averaging between 2 percent and 3.5 percent a year.

All of them had worse experiences in the 1970s than in the 1960s; indeed, inflation was the most serious problem of the decade for the Pacific basin. The worst performance early in the decade was shown by the Philippines and later in the decade by Korea and Australia. As demonstrated by the experience of the Philippines and Australia (and possibly Japan and the United States), the timing of an inflation episode is related to when the government chooses to adjust its exchange rate rather than solely to demand management of the moment. But external factors also play an important role.

The acceleration of inflation from 1972 to 1974 in all six countries was related to the commodity boom and oil crisis and thus all of them imported inflation directly through their merchandise trade. However, inadequate domestic policies contributed to the virulence of inflation in many of the countries.

The reaction to the inflation that occurred after the oil crisis was most pronounced in Japan, where an aggressive policy was remarkably successful. Price stability at the wholesale level was restored very quickly and consumer prices also responded, albeit with a lag. In the Philippines and Thailand, reasonable price stability was also restored fairly rapidly. In Australia, the deceleration was slow and painful in part because anti-inflation policy was delayed, but by 1978 the policy of restraint was having some success. The situation in the United States and Korea, however, was very different. In the United States some deceleration of inflation did occur in 1976 and 1977, but as the economy began to approach full capacity, inflation once again headed for a double-digit range indicating that the policy response was inadequate. Korea also experienced some decline in inflation in 1976 and 1977, but the level remained very high and began to accelerate again in 1978 (it may be that the Korean government does not consider a high inflation rate alarming).

Equilibrium in the balance of payments is so elusive that no set of criteria fits all countries at a single moment or even one country at all times.

However, serious disequilibriums are generally recognizable. Balance in its external accounts should be considered a goal of policy, since no country can be indifferent about its foreign borrowings—they affect future obligations and determine whether the country is fulfilling its proper role in the world economy. When a rich country where returns to capital are low borrows from a poor country with higher real returns to capital, neither is achieving its goals.

The United States only approached balance-of-payments equilibrium in one year, 1973; in all other years it was in actual or potential deficit. In 1973 the U.S. economy was operating slightly above its potential, but nevertheless the current account surplus was of the same dimension as its long-term capital lending (table 8-3) and short-term capital movements were consistent with relative monetary conditions. Thus the devaluation of the dollar in 1971 and 1973 had its intended effect. In the other years, the current account surplus was too small and by 1977 was actually in substantial deficit.[4] Domestic absorption of resources for consumption and government expenditure was too large relative to domestic production to permit balance in the U.S. external accounts. In time the imbalance forced a reduction in the value of the dollar which was further undermined by a loss of confidence in the currency. If American domestic policy had been more restraining, then the devaluation would have helped transfer resources from domestic absorption to net exports, but that policy was not taken until November 1978, by which time the U.S. balance-of-payments deficit had become huge.

In contrast Japan's balance of payments was in surplus for most of the decade. As a result of the earlier yen appreciation, the surplus was being corrected after 1972, but then the oil crisis intervened to confuse the situation. Japan had a current account deficit in 1973–75, but in 1973 economic growth was very high and in 1974–75 very low in response to the oil crisis. Massive inventory changes were involved which, because of their distorting effect on imports, confused the underlying balance-of-payments situation.[5] Nevertheless, it was clear by 1976–77 that Japan's balance of payments was back into surplus. The yen responded in 1977 and most of 1978 by rising in value and Japan's domestic policy was made more stimulative to support the adjustment; however, the amount of stimulation proved inadequate.

4. The large U.S. current account surplus in 1975 was caused by the very deep recession in that year and was still less than long-term capital outflows.

5. The value of the yen cycled in response to the uncertainty which itself confuses balance-of-payments numbers measured in a foreign currency.

Table 8-3. *Balance of Current and Capital Accounts of Six Pacific Basin Countries, 1970–77*
Millions of dollars

Country and account	1970	1971	1972	1973	1974	1975	1976	1977
Japan								
Current account	1,970	5,797	6,624	−136	−4,693	−682	3,680	10,911
Long-term capital	−1,464	−958	−3,016	−8,453	−3,596	−82	−728	−2,310
Short-term capital	287	4,903	−1,275	5,023	9,596	665	723	−2,329
Errors and omissions	n.a.	527	534	−2,762	−66	−492	125	248
Total	n.a.	10,269	2,867	−6,328	1,241	−591	3,800	6,520
United States								
Current account	2,383	−1,410	−5,989	6,881	1,720	18,456	4,339	−15,207
Long-term capital	−6,203	−9,047	−5,637	−6,733	−7,123	−19,551	−14,329	−12,486
Short-term capital	−6,486	−10,180	2,517	−2,784	−1,732	−9,000	−9,871	−6,542
Errors and omissions	n.a.	−9,819	−1,975	−2,719	−1,686	5,436	9,319	−1,015
Total	n.a.	−30,456	−11,084	−5,355	−8,821	−4,659	−10,542	−35,250
Australia								
Current account	−854	−816	557	465	−2,627	−603	−1,419	−2,544
Long-term capital	1,076	1,933	−1,663	−668	829	638	1,458	2,152
Short-term capital	−75	−86	40	156	−137	−57	379	−177
Errors and omissions	n.a.	265	470	−302	292	−921	779	−587
Total	n.a.	1,296	−596	−349	−1,643	−943	−361	−1,156

Korea

Current account	−623	−848	−370	−307	−2,027	−1,888	−308	12
Long-term capital	463	529	494	655	1,044	1,344	1,329	1,287
Short-term capital	224	261	−3	−6	696	1,123	535	−9
Errors and omissions	n.a.	12	39	11	115	−212	−242	81
Total	n.a.	−46	160	353	−172	367	1,314	1,371

Philippines

Current account	−43	−2	7	474	−207	−923	−1,105	−829
Long-term capital	130	−9	115	132	227	517	1,137	928
Short-term capital	83	251	168	80	640	596	58	45
Errors and omissions	n.a.	−142	−107	−19	−70	−187	−147	−170
Total	n.a.	98	183	667	590	3	−56	−26

Thailand

Current account	−47	−175	−51	−46	−87	−606	−436	−1,087
Long-term capital	110	81	156	80	388	255	314	446
Short-term capital	54	16	38	240	137	215	222	620
Errors and omissions	n.a.	60	53	−54	36	84	−21	30
Total	n.a.	−18	196	220	474	−52	79	9

Source: International Monetary Fund, *International Financial Statistics*, vol. 32 (October 1978).
n.a. Not available.

Australia's balance-of-payments surplus in the early part of the 1970s was a contributing factor causing inflation. When the Australian dollar was appreciated and tariffs reduced to cure the surplus, the inflation was already under way and the balance of payments went into deficit. Subsequently the deficit was attacked through domestic restraint and currency changes, but unfortunately also through increased trade protection.

The balance of payments received constant attention in Korea and did not swing greatly out of balance, possibly because of prompt policy responses. The deficit in 1974–75 caused by worldwide recession was cured and some surplus appeared in 1976–77. Equilibrium was maintained by the balancing of high domestic inflation against rapid productivity growth in traded goods industries. Both the Philippine and Thai payments balances had difficulty recovering from the commodity boom and worldwide recession; by 1977 the Philippine deficit was getting a bit smaller, the Thai deficit was growing.

Interaction among Pacific basin countries is most noticeable in the balance of payments. The U.S. and Japanese accounts are almost mirror images of each other (after correcting for the OPEC surplus). If American policy had been more effective in curing the U.S. deficit, then the Japanese surplus would have been smaller, and conversely for Japanese policy and the U.S. deficit. Given the problem of inflation, the inadequacies of U.S. policy were more to blame. Clearly the payments balances of the other four countries are greatly affected by what happens in Japan and the United States and in the Pacific basin as a whole.

The Philippines and Thailand came closer to satisfying their growth, inflation, and payments needs during the 1970s than the other four Pacific basin countries. Korea achieved truly outstanding growth with balance-of-payments equilibrium, but its inflation performance was poor. Japan had slightly more success than the United States, while Australia's economic performance was inadequate in all three areas. Australia was, however, making some progress in 1978.

The natural question to ask is why the economic performance of the three developing countries was better than that of the three advanced countries. Superior policy decisions do not appear to be the primary answer. One factor may be the ability of advanced developing countries to adjust to massive disruption in the world economy. Rich countries with highly developed industries adjust less easily (as do underdeveloped poor countries). Only wealthy countries have the resources and reserves to postpone an adjustment; poor countries must do it more rapidly, and delay makes adjustment more difficult. When economic difficulties require a decline in real income, it is very difficult to accomplish in rich countries because of institutional rigidities ranging from labor contracts, especially with cost-of-living escalator clauses, to legislation that protects civil servants, the poor, the aged, and the retired. The structural changes in industry that change in the relative price of energy dictates are easier to accomplish when industries are being created than in facilities that have to be refitted. The same could be said for meeting the challenge of environmental deterioration. Government regulations and the like introduce inflexibilities in the labor and product market of advanced countries that are not duplicated in developing countries. Thus a difference in adjustment capacity appears to be the principal factor behind the difference in macroeconomic performance.

But none of the six countries recognized the significance of economic interdependence in its policies even when their impact was mainly within the Pacific basin. The United States gave no greater weight to the needs of its trading partners when it embargoed soybeans than did Thailand when it embargoed rice. Japan was as irresponsible in limiting silk textile imports as was Australia in limiting labor-intensive manufactured goods. Korea showed no greater sensitivity to fallout on others from its large currency devaluation than did the United States in not moderating the swings of the dollar. Such a small-country approach to policymaking—that is, attempting to cure domestic problems through forcing the adjustment onto the rest of the world—will not work in an interdependent world without severe repercussions on others and ultimately on the offending nation itself.

CHAPTER NINE

Dealing with Change

THE PACIFIC BASIN is the most dynamic region of the world. Economic growth and international trade in the region are advancing at rates not experienced elsewhere. Much of the success comes from positive stimuli spilling over from country to country. Thus benefits of economic interdependence are being captured. However, many economic stimuli in the region have been destructive, and governmental policies have more often promoted the negative than the positive. The countries of the Pacific basin have often taken a small-country view in their policymaking, disregarding the difficulties they were causing others, assuming their policies would do little harm outside their national economies.

The costs of inappropriate international economic policies have often fallen heavily on small developing countries of the Pacific basin. Barriers to international trade tend to stymie their economic advance. But the risks are equally large for the advanced countries of the region. During the 1970s it was only the economic performance of Australia, Japan, and the United States that deteriorated. If this deterioration is to be countered and reversed, much help will have to come from the fast-growing developing countries.

The policies that governments undertake are those they perceive to be in the national interest. International economic policymaking can best be improved by broadening governments' perception of their interests. If their field of vision can be extended to the indirect consequences of their measures, governments might, for example, forswear the practice of blaming foreigners for domestic economic difficulties. Against the domestic political gains of such claims they would have to weigh the costs of intergovernmental disputes and economic nationalism. Their perceptions might also be improved by lengthening the time span their policy evaluations cover. If the short-run gains of trade embargoes, for instance, had to be weighed against the eventual loss of markets and retaliation of trading partners, governments might decide against shifting a large part of their adjustment burden to others. The pattern of economic interaction in the Pacific basin in the 1970s confirms the need to broaden and lengthen governments' perspectives.

Just as shortsighted nationalism leads to more nationalism in retaliation, so success in international economic cooperation breeds further success. As trust among countries grows, the technical constraints on reaching balanced agreements lessen. When each country's gain must always equal that of others, negotiating efforts are protracted and gains less than optimal. Where mutual trust exists, however, countries need not insist on gaining rightful shares on every issue, for the credits they accumulate can be honored in future negotiations.

The greatest challenge to international economic policymaking is to create a system that can operate efficiently without a single or hegemonial country at its center. In the past the world economy only made substantial progress when led by a hegemonial country such as Great Britain before World War I and the United States for two decades after World War II. The United States is no longer powerful enough to control the system. Until August 1971 it was the primary stimulator of growth in the Pacific basin. Subsequently Japan and Australia filled the vacuum created by the retrenchment of the United States. When those economies faltered at the onset of the oil crisis, the region's forward momentum was sustained by demand from OPEC countries, recovery in the United States, and the individual efforts of Pacific basin countries.

Lessons of the 1970s

The experience of individual countries in the Pacific basin during the turbulence of the 1970s offers some policy lessons that will be helpful in the future, but also examples of things to avoid.

The United States can no longer afford to make domestic policy decisions that ignore policies of other governments. While U.S. policy served as a fixed point in the world economic system, the independence of the United States may have worked to convert an inherently chaotic decisionmaking system into an orderly sequential process. But the United States disregarded the rest of the world to a fault. The United States must design and effectuate policies that improve its international position. Furthermore, information on developments in international trade and exchange rates is an important source of information about the United States itself, of critical importance to American policymakers simply because the U.S. economy is part of an interdependent world economy and is greatly affected by policy decisions taken abroad.

No government can afford to overlook the distributional consequences of its policies; particular groups should neither be forced to accept unusually large burdens nor be given undue windfalls. Furthermore, government cannot be seen as taking most of the rewards of individual effort from the productive members of society and wasting them through useless expenditures or largess to the unproductive members of society. Economies are most likely to weather economic crises successfully if they have strong political leadership. Effective leadership seems to be the necessary element in establishing confidence in the society's basic fairness.

Government fiscal policy (in conjunction with monetary policy) was for the countries in this study a powerful instrument for influencing economic outcomes. It was not always well designed, however. Thailand, for instance, long failed to take the overall fiscal impact of its actions into account when drawing up its budget, and Japan geared its fiscal plans to the realized government deficit. The macroeconomic performance of both countries could have been improved if their fiscal stimulus had been aimed at a high employment budget (or high capacity utilization).

The most imaginative attempt to counter inflation was the Republic of Korea's increases in supply rather than reductions in demand. The Koreans had some success with this strategy, although their inflation rate remained quite high. France tried a similar strategy in 1968 but quickly discarded it for more traditional policies when the inflation it sought to counter seemed to be getting out of hand. An exceptionally good crop is a natural application of the strategy of reducing inflationary pressure by increasing supplies; doing so in industry requires an autonomous increase in productivity. The trick is to achieve better balance by adding more to supply than to demand, which a government may do if it can improve its fiscal balance sharply as output rises (without creating excess liquidity through monetary ease). The government must stimulate the economy through structural policies such as investment incentives, but keep its principal macroeconomic policies moderately restrictive. Clearly the success of such a policy depends on a receptive world market for the output of new industries so that an internal balance of supply and demand by product need not be maintained. Despite international complications, inflation in all six Pacific basin countries in the 1970s was the result primarily of domestic policy mistakes, and better domestic policies must be devised to deal with it. Supply-promoting policies of different sorts should clearly be part of the anti-inflation strategy. Korea's moderate success in its strategy is possibly worthy of emulation.

The Philippines suffered from the side effects of a persistent balance-of-payments disequilibrium because it erected a set of inefficient defense mechanisms, the most damaging of which were import controls. Deficits are best attacked by devaluing the currency while restraining domestic demand to permit resources to be transferred to tradable goods industries. It is important that trade restrictions be retracted when currency changes are made. While the Philippines did devalue the peso in 1970, it did not liberalize trade. Thus the country suffered more domestic inflation than was necessary and perpetuated the misallocation of resources by protecting investment in less efficient industries.

Korea, the Philippines, and Thailand took a variety of approaches to the problem of imported inflation. In 1972–73 during the commodity boom and again in 1974 in the oil crisis, inflation seemed not to inhibit the growth of real economic activity in Korea. The private sector apparently found ways to adjust to the rise in costs without limiting output. However, when Korea put on selective price controls to contain inflation, real economic activity did suffer. The Philippines had a similar experience. And Thailand found that freezing the price of cement to contain inflation slowed domestic cement production but did little to stop inflation since higher priced imports were required to meet growing demand. Selective inducements to increase production appear to be successful, but selective efforts to stop inflation are frustrated.

Both Korea and Japan found that structural policies designed to promote production capability were extremely effective in increasing exports of specific goods. Competitiveness in those industries was so substantially improved that international comparison of price or cost developments was totally misleading. It appears that for many industries international competitiveness can be established by having the newest facilities embodying the most up-to-date technology. Furthermore government research into new geographic markets not only opened up new trade for Japanese and Korean industries by providing market information but helped to overcome the substantial inertia that limits export efforts. Large countries such as the United States can benefit as much as small ones from such governmental investments.

In the Philippines and Thailand—predominantly exporters of raw materials and food—the exports that responded most readily to actions such as devaluation of the currency were manufactured goods. Policies in primary producing countries that promote the development of manufacturing solely to replace imports may therefore be shortsighted and possibly seriously deficient. The fact that Thailand found markets for some of its manufactured goods in other developing countries further suggests that exploitation of export opportunities depends on a broad view of possible markets.

National Policies and International Markets

Though every country can be expected to adopt the macroeconomic policies it deems best for its own interest despite the advice, suggestions, and even cajoling of other countries, there are limits on its freedom to set targets and utilize economic instruments. These limits were abused by both Japan and the United States in the 1970s.

Following the inflation-recession problems of the first half of the 1970s, Japan chose to fight inflation, the United States to fight unemployment. But extreme targets are unlikely to be met. The country that chooses, for instance, to crush inflation regardless of its side effects will not only cause unemployment for itself but unemployment and trade deficits for its trading partners. The likelihood of a rise in pressure for protection in these circumstances should serve as a moderating force in limiting a country's choice of targets.

The monetary system also imposes limits on such decisions. For example, the country that chooses maximum output as a target, completely ignoring the inflation that results, will soon find that its currency is falling in value in the foreign-exchange market, which will upset its own financial markets. If no end to the inflation is anticipated, then confidence in the currency will be destroyed and the currency will no longer be accepted in international transactions. If this should happen to a large country such as the United States, then the monetary system will be destabilized and will soon become encumbered with exchange controls or other devices as other countries attempt to defend themselves. A small country courting inflation must be prepared to bear the tremendous burden of using foreign currency for all of its international transactions and eventually even its domestic transactions. Thus either concern over the monetary system or the actions of the system itself constrain countries in their inflationary behavior. Realization that there are constraints in the world economy should encourage countries to cooperate in the system despite the loss of sovereignty that seems to be implied.

The failure of Japan and the United States to respect limits on their macroeconomic policies was the major cause of the economic problems that surfaced between them in the 1970s and caused severe problems for other countries both in and outside the Pacific basin. The challenge for the future is to identify and publicize the limits of national policy. Governments will avoid policy excesses if they know they are going to fail. Limits must also be placed on the frequency with which countries change targets. If, for instance, the United States and Japan were synchronized in their economic behavior and they chose to shift frequently between stimulation and restraint, the results would be transmitted in magnified form through international trade and could be catastrophic for the raw material suppliers of the Pacific basin. The experiences of Australia, the Philippines, and Thailand indicate how destabilizing such cycles can be. Without full access to international capital markets, the smaller countries would be unable to dampen the destabilizing impact on their economies. The larger countries of the Pacific basin thus have an obligation to maintain some stability in their macroeconomic targeting even if it is not forced on them by the economic system.

Export-led Growth, Payments Balances, and the Exchange Rate

Most countries when entering the international market in a big way for the first time receive a substantial boost in their rate of economic growth. Large gains in productivity are recorded in export industries as static and dynamic benefits from international specialization are captured. Despite the obvious benefits of such export-led growth, there are dangers if imports do not rise as fast as exports. The experience of Japan and West Germany should be a warning to Korea and other Pacific basin countries of the excesses that should be avoided. There is a limit to the speed with which countries whose markets are being penetrated can adjust. Attempts to force the pace will lead to unnecessary economic dislocation and destructive political resistance. The larger the country that is exporting, the greater the difficulties it causes other countries.

The currencies of countries experiencing export-led growth often become undervalued (even if they are periodically revalued) because governments and even the market rely on measures of inflation that do not reflect the growing competitiveness stimulated by new export industries. Undervaluation of the exchange rate, if long maintained, leads to both internal and external distortion. Internally, too much investment is committed to traded goods industries, as Japan learned in the early 1970s when it had surplus production capacity but was unable to satisfy popular demand for schools, hospitals, housing, clean air, and the like. Externally, Japan developed a chronic balance-of-payments surplus which became a depressant for, and an irritant to, its trading partners.

Inappropriate exchange rates, whatever their origin, cause structural problems for countries. However, sudden and large shifts of supply and demand in almost any sector can also create structural problems, even if the exchange rate does adjust. Indeed the structural problem in Australian secondary manufacturing came to light when the exchange rate appreciated to more properly reflect Australia's new mineral wealth. Since structural distortions in one country necessarily affect other countries, their correction is a matter of international interest. Maintaining a disequilibrium exchange rate to ease a structural problem is both unhelpful to the initiating country and a disservice to others. Correcting the exchange rate may not be sufficient, however, in which case other policy instruments tailored to the specific situation will be needed.

Governments usually recognize the need for adjustment to correct structural or even cyclical disturbances, but they may be reluctant to undertake necessary measures, in the belief that the economy is too weak to accommodate an adjustment—particularly before an election—or that the disturbance is temporary and will correct itself. The experiences of Australia and Japan in adjusting exchange rates point to the dangers of attempting to avoid taking unpleasant measures. A case can be made for cushioning disturbances, if an immediate adjustment would exceed the speed at which a country and its trading partners can absorb the changes. All six countries in this study cushioned the shock to their economies of the oil crisis. They cannot be faulted on this score. However, excessive cushioning can delay adjustment for so long that the underlying problem is made worse—as the U.S. tardiness in adopting a comprehensive energy policy proves. Most problems require a policy response, and a prompt one is usually the most effective.

The question of the exchange rate and what to do about it under a floating-rate system is one of the most important policy choices of governments and has been a vexing one for every country in the Pacific basin. Conceptually the problem is simple: a country should maintain an equilibrium value for its currency. The difficulty comes in discovering what the equilibrium value is and maintaining it. Too frequently governments confuse an equilibrium exchange rate with a stable exchange rate, but too stable a rate when change is needed causes disruption and appears as excessive instability later. The U.S. dollar was too stable in 1976 and 1977 when it should have fallen, while the Japanese yen and Korean won were too stable during these same years and should have risen. Though there is no mathematical formula that yields the equilibrium value of a currency, there are clear signs that a currency is not at its equilibrium level. Persistent upward or downward pressure on the currency in the exchange market, which the government resists through market intervention, is an indication that a currency is not properly valued. A sure sign of improper intervention is the massive accumulation or depletion of a country's international reserves over time. The market is the best test of the proper currency value for a major country when it is supported by indications from the balance of payments. For smaller countries, the exchange market is generally made by the government and thus changes in reserve levels must be relied on as an indicator of an inappropriate exchange rate. Unusual transactions can of course distort the picture. Thus only a thorough analysis of the balance of payments will suggest whether it is sustainable without a currency change—that the currency has not strayed from its equilibrium value.

Exchange-rate changes can be misused. In particular, changes or resistance to change designed to stabilize domestic prices can cause disturbances in the balance of payments. It is inflation that causes depreciation, not a depreciating exchange rate that causes inflation. A country that prevents the depreciation of its exchange rate and does nothing else in order to stop inflation only makes the problem worse.

The exchange rate between the U.S. dollar and the Japanese yen is of particular concern not only because of its effect on the economies of these two countries. Major changes in the yen-dollar rate have forced adjustment on other countries in the Pacific basin. Changes in this rate should be carefully managed, and small changes encouraged to preclude the need for massive changes. A small change that is reversed has little long-term impact, but a cumulating disequilibrium is very disturbing. When a major change is necessary, care should be taken to control the natural tendency of markets to overshoot. The two governments will have to cooperate to prevent disorderly exchange markets from developing since the difference in time zones prevents either from managing the entire market.

Commercial Policy and Tariffs

The most economic progress in the Pacific basin in the 1970s was made by those countries that experienced rapid growth in international trade. Each of the six countries in this study benefited from policies liberalizing trade and lost from those restricting it. International trade was also most responsible for causing tension among nations, but that only suggests that care must be taken in liberalizing trade.

The developing countries in the Pacific basin appear to have the potential to industrialize very rapidly, as Korea is doing. Realization of that potential depends on the maintenance of a permissive international market that new producers can enter without discrimination. If the markets of the advanced countries of the Pacific basin, which include the United States, Japan, and Australia, are to be receptive to new imports, they must have sustained and general economic prosperity. To prevent undue hardship and public demand for protectionist policies, adjustment assistance must be available for their domestic industries so that factors of production that are displaced by imports can be maintained and used elsewhere.

Developing countries are equally obliged to liberalize access to their markets. The markets of developing countries, including Korea, the Philippines, and Thailand, are more highly protected than those in advanced countries (with such notable exceptions as Hong Kong and Singapore). Protectionist measures make it almost impossible to determine which developing country has a comparative advantage in a particular industry. Inefficient duplications are the result. And since the development of normal trade relations among developing countries is hindered, they fail to reap many of the advantages of international specialization. The Association of Southeast Asian Nations (ASEAN) would not have to be searching for artificial ways to stimulate trade among member countries such as the Philippines and Thailand if they had not earlier raised restrictive trade barriers.

Korea and many other developing countries have utilized incentives to promote the exports of newly created manufacturing industries. Governmental aid has been made available to compensate for inexperience in handling sophisticated international commerce and ignorance of marketing opportunities. Such ancillary services as banking and transportation have been created. New, comparatively small competitors encounter little resistance or resentment in entering markets. But as their share of the world market grows, their competitors complain of the unfair advantages of the not-so-new and not-so-small exporters from developing countries. Export incentives obviously can become counterproductive. Subsidies once in place are hard to withdraw. To avoid conflicts with trading partners, and to prevent domestic distortions as well, Korea and the other advanced developing countries in the Pacific basin should provide only incentives that are self-liquidating. And they should resist the temptation to increase export subsidies when world markets are weak, for unfair policies lead to retaliation and the net result is the aggravation of recession.

A similar hazard is the temptation of exporters to excessively diversify their markets and importers to diversify their sources of supply. The Philippines, and to a lesser extent Korea, have followed a diversification strategy. While the desire to allay the risk that catastrophe will strike all markets or all suppliers simultaneously is admirable and achieving it worth accepting some costs, the benefits do not necessarily outweigh the costs. Diversification could require an exporter to absorb tremendous transportation costs or force a country to buy from a very high-cost supplier. Furthermore, diversification can have a negative effect on trading relations and domestic harmony if it involves overt discrimination.

Export controls are another instrument that acts to undermine the international trading system. Though use of export controls has become fairly common, the General Agreement on Tariffs and Trade has no explicit rules proscribing such hindrances to trade. The United States and Thailand both attempted in the 1970s to insulate domestic markets against rising world commodity prices through export controls. The Philippines used them in an effort to replace raw material exports with manufactured products made from those raw materials and Japan used them to help correct a balance-of-payments surplus. The Philippines' desire to restrict the export of logs in order to promote the export of lumber and plywood is easily understood. Its natural comparative advantage in exporting processed wood products is possibly being subverted by Japanese tariffs, which escalate rapidly from raw material to processed products, providing excessive protection for domestic producers in the Philippines' major market. But the Philippine response to the problem is appropriate only if it is impossible for the government to induce Japan to reduce its tariff escalation and if other log exporters to Japan follow suit. Rather than acting unilaterally, the Philippines should work to convince all log exporters (including the United States) to bargain on a reciprocal basis with Japan for a reduction in its tariffs.

Japan's effort to subdue the massive increase in its current account surplus in fiscal 1977 by controlling exports of those products such as automobiles and television sets that had been the centerpiece of its exports was not an appropriate remedy. Selective export controls cause serious distortions for everyone. In Japan, efficient export industries are sacrificed to maintain other export and import-competing industries that are inefficient. This not only hurts Japan, but it prevents the normal development of export industries in other countries, especially developing countries. Furthermore, it doubles the chances for success of protectionist forces in importing countries—their own governments might restrict imports or the Japanese might restrict exports. Normal development of international commerce will be seriously impeded if such actions become widespread.

The improper use of tariffs is a further factor that has confused commercial policy. The proper role for import tariffs is to protect domestic industries from foreign competition. Indeed, tariffs always provide some protection, whether intended or not. Under some circumstances, they are also a proper means of raising government revenue—the customs house may be the easiest place to collect the revenue if a corresponding fiscal burden is placed on actual or prospective domestic production. However, changes in tariffs are not properly used for such purposes as correcting balance-of-payments disequilibriums, redistributing income, and controlling inflation. There is a temptation to applaud tariff reductions regardless of their purpose because they promote trade and usually (but not always) reduce the degree of protection in the economy. But if tariff reductions are justified as a proper way to reduce balance-of-payments surpluses, then tariff increases must also be approved as a means of correcting deficits. Neither change is appropriate. The Australian manipulation of tariffs to correct payments imbalances clearly indicates that disequilibriums are best treated with exchange-rate changes supported by monetary and fiscal policy.

Similarly, tariff reductions are not a proper way to fight inflation. While they do reduce inflation, they also reduce domestic protection. As Australia learned, tariffs will have to be raised to redress the unintended loss of protection when the market weakens and inflation subsides. This cyclical use of tariffs tends to exaggerate fluctuations in supplier countries. Only if a country wants both to fight inflation and to reduce protection are tariff reductions appropriate. Otherwise, other anti-inflation instruments are better.

In Thailand (and other countries) tariffs have been used to redistribute income by raising tariff rates on luxury items more than those on necessities. However, this effective protection of domestic industries encourages production of luxuries such as jewelry and high-fashion clothes rather than utilitarian goods. Income redistribution is better accomplished by use of a progressive income tax or even a differentiated consumption tax.

Commodity Policy

Fluctuation of commodity prices causes difficulties for both exporting and importing countries. Ideally, such disturbances should not be allowed to occur in the first place. The destructive consequences of ex post adjustment policies were apparent during the 1972–74 commodity boom and the 1974–75 collapse. Neither the physical controls that Thailand used on rice, nor the price controls the Philippines placed on certain wage goods, nor manipulation of exchange rates can insulate an exporting country from such a disturbance. The disturbance of commodity prices has both real and monetary aspects that cannot be fully neutralized and that even a complex, perfectly orchestrated set of policies can at best only moderate. Crude attempts to deal with price fluctuations simply shift more of the burden onto importing countries and cause greater inefficiency in the long run. Efforts to moderate disturbances can be marginally useful, but those aimed at insulating a country from the market are bound to fail.

Neither exporting nor importing countries are satisfied with existing commodity arrangements. The market has been characterized by booms and busts—booms in which the volume of trade and prices rise sharply, and busts when both are reversed. In Australia this cyclical instability appears to have added to overall inflation (because of asymmetries in labor and product markets), distorted investment decisions, and thereby reduced growth potential. Both exporters and importers of commodities in the Pacific basin are adversely affected by these cycles. Unusually stable prices from 1953 to 1971 obscured the problem, but during the 1970s the pre-1953 pattern of instability returned. The unilateral actions that the six Pacific countries took to insulate themselves from this instability only achieved a modicum of success in return for worsening the problem for other countries in the short run and for themselves in the long run.

The optimum solution of the commodity problem is a world commodity agreement in which buffer stocks are held under international control. Sales of commodities from buffer stocks would prevent excessive price rises and purchases prevent undue falls. A successful commodity agreement—and those that have been tried have only been failures—would have to meet a number of stringent requirements: its sole purpose must be to stabilize prices (rather than to raise or lower them); its funding must be generous; its managers must be honest and wise and have the power to raise and lower target prices, but only in response to underlying shifts of supply and demand; and its managers must have full information on commodity supplies along with standby power to limit the speed of investment in new production. A well-managed buffer stock should be able to accumulate sufficient stocks during periods of excess supply to service the market during times of excess demand. Market prices would fluctuate, but within a narrow range and with few negative consequences, and export volumes would not vary widely. Obviously these conditions are not easily met, but buffer stocks are possible for some commodities such as rubber and tin which are of great importance for the Pacific basin and they should be attempted.

Buffer stocks controlled by individual countries, but subject to some international coordination, are a second best solution. The United States already stockpiles many domestically produced agricultural products to support American agricultural policies and it also maintains stocks of both domestically produced and imported materials for strategic purposes under the control of the General Services Administration (GSA). Inventories of commodities are also held by the private sector in the United States. Japanese business firms and associations of firms with some government guidance and support also hold inventories of commodities. In fact all producers and consumers of commodities hold inventories of some sort; Australia's holdings in certain domestically produced commodities such as wool are particularly important. If the policies of these stockpiling groups could be coordinated, then some of the objectives of a jointly controlled buffer stock could be achieved. Of course, ideas about the proper targets and market strategy would vary. Some producers will resent releases from stockpiles regardless of how high the price rises (as seen by the criticism of American GSA sales of tin), but international discussions might improve the atmosphere for such national actions.

At times of great stress in commodity markets, however, it is extremely hard to get cooperation and inventory behavior is often perverse. For instance, during the height of a boom where current demand exceeds current production by its greatest margin, inventory managers are reluctant to reduce stocks for fear of exhausting supply; indeed they sometimes even try to increase their holdings. And when prices are at their lowest point, some inventory managers try to dump their holdings for fear of further inventory losses. Despite these difficulties, some gains could be obtained through international cooperation.

The market as it now works tends to equate supply and demand, but does so less than perfectly. The stockpiles that are maintained and controlled by individual countries usually serve the interests of all countries, but sometimes do not. Governments on occasion intervene in commodity markets, but (except in the case of oil) they are generally responding to, rather than causing, price instability. The bilateral agreements between Australia and Japan combining direct investment with long-term supply contracts have both good and bad consequences.[1] By guaranteeing future markets, they make possible large-scale natural resource projects that might otherwise not be undertaken. And they have managed to moderate the fluctuations in the realized prices and volumes of trade among the parties to the agreement. However, during times of market stress, one side or the other has tended to unilaterally modify agreements in its own favor causing significant tensions between the countries. Thus the market and current arrangements might well be improved upon.

Capital Flows and Capital Markets

Direct investment is the most beneficial and most controversial form of international capital movement because it transfers technology, management

1. See Kiyoshi Kojima, "Japan's Resource Security and Foreign Investment in the Pacific," and Ben Smith, "Australia's Mineral Production and Trade: Case Study of a Resource-Rich Developed Country," in L. B. Krause and H. Patrick, *Mineral Resources in the Pacific Area, Report of the Ninth Pacific Trade and Development Conference* (Federal Reserve Bank of San Francisco, 1978).

skills, marketing outlets and strategies, and other things in addition to funds. Japan and the United States have been the major sources of direct investment in the Pacific basin and have also been hosts for direct investment. A reasonable economic and political climate in the host country is essential to induce foreign business firms to accept the risks involved in making and sustaining direct investment. Artificial incentives are both unnecessary and undesirable where policy for direct investment is reasonably congenial. In particular, international competition based on subsidies distorts normal international capital flows. Furthermore large subsidies deprive host countries of benefits they should enjoy. Modest subsidies from their own government may be necessary to help businesses overcome irrational fears and lack of information about undertaking foreign investment, but they may also be undesirable if they are large and selective (either by industry or by area). Direct investment is in general a mutually beneficial channel between countries that adds to the stability of their economic relations.

The totality of financial relations between countries is very complex and at times has raised concerns of excessive borrowing or lending, particularly between developed and developing countries. Such rules of thumb as the debt-service ratio[2] that are used to forecast difficulties are inadequate and can be misleading. For example, Korea's supposed overborrowing in 1975 occurred just when it experienced a renewed burst of growth and simultaneous improvement in its balance of payments. Because the debt-service ratio merely reflects the past, it does not consider ingredients that may be important in determining whether or not a country will face financial difficulties in the future. Timely, complete, and accurate data on investment positions, including assets as well as liabilities, can improve investment prospects for both lenders and borrowers.

A greater variety of official and joint private-official sources of finance available to developing countries could also improve capital markets. The experience of the borrowing countries in the Pacific basin indicates that gaps exist between very short-term trade credits (which are readily available) and long-term development loans (which may be available under certain circumstances). If the maturity structure could be filled in from a combination of private and official sources, then greater efficiency would be achieved. Borrowing countries would have to exercise self-discipline in utilizing such financing—as the Philippines learned in the latter 1960s, balance-of-payments deficits that are financed for too long make the inevitable correction more difficult. A properly functioning capital market would promote healthy

2. The numerator of the debt-service ratio is the sum of interest and principal payments due in a particular period and the denominator is the value of exports of goods and services in that period.

international interchange, yet it would not remove the necessity of making adjustments when they are required. Because capital expenditures for certain vital social purposes in developing countries are not likely to be recovered, developed countries should support them with concessional loans or grants. The United States and Japan's lack of generosity in recent years shows a lack of foresight on their part given their substantial interest in the Pacific basin.

The efficiency of capital markets has been sacrificed at times for other short-term goals such as the elimination of balance-of-payments surpluses or deficits. And governments have instituted exchange controls to force capital into or out of their countries. Japan has used capital controls extensively for various ends depending on the state of the Japanese balance of payments. Also Australia has maintained controls on the outflow of capital. Not only is the efficiency of the market undermined by capital controls, but the incidence of loss is discriminatory since it is not spread evenly over all borrowers and lenders in all countries. Moreover the speculative borrowing and lending which occur in anticipation of the imposition of controls add to market instability. Over time, the effectiveness of capital controls weakens as firms transfer their financing function to foreign subsidiaries and as offshore banking facilities in the currency of the controlling country are established. Where capital restraints appear to be necessary, outright prohibitions are much more destructive for financial institutions than are rules that affect the cost of borrowing such as reserve requirements and variable deposit rates.

Capital markets could also be improved if competition among financial institutions were increased. Often governments fail to recognize the importance of competition in banking since the smaller the number of institutions, the easier it is to regulate monetary policy through nonmarket instruments such as administrative guidance. It may be reasonable to encourage a viable domestically owned banking sector before opening the doors fully to foreign institutions, but as Australia found, such protections maintained for too long can lead to oligopolistic control of financial intermediation and be very damaging to the economy. Having foreign-owned financial institutions can be very beneficial to the host country, as has been recognized by Korea and the Philippines (as well as Hong Kong and Singapore). Since the linkage of national capital markets is mutually beneficial for countries, the better the competition among financial institutions, the greater the efficiency of the market and the larger the gains for society.

Sectoral Policy

Despite the importance of agriculture in the economies of all six Pacific basin countries, their agricultural policies are in general ill-designed to promote economic efficiency. The reasons are understandable. Fear of starvation and the political power of rural areas encourage governments to promote domestic production even at very high costs, as in Japan. Food commands such a large part of the household budget that governments are not prepared to let markets determine prices of food for social reasons as well as concern over inflation, as in the Philippines and Thailand. Once the government becomes deeply involved in the domestic market for agricultural products, it must necessarily interfere in the international trade of agricultural products in order to sustain domestic policy. Thus agriculture is the stepchild of international trade, ignored when trade liberalization is undertaken and abused when trouble occurs.

Agricultural policy is of overwhelming importance for the economic performance of Thailand and the Philippines, of considerable importance for Korea and Australia, and of more than passing interest for the United States and Japan. In the developing countries, productivity growth in agriculture has been one of the major determinants of aggregate economic performance, and in the advanced countries the movement of labor out of agriculture into higher productivity sectors has contributed to economic advancement. It thus seems strange that governments have acted as if they could distort the economics of agriculture without causing repercussions in the economy. Agricultural efficiency must be encouraged to improve economic performance, which means more production in countries such as Thailand and less production in countries such as Japan. The international implications of agricultural policy should also be given greater attention. However, efficiency cannot become the dominant consideration in determining location of agricultural output unless importing countries feel secure that they will have equal access to world supplies in times of shortage. In international trade negotiations, both exporting and importing countries must learn to treat agricultural products the way they do other goods.

Since the oil crisis it has been clear that the oil market cannot be expected to work perfectly nor the transition from one energy source to another to take place without sharp price rises. A conscious policy is necessary therefore to establish energy conservation programs and to promote energy production at the lowest possible cost. The uncertainties of scientific advance and technological development, as well as the actions of the OPEC cartel, demand that no potential source of energy be overlooked. Thus nuclear, solar, geothermal, and other esoteric sources of energy should be given support and the research capabilities of many countries, particularly the United States and Japan, should be coordinated. While the objectives of an energy policy are straightforward, the translation of those objectives into effective policy is exceedingly complex and politically difficult but must be given highest priority because of its great importance.

The international consequences of the United States' inability to resolve its domestic energy dilemma are grave. The strategic and economic power wielded by OPEC has been perpetuated by continued U.S. imports of petroleum which have created energy shortages and forced up the price of oil. The failure of the United States to enact promptly an energy policy had consequences for the entire Pacific basin, particularly Japan. American inaction caused an ineradicable sense of insecurity in Japan. Many Japanese believe that Japan could run out of energy and that the whole postwar economic miracle could dissolve. Such fears have had a role in perpetuating Japan's economic stagnation.

Regional Cooperation

That the countries of the Pacific basin during the 1970s failed to take certain actions that now seem plausible is both understandable and inevitable. But all of them took unilateral actions that had profound effects on their trading partners without consulting them or even giving consideration to the problems they might be causing for them. The U.S. export embargo on soybeans, the Japanese import embargo on meat and naphtha, the tightening of Australian import restrictions on labor-intensive manufactured goods, the Thai export embargo on rice, all have a symbolic importance beyond their actual economic impact, for they demonstrate the scant recognition of economic interdependence in policymaking. If the circumstances were repeated, there is every reason to expect similar unilateral actions in the future.

The justifications for unilateral action are easy to produce: the need to find a compromise among many domestic interests precludes the consideration of foreign interests; the need to maintain secrecy to prevent anticipatory market reactions means that only a few people can be involved in making a decision; the smallness of a country means that the external impact of its actions is expected to be small. All of these reasons for unilateral action have some legitimacy, but that does not make them desirable or even acceptable to other countries. A unilateral action of this kind taken by any country is deplorable, but such actions taken by the United States—which is still the recognized leader among market economies—undermine international cooperation even more than those of other countries. Policymakers must move to change the way in which international economic policy is made.

The challenge is formidable. They must seek ways to build mutual trust, find a surrogate for hegemonial power, design mechanisms to make countries aware of the limits to their macroeconomic goals, make countries aware of the implications of their macroeconomic policies on others, avoid excesses of export-led growth, face up to cyclical and structural problems, improve the functioning of the exchange-rate market, promote international trade and contain protectionism, put limits on export promotion efforts and export controls, and design a system to reduce price fluctuations of commodities.

If any of these goals are to be reached, a regular and continuous procedure for consultation among governments of the Pacific basin must be created. International cooperation will help to broaden and lengthen policy horizons of national governments. International consultations can help resolve economic problems in the Pacific basin if they encompass all of the interacting and overlapping aspects of economic issues and bring together both developed and developing countries. None of the international economic institutions, agencies, and forums created in the twentieth century has been able to accomplish this task. Functionally narrow institutions such as the International Monetary Fund and the World Bank that perform well in their own field do not provide the basis needed for broader cooperation. The Organization for Economic Cooperation and Development, though it has had some success in promoting cooperation, has a membership limited to advanced countries. Those institutions that have a universal mandate with respect to both countries and problems have not been successful. Their deliberations tend to degenerate into a morass of negative coalition politics in which it is easy to prevent progress and impossible to create it. The secretariats that governments have generously funded to search for the solutions that the countries could not find have soon become bloated bureaucracies, with ideological programs often completely removed from the political reality of the member governments.

To meet the need for greater economic cooperation in the Pacific basin, a group of experts has proposed creating an Organization for Pacific Trade and Development.[3] The institution would at a minimum provide an efficient mechanism for transmitting information concerning economic developments and government policies and plans among its members on a regular basis. By providing a forum for the discussion of economic issues, it would make

3. Peter Drysdale, "An Organization for Pacific Trade, Aid and Development: Regional Arrangements and the Resource Trade," in Krause and Patrick, *Mineral Resources in the Pacific Area;* and Peter A. Drysdale and Hugh Patrick, "Evaluation of a Proposed Asian-Pacific Regional Economic Organization," in *An Asian-Pacific Regional Economic Organization: An Exploratory Concept Paper,* Committee Print, prepared by the Congressional Research Service, Library of Congress, for the Senate Committee on Foreign Relations, 96 Cong. 1 sess. (GPO, 1979).

governments more aware of the implications of their policies for other countries. Eventually it might become the catalyst for the coordination of economic policies among the governments of the Pacific basin and might even perform certain limited tasks for member countries.

Among the substantive issues that a regional organization should discuss are the macroeconomic conditions and policies of the countries involved. Disclosure of economic information in itself should improve demand management, particularly in the smaller countries. The international implications of actual or threatened structural imbalances might also be examined and discussed. If particular causes of imbalance were identified—such as inappropriate exchange rates or improper investment policies—cooperative solutions could be encouraged. National development plans (like those drawn up by Korea) might be jointly reviewed to determine their implications for other countries. Through careful analysis, problems might be identified early enough to enable countries to act to accommodate or forestall them. Identification of a member's emerging balance-of-payments problems, for example, might lead to the provision of bridging finance beyond that extended by the IMF. Much of the effort of a regional institution would be devoted to improving macroeconomic performance.

The organization could also focus attention on certain policy issues and use of particular instruments. Full discussion of the use of export incentives, for instance, would help determine the economic and political limits on their use that all countries should recognize in order to avoid disputes. Examination of commodity policy within the context of the Pacific basin would be logical since countries in the region are major producers and consumers of many commodities, especially minerals.

Even worldwide issues can be profitably discussed within a regional context. For instance, the danger of nuclear proliferation that nuclear power and fuel reprocessing pose might be effectively dealt with through regional facilities of international agencies, but the drafting of solutions might only be realized through the discussions and actions of a regional institution. Discussions on the regional implications of developments such as the extension of national jurisdiction over the ocean's economic wealth to the two-hundred-mile limit might also be beneficial. The purpose would not be to form a regional caucus to influence the Law of the Sea Conference, but rather to explore regional solutions to regional problems when universal policies are unattainable.

Countries of the Pacific basin choose to take essentially pragmatic approaches to economic issues. Hence a regional institution could be successful despite the different economic structures and levels of economic development of its member countries. All the countries of the Pacific basin should have an interest in such an institution, although some might not participate in launching a joint venture. Either an institution such as the Asian Development Bank could be reorganized to perform a broader function, or something new could be created to foster regional cooperation. In any event the institution's mode of operation requires careful thought. The purpose is to improve interstate relations, not replace them, so the secretariat should be small and its functions limited essentially to research and dissemination of information. The institution might perform certain functions for member countries, but only in response to requests, and never in anticipation of a need.

Such an institution should neither threaten nor compete with existing institutions. The functions of the Asian Development Bank would not be usurped, nor those of ASEAN undermined. Indeed the existence of the larger institution would give ASEAN the added purpose of amassing the power of its members to enable them to meet with the big countries of the region on a more nearly equal footing. In a world in which global solutions to problems seem less and less promising, regional approaches must be given consideration.

During the 1970s the countries of the Pacific basin had many policy successes, but quite a few failures as well. In none of their common experiences did the importance of their economic interaction seem to be recognized by these countries. This lag in perception is serious. The Pacific basin holds great promise of economic gains, but the promise will not be fulfilled if government policy is not addressed to promoting it. The problem goes beyond correcting individual policies, however. The policymaking mechanisms of Pacific basin countries must be altered. Possibly the only way to do this is by creating a cooperative economic institution for the Pacific basin. Any country in the region might take the initiative in forming such an institution, but it will not get very far unless it has the strong support of the United States. Thus the challenge is greatest for the United States.

Index

263